THE HEART OF THE DRAGON

THE HEART OF THE

HOUGHTON MIFFLIN COMPANY/BOSTON/1985

DRAGON

Alasdair Clayre

Patrick Procktor

First American Edition 1985

Copyright © 1984 by Dragonbook ApS

Library of Congress Cataloging in Publication Data
Clayre, Alasdair.
The heart of the dragon.
Includes index.
1. China—Social life and customs—1976–
I. Title.
DS779.23.C55   1984   951.05   84-10806
ISBN 0-395-35336-X

Printed in the United States of America

R 10 9 8 7 6 5 4 3 2 1

Designed by Barney Wan
Picture research by Anne-Marie Ehrlich
Picture Editor Patrick Lui
Based on the television series produced by
Antelope-Sino-Hawkshead Films Ltd

回顾　信仰　婚姻　调解

饮食　古法　工作　改正

理解　创作　贸易

磊怀

CONTENTS

ACKNOWLEDGEMENTS

In writing this book I have been deeply indebted to many people and there is no way in which they can all be thanked enough. The most immediate thanks are due to my partner Peter Montagnon, executive producer of the series, to my fellow producers and directors Patrick Lui and Nigel Houghton, Mischa Scorer and David Kennard, and to all the rest of the production team of the television series, especially to the camera crews, led by Mike Fox, Chris O'Dell and Peter Mackay, and to the film editors, Anne Chegwidden, David Hope and Laurence Williamson. Thanks are equally due to our colleagues in the China News Bureau and China Television, who saw the series through from the start and made possible the complex task of filming throughout the length and breadth of China.

On the academic side the series was fortunate to have, from the start, the help of Dr Hugh Baker of London University, and, as it progressed, of an international team of sinologists of great distinction, who made many contributions in their specialist areas, and who warmed to the challenge of television and of a book less academic than their own, yet requiring perhaps as much accuracy of detail. Where that is lacking, the fault is the author's; where it is present, it is largely due to the pasting, in both senses, taken by early drafts at the hands of these masters. Particular thanks are due to Denis Twitchett, Stuart Schram, Arthur Waldron and Jacques Gernet for their help in connection with 'Remembering'; Wolfgang Bauer, Ho Peng Yoke and Guiliano Bertuccioli with 'Believing'; C.P. FitzGerald, Hugh Baker and Sukie Colegrave with 'Marrying'; Sheila Hillier, Elizabeth Wright and James Geiss with 'Mediating'; Eugene Anderson Jr and Kenneth Lo with 'Eating'; Elizabeth Wright (especially for her help with the study of Maoping village), C.P. FitzGerald, Irene Andreae and Jack Gray with 'Living'; Christopher Howe, Dwight Perkins, Jack Gray, François Godement and Susan Shirk with 'Working'; Herbert Franke, Denis Twitchett, Paul Ch'en and Brian Hipkin with 'Correcting'; Christopher Cullen, Joseph Needham, Nathan Sivin and Jacques Gernet with 'Understanding'; Michael Sullivan, Roderick Whitfield and Anne Farrer with 'Creating'; and Irene Andreae, Wang Gungwu, Endymion Wilkinson and Seth Masters with 'Trading'. The series and the book were valuably advised at various times by the late Sir John Addis, William Atwell, Marianne Bastid, Francesca Bray, K.C. Chang, Cheng Te K'un, Jean Chesneaux, Joan Lebold Cohen, Charles Curwen,

John K. Fairbank, Else Glahn, Lionello Lanciotti, Lucy Lo, Lu Gwei-djen, Shigeru Nakayama, Robert Oxnam, William L. Parish Jr, Jessica Rawson, Mary Tregear, William Watson, Wen Fong, Arthur Wolf and Margery Wolf. In addition Denis Twitchett, C.P. FitzGerald, Herbert Franke and Arthur Waldron, together with the chief editorial consultant, Hugh Baker, took a close interest in the development of the book as a whole, and Irene Andreae gave invaluable and generous help, particularly over the final stages.

In an illustrated book of this kind, there is an unusually heavy debt to those who worked on the pictures and the design – to Patrick Lui, the stills photographer and picture editor, Anne-Marie Ehrlich, the picture researcher, Deirdre McGarry, who helped with the captions, and Barney Wan, the designer – and, over the text as well as the pictures and design, to the publishers, Adrian House, Mark Bonham-Carter and Carol O'Brien at Collins/Harvill, to Helen Renwick, the copy editor, and to Nan Talese at Houghton Mifflin.

The debt closest to the author is to the small team who worked on the research and word-processing of the book in the production office, especially to Lillian Chia, who turned Daoist manuscript into Confucian typescript and helped to prepare the date chart; and to Jenny Lanning, who dealt with the organization of the book and with all the academic consultants, taking calls from different continents and in different languages, sometimes simultaneously, with unruffled ease.

The series could not have existed without the extraordinarily active participation of Stephen Keynes and The English Association Trust, the merchant bankers, supported by their solicitor, Keith Allison, who approached without blanching the task of raising the entire budget for the series through risk capital in the City of London, and secured the participation of Refuge Assurance, The Equitable Life Assurance Society, Sun Life Assurance Society, Guardian Royal Exchange Assurance Group, London Trust, Andrew Weir and Company, United Media and the Caparo Group. In addition the participation of Channel Four, and its confidence in the project at an early stage, were decisive.

Last, and certainly not least, our deepest thanks go to the Chinese people, for sitting for this portrait with friendliness, patience and humour.

Alasdair Clayre

CHRONOLOGICAL TABLE

PERIODS	CHINA	ELSEWHERE
PREHISTORIC/LEGENDARY PERIOD to c.16th century BC Prehistoric Period	Peking Man (500,000-210,000 BC) Neolithic villages: Hemedu, south-east China: rice (c.5000 BC); Banpo, north-west China (Yang Shao culture): millet, silk (c.4800 BC) Longshan culture, north-east and north-west China (c.2500 BC)	Old Kingdom in Egypt (3100-2160 BC)
Legendary Period Xia (c.21st century-c.16th century BC)	Mythical 'sage-emperors': Fu Xi, inventor of the eight trigrams; Shen Nong, inventor of agriculture and herbal medicine; Yellow Emperor (Huang Di), inventor of writing and weapons; Virtuous Emperor Yao, who abdicated in favour of the wise commoner Shun; Yu the Great (d.2197 BC), tamer of floods Xia 'Dynasty' identified by Chinese archaeologists with a late stage of the neolithic Longshan culture	Rise of Sumerian civilization (c.3000 BC) Height of Minoan culture on Crete (c.1700-c.1500 BC)
SHANG c.16th century-c.11th century BC	Jie, 'wicked' last ruler of Xia, said to have been killed by Tang, legendary founder of Shang Bronze age: fine bronze vessels and weapons, carved jade ritual objects Capital moved to Yin (modern Anyang) (c.1300 BC) Historical records on oracle bones in early form of Chinese script; use of silk; rich royal burials with human sacrifice	Height of Egyptian empire (c.1300 BC) Exodus of Jews from Egypt (c.1240 BC) Trojan War (c.1200 BC) King David of Israel Height of Assyrian empire (c.900-c.600 BC)
ZHOU c.1027-256 BC Western Zhou (1027-771 BC) capital: near Xi'an Eastern Zhou (771-256 BC) capital: Luoyang Spring and Autumn Period (771-476 BC) Warring States (475-221 BC)	Zhou Xin, 'wicked' last ruler of Shang, overthrown by King Wu of Zhou (c.1040 BC) *Yijing* (*Book of Change*) Rong nomads overrun Western Zhou (771) Period of *Spring and Autumn Annals*, said to have been composed by Confucius (c.551-479 BC) Feudal states no longer under central control Schools of philosophy flourish: Confucius (c.551-c.479 BC); Lao Zi, possibly mythical contemporary, Daoist; Zhuang Zi (4th century BC), Daoist; Meng Zi (4th century BC), Confucian; Han Fei Zi (4th century BC), Legalist; compilation of the Daoist book, *Daodejing* (probably 4th century BC) Wars among states of Qin, Qi, Chu, Zhao, Han, Wei, Yue, Yen Shang Yang (d.338 BC), Legalist chief minister of Qin (c.360 BC) King of Zhou dethroned by King of Qin (256 BC)	Age of Hebrew prophets (c.875-c.520 BC) Height of Etruscan empire (c.800-c.500 BC) Rome founded (753 BC) Buddha (c.563-c.483 BC) Persian empire (538-333 BC) Golden age of Athens (c.500-c.350 BC) Alexander the Great conquers Egypt, western Asia (336-323 BC)
QIN 221-207 BC capital: Xianyang	Qin Shihuangdi, the 'First Qin Emperor' (221-210 BC) Work begun on 'Great Wall' (214 BC) Li Si (d.208), minister of state Standardization of script, weights and measures Attacks on opposing philosophies	Hannibal crosses Alps (218 BC) Carthaginians at gates of Rome (211 BC)
WESTERN or FORMER HAN 206 BC-AD 9 capital: Chang'an	Liu Bang, called Emperor Gaozu (202-195 BC) Emperor Wu (Han Wudi) (140-87 BC) Sima Qian (145-90 BC), historian Zhang Qian's expedition to western Turkestan (138 BC) Beginnings of paper-making (1st century BC) Territorial expansion into central Asia, north Korea, south and south-west China and North Vietnam	Height of Roman empire (c.100 BC-AD 200) Augustus, first Roman emperor (27 BC-AD 14) Jesus Christ (?4 BC-?AD 29)
XIN 9-23	Emperor Wang Mang, the 'Usurper' (9-23)	
EASTERN or LATER HAN 25-220 capital: Luoyang	Emperor Guang Wu (25-57) Buddhism probably introduced Cai Lun produces fine paper for government use (105) Chinese victories over Xiongnu tribes of central Asia (124-6) Silk Route developed Eunuchs gain power under Emperor Ling (167-89) Yellow Turban rebellion (184) Massacre of eunuchs by troops of murdered general He Jin; emperor deposed (189) Emperor Xian (190-220)	Roman invasion of Britain

PERIODS	CHINA	ELSEWHERE
THREE KINGDOMS (Shu, Wei, Wu) 220-65	Period of political disunity Pilgrimages to Buddhist sites in India	Sassanian empire in Persia (226)
NORTHERN AND SOUTHERN EMPIRES 265-589 Six Dynasties (Western Jin, Eastern Jin, Former Song, Southern Qi, Southern Liang, Southern Chen) (265-589) Northern Dynasties (Northern Wei, Northern Qin and Northern Zhou) (386-587)	Buddhist influence on art and literature Barbarians invade north China (early 4th century) Gradual colonization of south China Emperor Wu (502-49) of the Southern Liang Dynasty Military aristocracy dominant (5th-6th centuries) North unified under Northern Wei, divided after 530, and reunified under Northern Zhou in 578	Rome falls to the barbarians (410) Justinian, ruler of Eastern Roman empire (527-65) Buddhism reaches Japan (c.550) Prophet Mohammed (570-632)
SUI 590-618 capitals: Yangzhou, Luoyang, Chang'an	Yang Jian, called Emperor Wen (581-604) Reunification of China (589) Yang Guang, called Emperor Yang (605-18) Grand Canal constructed Civil service examination system	
TANG 618-906 capital: Chang'an	Rise of scholar-officials Period of territorial expansion into Manchuria, Korea, central Asia Contacts with Japan, south-east Asia, Sassanian and Arab empires, Byzantium Emperor Taizong (626-49) Empress Wu (690-705) Emperor Xuanzong, sometimes called Ming Huang (712-56) Rebellion of An Lushan (755) Wang Wei (699-759), poet and landscape painter Great age of poetry: Li Bai (Li Po) (705-62); Du Fu (712-70) Oldest book with a printed date, *The Diamond Sutra* (868) Great age of figure-painting: Wu Daozi (c.689-758); Zhang Xuan (713-42); Zhou Fang (c.740-800) Rise of landscape-painting Foreign religions in China: Zoroastrianism, Nestorian Christianity; Manichaeism; Islam Rebellion of Huang Chao (878-84), breakdown of central government	Kingdom of Ghana established (c.600) Golden age of Maya civilization Rise of Arab empire (635-715) Founding of Turkish empire (760) Charlemagne (768-814) Arabs sack Rome (846)
FIVE DYNASTIES (Later Liang, Later Tang, Later Jin, Later Han, Later Zhou) 906-60	Period of upheaval: China divided into 9 or 10 independent kingdoms Non-Chinese peoples dominate parts of north China First military use of gunpowder	
NORTHERN SONG 960-1126 capital: Kaifeng	Zhao Kuangyin, called Emperor Taizu (960-76) Reunification of China (960-79) Large parts of north-east and north-west remained under alien rule Wang Anshi, prime minister (1069-86) New laws created to reform Chinese economy and government, withdrawn after conservative opposition, decades of factional disputes Su Dongpo (1036-1102) Zhang Zeduan paints 'Qing Ming Shang He Tu' Great age of landscape-painting: Fan Kuan (c.960-1030); Guo Xi (c.1020-90) Emperor Huizong (1101-25) Dominance of neo-Confucian philosophy Jurchen conquer north China (1127) Footbinding becomes general in north and central China Firm evidence of use of lodestone and magnetic compasses	Norman conquest of England (1066) First crusade (1096-9)
SOUTHERN SONG 1127-1279 capital: Hangzhou	Song Dynasty controls the south, north remains under Jurchen domination Genghis Khan (c.1167-1227): Mongol conquest of north China Mongols begin invasions of south (1234)	Mongols conquer Russia (1237-40)

PERIODS	CHINA	ELSEWHERE
YUAN or MONGOL 1279-1368 capital: Dadu (Peking)	Kublai Khan (1260-94) Final Mongol conquest of all China (1279) Marco Polo in China (1275-92) Mongols attempt to invade Japan (1274-81) and Java Drama flourishes	Mamelukes (Arab Moslems) conquer Acre, end of Christian rule in the Middle East (1291)
MING 1368-1644 capitals: Peking, Nanjing	Zhu Yuanzhang, the Hongwu Emperor (1368-98) The Yongle Emperor (1403-24) Peking becomes capital of Ming China (1421) Naval expeditions to Indian Ocean (1405-33) and Africa Portuguese traders arrive at Guangzhou (1514) Matteo Ricci, Jesuit, received at Chinese court (1582) Novel flourishes; *The Water Margin* edited from traditional sources Widespread export of porcelain (as far as Africa)	Turks conquer Constantinople (1453) Discovery of America (1492) Protestant Reformation inaugurated by Martin Luther (1517) Queen Elizabeth I (1558-1603)
QING or MANCHU 1644-1911 capitals: Mukden (Shenyang), Peking	Dorgon (1612-50), founder of Qing Manchus conquer China (1644) Pigtail forced on Chinese as sign of submission The Kangxi Emperor (1662-1722) Russia establishes trading rights in Peking (1689) The Qianlong Emperor (1736-95) Cao Xueqin's *The Red Chamber Dream* (1754) Macartney's meeting with the emperor (1793) Opium War (1840-2) Five 'Treaty Ports' opened to foreign trade and China opened to Christian missionaries (1842) Taiping Rebellion (1850-64) British and French take Peking (1860) The Self-Strengthening Movement (1861-95) Empress Dowager Cixi (1862-1908) The Tongzhi Emperor (1862-75) Programme to modernize China War with Japan (1894-5) Hundred-Day Reform (1898) Boxer Rising (1900-1) Belated reforms of government and army (1903-10) Republican revolution (1911)	Chinese art and thought influential in Europe (18th century) American Declaration of Independence (1776) French Revolution begins (1789) Queen Victoria (1837-1901) European nations compete for colonies Industrialization of Japan (1868-1912)
REPUBLIC 1911-1949 capitals: Nanjing, Chongqing	Sun Yat-sen (1866-1925), founder of Guomindang, provisional president Yuan Shikai, first president (1912-16) Warlord era (1916-26) Northern Expedition (1926): Chiang Kai-shek (1886-1975) emerges as dominant, becomes president (1928) Japan occupies Manchuria (1931) 'The Long March' (1934-5) War with Japan (1937-45) Defeat of Japan (1945), followed by Guomindang-Communist civil war Communist victory (1949)	World War I (1914-1918) Bolshevik Revolution in Russia (1917) World War II (1939-45) Japan and USA enter World War II (1941) Establishment of United Nations (1945)
PEOPLE'S REPUBLIC 1949- capital: Beijing	Mao Zedong (1893-1976), chairman of Communist Party (1949-76) Liu Shaoqi (1898-1969), head of state (1959-66) Zhou Enlai (?1898-1976), prime minister of People's Republic (1949-76) Deng Xiaoping (1904-), secretary-general of Communist Party (1956-66) Five Year Plan for industry (1953) Great Leap Forward (1958) Growing tension between China and Russia: withdrawal of Russian technicians (1960) The 'Three Years of Natural Disasters' (1960-2) Cultural Revolution (1966-76) Hua Guofeng (1920-), chairman of Communist Party (1976-80) Deng Xiaoping emerges as leader (1978) New legal system (1980) Trial of the 'Gang of Four' (1981) Responsibility System in agriculture and in industry	Independence of former European colonies Korean War (1950-3) Death of Stalin (1953) First man in space (1961) First man on moon (1969) Nixon visit to China (1973)

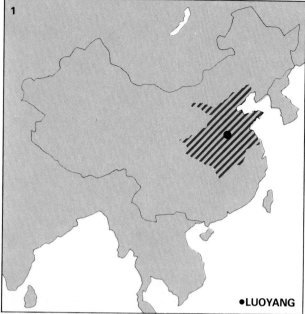

Zhou Dynasty 1027 – 256 BC

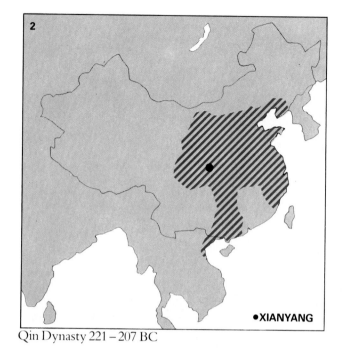

Qin Dynasty 221 – 207 BC

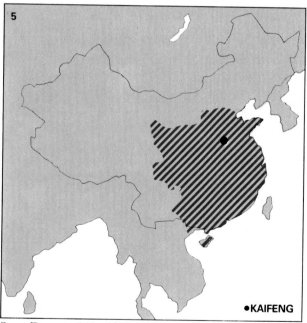

Song Dynasty 960 – 1279

Ming Dynasty 1368 – 1644

●   Capital

  Boundary

—   China's present boundary

Han Dynasty 206 BC – 220 AD

Tang Dynasty 618 – 906

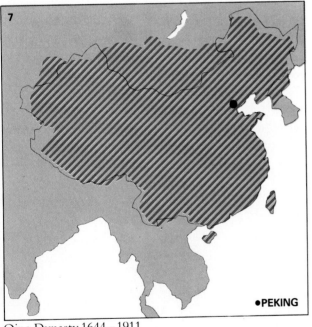

Qing Dynasty 1644 – 1911

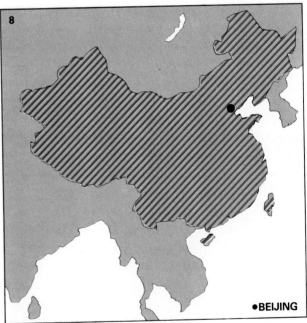

People's Republic of China 1949 –

CHINA'S BOUNDARIES FROM THE ZHOU DYNASTY

NOTE ON CHINESE NAMES AND TERMS

Chinese names are written in the roman alphabet in this book in the system used in mainland China, pinyin, with the exception of a few familiar names which have been retained in older forms: Confucius, Sun Yat-sen and Chiang Kai-shek, the Yangtze River, and Peking for the capital of China up to 1949, the pinyin form, Beijing, being used for it after that date.

Pinyin is pronounced phonetically with a few idiosyncracies, chiefly these:

Consonants

c is pronounced like the *ts* in *tsetse fly*.

q is pronounced like the *ch* in *chin*.

x is pronounced like the *sh* in *sheen*.

zh is pronounced like the *j* in *jump*.

Vowels

e is pronounced like a dull *er* without the *r* being sounded, like the *e* in *talent*.

e before *ng* is pronounced like the *u* in *rung*.

o is pronounced like the *aw* in *jaw*.

ou is pronounced like the *o* in *go*.

Some names are given below in pinyin and in their equivalent in the more familiar older forms of romanization, mainly the Wade-Giles system:

PEOPLE

Pinyin	Wade-Giles or other older romanization
Cao Xueqin	Ts'ao Hsüeh-ch'in
Empress Dowager Cixi	Tz'u-hsi
Deng Xiaoping	Teng Hsiao-p'ing
Hua Guofeng	Hua Kuo-feng
The Kangxi Emperor	The K'ang-hsi Emperor
Lao Zi	Lao-tze (more familiar) or Lao-tzu (more correct)
Li Bai or Li Bo	Li Po
Liu Shaoqi	Liu Shao-ch'i
Mao Zedong	Mao Tse-tung
Meng Zi	Mencius
The Qianlong Emperor	The Ch'ien-lung Emperor
Qin Shihuangdi	Ch'in Shih-huang-ti
Su Dongpo	Su Tong-p'o
The Yongle Emperor	The Yung-lo Emperor
Zhou Enlai	Chou En-lai

NB: In Chinese, the surname or family name precedes the given name.

PROVINCES AND 'AUTONOMOUS REGIONS'

Pinyin	Older romanization
Anhui	Anhwei
Fujian	Fukien
Gansu	Kansu
Guangdong	Kwangtung
Guangxi	Kwangsi
Hebei	Hopeh
Heilongjiang	Heilungkiang
Henan	Honan
Hubei	Hupeh
Hunan	Hunan
Jiangsu	Kiangsu
Jiangxi	Kiangsi
Jilin	Kirin
Liaoning	Liaoning
Nei Monggol	Inner Mongolia
Ningxia	Ninghsia
Qinghai	Kokonor
Shaanxi	Shensi
Shandong	Shantung
Shanxi	Shansi
Sichuan	Szechwan
Xinjiang	Sinkiang
Xizang	Tibet
Yunnan	Yunnan
Zhejiang	Chekiang

OTHER PLACE NAMES

Pinyin	Older romanization
Beijing	Peking
Chang Jiang	Yangtze Kiang or Yangtze River
Chengdu	Chengtu
Chongqing	Chungking
Datong	Tatung
Dunhuang	Tunhuang
Fuzhou	Foochow
Guangzhou	Canton
Guilin	Kweilin
Hangzhou	Hangchow
Hankou	Hankow
Huang He	Hwang Ho or Yellow River
Lanzhou	Lanchow
Nanjing	Nanking
Ningbo	Ningpo
Qingdao	Ts'ingtao
Shaoxing	Shaohsing
Tianjin	Tientsin
Turpan	Turfan
Urumqi	Urumchi
Xiamen	Amoy
Xi'an	Sian
Yan'an	Yenan

MEASURES, WEIGHTS AND CURRENCY

A *li* is roughly a third of a mile or a fifth of a kilometre.
A *mu* is a sixth of an acre or a six hundredth of a hectare.
A 'catty' is 1.1 pounds or roughly half a kilogram.
A *yuan*, here often abbreviated to Y, is the Chinese unit of currency, divisible into 100 *fen* and exchangeable for roughly £0.30 or $0.45. It will currently buy six pounds of rice or wheat flour, a dozen eggs, $\frac{1}{160}$ of a bicycle, and $\frac{1}{2000}$ of a new house in a village.

PREFACE

Some time in 1980, several people had the idea of making a film series about China, on a scale that would in some way reflect that of the subject. This book was planned to accompany such a series.

At the time there were signs of a new openness on the part of the Chinese Government to impartial scrutiny of their country. It coincided with a new climate in British television in which several producers were leaving the large organizations and seeking finance from new sources to continue the tradition of documentary film series. Peter Montagnon, who, in the BBC, had produced *Civilisation* with Michael Gill and *The Long Search*, and between the two had been the first head of television and radio at the Open University, was approached by Nigel Houghton, a former BBC colleague, and Patrick Lui, an independent film producer in Hong Kong, who had already had long discussions about filming with the Chinese authorities. The author of this book, Peter Montagnon's partner, got in touch with Stephen Keynes, a merchant banker, who raised the not inconsiderable cost of the series, four million pounds, in the City of London. The team of producers and directors was completed by Mischa Scorer, who, among much documentary filming, had worked with Peter Montagnon on *The Long Search*, and David Kennard, who had worked with the author of this book on earlier programmes and subsequently on *The Ascent of Man, The Age of Uncertainty, Connections* and *Cosmos*. The team was supported by Dr Hugh Baker and other leading sinologists.

Two and a half years later, besides the series of edited programmes, there are some two hundred hours of film shot on location in China. The book draws on all the resources and research that went into the making of the films, and also on the insights that came through the work of the directors and the patience and skill of the camera crews and the film editors.

It was the feeling of those who worked on the project that, despite the old tags about their inscrutability, the Chinese are not difficult to understand, even though there remain areas of mystery and of reserve in them, as in other peoples. The main difficulty in portraying Chinese life is the variety within the vastness of the canvas. Here, as in the films, it has been divided according to different aspects of everyday life, such as eating, working and believing, with the present and the past of each considered together. It is to be hoped that the series and the book will do something to dispel myths, and to make Chinese civilization – the only surviving civilization to have grown up and flourished until recently in independence of the West – better understood among some of the three quarters of the people in the world who are not Chinese.

Alasdair Clayre

THE HEART OF THE DRAGON

REMEMBERING

迴
顧

EMPERORS AND REBELS

When the emperor of China received Lord Macartney, there were difficulties. Lord Macartney did not want to kowtow. A gentleman in knee breeches – it was 1793 – representing George III and with somewhat stiff joints, has several reasons for remaining upright. The emperor, on his part, was not impressed by the English court's presents, which included six hundred cases of scientific instruments. However he told Lord Macartney to reassure his sovereign. He would accept the gifts, though actually there was nothing he needed; and if the king of England continued to be as civil as he was evidently attempting to be, he need fear nothing: the emperor would consider his country a loyal tributary state of the Chinese empire, and would do nothing whatever to harm him.

For the Chinese, the emperor of China ruled the world; his power was over *tian xia*, 'everything under heaven'. Imperial dynasties stretched back through all known time. The first great men, who had given the world fire, agriculture and writing, were early emperors of China.

The Chinese have the oldest continuous civilization in the world – going back some four thousand years – and also the oldest centralized state, which has survived, with interruptions, since 221 BC. They also have far and away the largest population of any country in the world: more than a thousand million. It is as if the whole of eastern and western Europe, together with parts of Africa and the Near East, had been reunited under the rule of the Roman Empire, with all official business conducted in Latin, and the only major change a shift in the capital to somewhere near the Russian frontier, for much the same reason as Beijing is on the frontiers of Russia in north-east Asia: to face the great land mass with its millions of potential invaders.

China has traditionally attracted invaders. It has been the treasure house, the workshop and the garden of Asia, full of rich pickings for nomad horsemen. The Chinese called the northern tribes who harassed them in early centuries the Xiongnu, and described them as wearing animal skins, drinking blood out of their enemies' skulls and marrying all their father's wives except their own mother on their father's death. Genghis Khan and his Mongols, who conquered China in the thirteenth century from the north, are still remembered with hatred. But the Manchus, who did the same in the seventeenth century and ruled until 1911, adopted Chinese customs, and the period when Macartney visited China, with the Qianlong emperor on the

Chinese tourists contemplate gigantic memorials of their past,
Buddhist sculptures in the Longmen caves in central China.

throne, is one to which many Chinese look back as a golden age. He had been ruling since 1735. China's frontiers were wider in his time than they have ever been; he and his grandfather, the Kangxi emperor, had almost tripled the size of their empire to more than four million square miles. The population was already 310 million, more than twice that of Europe including Russia. The country's wealth was legendary: everyday products in China were luxuries elsewhere. But the Chinese did not welcome the traders who tried to penetrate their country. They were self-sufficient. As an act of compassion, so they felt, they allowed out a little of their silk and tea, and accepted a few trinkets in return from the barbarians who sailed into their waters; but they kept them firmly limited to two ports in the far south; all others were barred to them.

Neither the superiority of the Chinese in so many respects nor their sense of superiority in all respects was lost on Lord Macartney. The emperor, he noted, had a personal income of £10,000,000 a year, and it was disconcerting

The Forbidden City, the imperial palace in Beijing (Peking), was built in the Ming Dynasty by the Yongle emperor (1403-24). Though designed on a massive scale, it follows the same plan as many traditional houses in China, where rooms for married sons, concubines and servants, gradually added to the central building, have been closed off to form courtyards. This picture shows the central courtyard with the Hall of Supreme Harmony, where the emperor gave formal audiences.

A painting entitled 'Ten thousand countries coming to pay tribute to the Qianlong emperor' gives a bird's eye view of the splendours of the Qing (Manchu) imperial court at Peking. Crowds of envoys await the arrival of the emperor.

Eighty per cent of China's people are farmers, yet less than 30 per cent of China's land is suitable for agriculture. Most of it is either too dry or too mountainous. In Shanxi Province over the centuries peasants have constructed terraces to increase the area of productive land and to prevent erosion of the fine soil.

to discover that he already possessed clocks and other Western wonders more remarkable than those Macartney had expected to dazzle him with, yet regarded his own and Macartney's alike as worthless, and wrote a poem, or commissioned one from a civil servant, to say so. His income, Macartney calculated, amounted to two thirds of the entire revenues of Great Britain; while those of the Chinese state were four times Britain's. Macartney, propelled to China by trade winds and representing the nation of shopkeepers, had come to propose that the Chinese should open their ports to trade and accept a British ambassador to oversee it at Peking. Both requests were refused, and he was sent back via Guangzhou (Canton), a journey of some three months overland, first across the vast North China Plain, then through the rice-growing valley of the Yangtze to the tropical heat of the far south, over twelve hundred miles of the emperor of China's territory. Even so, he had seen only a fraction of it.

For more than two thousand years successive Chinese empires had kept a kind of peace and civility over a vast area of eastern Asia. It is an area where, as time has gone by, every patch of land that can grow food has been cultivated, where every scrap of food has been used to nourish the maximum number of people the land can sustain, and where nothing has been wasted that could feed a pig, whose dung, mixed with human night soil, still fertilizes the land in an immemorial cycle.

Although some of China's cities may have had a million inhabitants as early as the Tang Dynasty (618-906), the country has always been mainly agricultural. Eighty per cent of the people live on the land today and the overwhelming proportion of their time is spent in growing food. Even the biggest cities have until recently been like sprawling conglomerations of villages, with single-storey houses and often with fields within their walls. They have never developed into independent city states.

Yet this centralized empire of villages was and is one of extraordinary diversity. The supposed uniformity of China and its apparent historic changelessness are both Western myths. Anything that is not looked at closely may seem featureless and unchanging. China has never been either. One historical period has been different from another, northerners are different from southerners, the majority, who call themselves the Han, contrast with thirty million members of the fifty-five 'national minorities' in China, and within each group individual character is as varied as anywhere in the world. Things hold together because of the closeness of ties within small groups of people, particularly families, and because of the overriding power of the centralized state, with its bureaucracy and its single written language.

Although the spoken language of China sounds so different in different parts of the country that a Cantonese cannot understand the speech of someone from Shanghai or Beijing, every member of the ruling bureaucracy throughout the length and breadth of China has used a single written language for two thousand years; and the script itself, though it has evolved, is continuous with the oldest known writing in China, found on the ancient 'oracle bones' which date back to the fourteenth century BC.

The language uses a unique ideographic script. Like much else in China it developed independently of other civilizations, though the Egyptians had writing earlier. In Chinese script every object and action has a separate picture; abstract ideas are built up mainly by combining concrete ones; there are almost no grammatical inflections; and every written character, like every court attendant on his separate flagstone in the imperial palace and every soldier of the imperial army on parade, occupies the same square space as every other character. To read a newspaper a Chinese needs to know about two thousand five hundred characters; six thousand would constitute a rich vocabulary; there may be fifty thousand in a comprehensive dictionary.

The China that this written language has held together is defined by two great rivers: the Yellow River and the Yangtze. From the Yangtze valley south is the China that Westerners often imagine to be the whole country: the land of paddy fields, water buffalo, tea, sub-tropical and tropical heat, people in shallow conical hats weeding by hand while standing up to their ankles in water, or carrying a pole that balances a pair of buckets between the shade of one bamboo and another. South China is the land of rice, of lakes and rivers and people who live by water. A thirteenth-century poet has left a beautiful pair of contrasting images for the boats of northern China and of the lower Yangtze valley (Wu): 'The boats of the Yellow River are like slices of cut melon,' and 'The boats of the Wu are oval, like turtles with tucked-in heads.' The northern craft are slender and shallow, built to carry light loads for short journeys on a river that may sometimes flow at great speed and at other times may be almost dry. The broad-beamed ships of the Yangtze, carrying heavy cargoes over many miles, are sturdier and function as homes for families who may spend most of their lives afloat. A northerner wrote of them in the

(Following page)
Villages and farmland surround the city of Guilin in the southern province of Guangxi. It is only in the last thousand years that the bulk of China's population has lived in the rice-growing areas of the south. The beginnings of Chinese civilization were in the north, in the valley of the Yellow River.

5

ninth century, 'Sailing along the creeks and waterways is their equivalent of cultivating vegetable gardens,' while another observed a little later, 'Almost half the people live by fishing . . . Their fields are, so to speak, the middle of the lakes.'

Many other things have bemused the northerners about their southern neighbours: they find them quick-tempered, noisy, volatile, devious and given to frivolous pleasures. To southerners, northerners are sturdy, dour, slow, tenacious, straightforward and devoted to garlic. The 'cradle of Chinese civilization' was in the north. The extreme south, Guangdong and its neighbouring provinces, was not fully integrated into the Chinese empire until Tang times (618-906), and it is only in the last thousand years that the bulk of China's food production and population has shifted to the rice-growing south, especially the Yangtze valley.

The north, which the Yellow River gives life and often death to, is a land of millet and wheat, of draught animals, of dusty farmlands petering out into desert to the west and pasturelands to the north. It depends on the rainfall that south China has not already taken from the Pacific winds, which blow all summer towards the more rapidly heated land mass of central Asia. Very often this rainfall fails; and in winter, when the sea cools more slowly, the winds blow from Russia across the dusty plateaus of central north-west China, carrying fine yellow dust, but no rain. The notorious Peking throat, and the spittoons that adorn even the most formal of Chinese official occasions, are the result of the dust in the northern air. The Yellow River and the Yellow Sea are named for the dust that travels by water. The dust that has settled lies over the north-western provinces of China on average a hundred and sometimes a thousand feet thick.

North China is a land where drought and flood are common. Everything depends on the vagaries of the Yellow River, 'the Sorrow of China'. In high summer, if the rains have been heavy, it can burst its banks, which in the eastern plains of China are levees like those of the Mississippi. In some places the river flows on a bed that is twelve feet above the surrounding countryside. The city walls, thirty feet high and built of brick and tamped earth, have been barriers against flood waters as well as against enemies. In such conditions of flood and drought, alternating with rich harvests of millet and wheat, the peasants of the central plains developed those qualities of resourcefulness, frugality, regular labour and cohesion which were necessary to survival. The cohesion has not been spontaneous. Everywhere the power of the centralized state has been visible, mustering, cajoling and regimenting the people into orderly groups with collective responsibility, obliging them to deliver taxes or forced labour, and requiring unquestioning obedience to its officials.

For besides their more spectacular 'four inventions', gunpowder, printing, paper and the magnetic compass, all of which in their time have changed the rest of the world, the Chinese have had another discovery in reserve to transform it again after twenty centuries of their own experience: universal bureaucracy. For better or for worse, it was they who first

conceived the idea of a civil service staffed by literary scholar-officials. Those men (they were all men) who succeeded in the highly competitive examinations that came in time to be the only means of access to government posts, had to have fine, regular handwriting, a detailed knowledge of an established body of classical texts and an ability to write prose and poetry that contained elegant echoes of the past. Their advancement consisted of promotion through an intricate set of grades and orders of rank. There was no equally desirable career open to an educated man. Thus they had imbued in them a deep reverence for what had been written by their predecessors, a strong sense of hierarchy and a passionate tenacity in the retention of their jobs and the preservation of their investment in all this learning, useless materially speaking without the imperial structure which rewarded it.

The ideal scholarly virtues were defined in the sixth century BC by Confucius, the great sage of China. They included benevolence, gentleness and loyalty. These qualities were expected to maintain harmony and order and thus keep society together without the undue exercise of force, by swaying the hearts of the common people, 'making them bend', as Confucius put it, 'like grass before the wind'. However, in case these gentler means failed, the officials had others in reserve. Until the judicial use of torture was abolished in the early twentieth century, one of these delicate scholars, suspecting a man of crime, might have him beaten, or his fingers or ankle-bones crushed, as a mere preliminary to asking him a few questions about his activities on the night of the 25th.

The sanctions the rulers used in their harsher dealings with the common people derived from a rival tradition of government to that of Confucius: Legalism. This doctrine, which was based on a belief in strict laws and rigorous punishments, was adopted fully by the state that unified the empire in 221 BC and gave the West the name China: Qin (Ch'in). The contrast between the legacies of Confucianism and Legalism is not a matter of ancient history only: it is vividly alive in the present, in the most recent and terrible memories of the Chinese people, and in the speeches and actions of Mao Zedong (Mao Tse-tung), who compared himself to the man whose cruelty and vast power are proverbial even today: to Qin Shihuangdi, the first emperor to unite China.

Qin Shihuangdi had been a great warrior: 'Cracking his long whip, he drove the universe before him, swallowing up the eastern and western Zhou and overthrowing the feudal lords. He ascended to the highest position and ruled the six directions, scourging the world with his rod, and his might shook the four seas.'* He had thought nothing, so later historians wrote, of sending hundreds of thousands of labourers to their deaths linking the northern defences of the empire into a 'Great Wall'. The suffering of his people was proverbial, but the emperor was striving for something unprecedented. He 'believed in his heart that with the strength of his capital within the Pass and his walls of metal extending a thousand miles, he had established a rule that would be enjoyed by his descendants for ten thousand generations'. *

Qin Shihuangdi, the 'First Qin Emperor' (221-210 BC), founded the dynasty which unified the country and gave China its name in Western languages. He is infamous in Chinese history and legend for the suppression of schools of philosophy which he thought subversive. Here the emperor is depicted watching as the literature of earlier periods is burned and scholars are thrown into a pit to be buried alive.

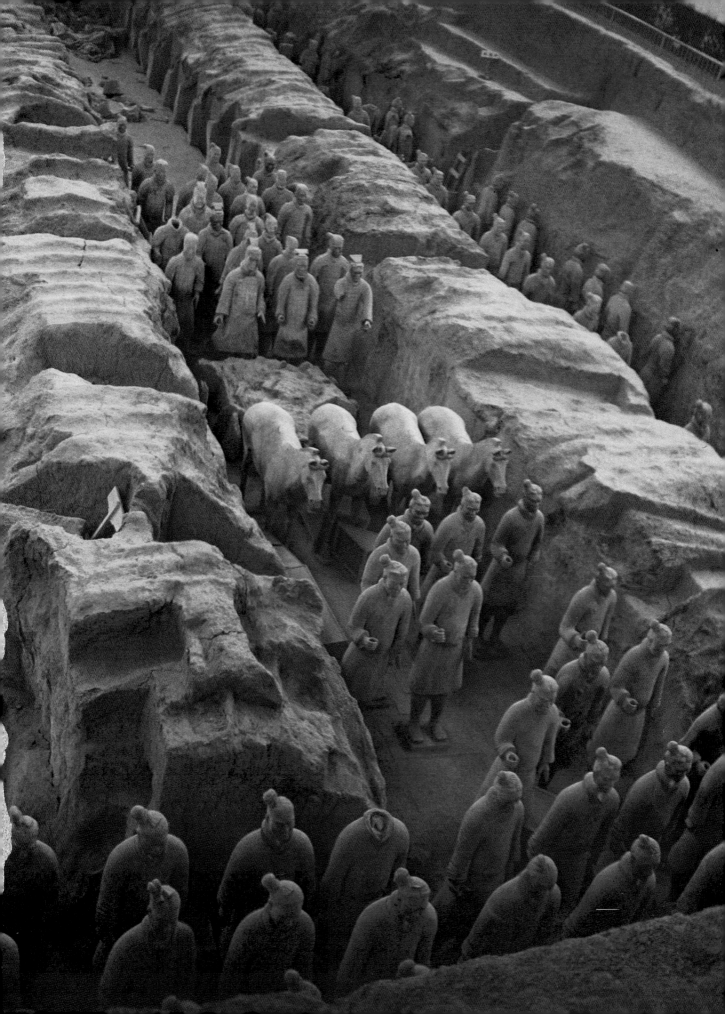

Under the Qin emperor, the whole of China was conquered and united into a centralized state. Qin Shihuangdi encouraged the mass-production of iron farming tools, made the axles of carts all the same width, made roads radiate from the Qin capital near modern Xi'an (Sian), deposed nobles and destroyed the ancient field system of landholding, giving land directly to peasants who were themselves taxed by the emperor. He unified the laws and imposed savage penalties. Mutilations, brandings, the chopping off of hands or feet, castrations, strangulations and decapitations multiplied. There was no other authority than Qin Shihuangdi's law.

The emperor's power was manifested in great construction projects, among them the building of the imperial tomb. Work on this proceeded for many years. It covered a vast area of countryside, was filled with an army of amazingly sculpted terra cotta soldiers, and was said to contain a map of China with moving rivers of mercury in its floor and a map of heaven with all the known stars in its ceiling. Crossbows were set to shoot automatically at tomb robbers; and the artisans who knew these secrets were walled up when the tomb was closed, as were all Qin Shihuangdi's many concubines.

Ironically, this man, whose tomb had cost so many lives, himself died in grotesque circumstances. It is said that his chief of chariots, Zhao Gao, conspired with his prime minister, Li Si, to conceal his death while they arranged the succession: in his name they issued proclamations and letters calling for the suicide of their rivals, passing them through the curtains of a litter to the corpse, and buying a cargo of fish to heap alongside it because, after two months in the summer heat, the smell left something to be desired.

The Qin empire had been built to last ten thousand generations; it lasted fourteen years. The conquerors who founded the next dynasty, the Han (206 BC–AD 220), were rebels. Han Gaozu, the first emperor of the new dynasty, was the son of a minor official. The Han rulers denounced their predecessor for his cruelties, but kept almost all his harsh laws, together with the Qin code of collective responsibility and the labour services system whereby each peasant was obliged to perform labour for the imperial state. At the same time they encouraged the Confucian tradition of humane statecraft and their reconciliation of Confucian 'humanity' with Legalist severity and central-

Chinese emperors, flanked by their attendants, portrayed in a silk scroll painting of the Tang Dynasty. The emperor Wu of the Northern Zhou Dynasty, second from right, was a strong military commander who ruled northern China. Behind him is the emperor Wen, founder of the Sui Dynasty at the end of the 6th century AD, who reunited the empire after three centuries of political turmoil.

(Previous page)
A vast terracotta army guards the grave mound of Qin Shihuangdi, the first emperor of China. The burial complex in Shaanxi Province, discovered by archaeologists in 1974, is on a fitting scale for a man who believed he had founded a dynasty that would last 10,000 generations. It fell three years after his death.

ization set the pattern for Imperial China for more than two thousand years.

The idea of a succession of imperial dynasties has given the Chinese their main framework for thinking about the past. If a Chinese is asked to date a building or a poem, he is unlikely to place it in a particular century; rather in a given dynasty, even if he is asked to think of the very distant past. Before 1911 the system of centuries revolving round the birth of Christ was almost completely alien to the Chinese. They counted in sixty-year cycles; and they dated particular years from the accession of the current emperor.

For most of the thousand years following the Qin unification China was not the closed and self-sufficient 'Middle Kingdom' of the European imagination. From the fourth to the sixth centuries a great variety of tribes – Tibetans, Turks, Mongols and Tungus – overran north China, bringing with them many influences from central Asia. The rulers of the next great dynasty, the Tang (618-906), came from near the northern borders, and China in their day was an open, even a cosmopolitan society: Chinese pilgrims and monks travelled to India, Ceylon, Sumatra and Samarkand; students and envoys came from Korea, Japan and Tibet; and traders from the Middle East visited and settled in the great cities of China. A young man on a night out eleven hundred years ago in the Tang Dynasty capital of Chang'an might have had dinner at a central Asian restaurant; the musicians might have come from Samarkand; there would perhaps have been wine from the grapes of Turpan in modern Xinjiang. If he had visited a Buddhist temple the ceremonies he took part in would have been originally Indian. If he had had eye trouble his doctor would probably have been a Persian. At the market he could have seen Iranian, Turkish, Uyghur, Indian, Korean and Arab merchants.

The emperor Taizong (626-49) was the son of the founder of the Tang Dynasty. He was a great military commander who extended Chinese influence far into central Asia, and also re-established civil order throughout China.

The Chinese seem to have become increasingly turned in on themselves and their past over the last thousand years by a loss of confidence after a succession of rebellions and foreign invasions. The loss of their north-west frontier territories in AD 755 during a great internal uprising, the An Lushan Rebellion, brought the borders within sixty miles of their capital. From then on and throughout the succeeding Song Dynasty (960-1279), the period that most Chinese regard as artistically the highest point of their civilization, parts of China were under alien rule, and they were constantly on the defensive against northern invaders. They held on to their northern capital of Kaifeng until all north China was lost and the imperial family was captured in 1126; then a new capital was established for the Southern Song Dynasty (1127-1279) at Hangzhou.

Before that flight to the south, the painter Zhang Zeduan made a painting of Kaifeng called 'Life along the River on the Eve of the Qing Ming Festival' (*Qing Ming Shang He Tu*) which, perhaps more than any other picture, records the vividness and bustle and also the profound ease of Chinese city life. It shows something of the power of markets and commerce in the life of the Song period. Though many other scenes are visible – people drinking tea in tea-houses, people giving money to beggars, someone addressing a crowd – the dominating impression is of activity in pursuit of money: cargo ships dipping their masts to pass under the city's bridges, shops and bankers' stalls, and processions of beasts of burden laden with goods.*

Many of the customs, institutions and ways of thinking that persisted into the twentieth century took shape at that time. China was then the wealthiest, most populous and luxurious society in the world: a society of many small farmers who were far better off than their contemporaries elsewhere. During the Song period the government of these huge territories was carried on in much the same way as in the Qin and the Han, with one major exception. From the third to the ninth century China had been an aristocratic society. It was now that the government began to be preponderantly staffed not by a mixture of aristocrats and their relations with a minority of examination scholars in a subordinate position, but by a professional civil service recruited almost completely through the examination system.

But neither the enormous wealth of the empire nor the sophistication of its administrators was able to prevent the overthrow of the Song Dynasty by the Mongols from the north. The Mongols who ruled China as the Yuan Dynasty (1279-1368) were ousted in their turn by a new Chinese ruling house: the Ming (1368-1644). That dynasty fell to the Manchus from the far north-east, whose dynasty was called the Qing (1644-1911). China has in fact been united under Chinese rule only for a third of the last millennium, fragmented for another third, and otherwise united under foreign rule.

In the course of successive regimes the boundaries of the Chinese world

A group of scholars, gathered to collate the best in classical literature for the education of the emperor's son. A knowledge of Confucian texts gradually became essential for anyone wishing to gain a public office. From the Tang Dynasty (618-906) onwards the government came to be staffed not by the aristocracy but largely by men appointed through examination.

were constantly moving: a single empire under the Qin, partitioned between Chinese and steppe conquerors from the fourth to sixth centuries and again in the tenth to the thirteenth centuries, part of a universal world empire under the Mongols, a truly Chinese and inward-looking state under the Ming, and then again, under the Manchus, part of a great expansionist empire. The People's Republic has generally treated the Manchu conquests as included in its natural territory and has sent its armies and its administrators into Tibet. Part of its territory is contested by the only other large empire that has survived in the modern world, the Russian, although both profess the same anti-imperialist creed.

The Manchus were great lovers of architecture and of hunting. They spent much of their summer each year at Jehol, their hunting preserve to the north of Peking. It was here that Qianlong deigned to receive Lord Macartney. In his time also the Summer Palace, the Yuan Ming Yuan, was designed by the European Jesuits. Through successive reigns they had maintained a presence at court, hoping to convert the Chinese by first converting their emperors. The rulers of China kept them as advisers and for their technological and mathematical skills; as to matters of religion, they expressed polite interest but were never 'converted'.

Although the empire reached the peak of its power in the Qianlong reign it was already being undermined in the last decades of that sixty-year period by the expense of its imperial conquests and of maintaining massive armies, by a

vast population explosion and by the all-pervading bribery and corruption. This was apparent even to an outsider like Macartney, who wrote in a letter to the East India Company, 'The Empire of China, is an old, crazy, first rate Man-of-War, which a fortunate succession of able and vigilant officers have contrived to keep afloat for these hundred and fifty years past, and to overawe their neighbours merely by her bulk and appearance.'

The scale of the problems facing any ruler wanting to control this empire was extraordinary. For example in the eighteenth century a routine order from Peking took fifty-six days to reach Guangzhou in the far south; even the fastest express courier took thirty-two days, an average speed of sixty-three miles a day. An ordinary message to Chengdu in the far west took forty-eight days, an express courier twenty-four. Even between Peking and Nanjing (Nanking), routine orders took three weeks. There was no question of immediate response by the central government to an emergency on the remote frontiers.

Since military threats in most centuries came from the north or north-west, the centre of government had generally to be in the north: in Xi'an from the third century BC to the tenth century AD or in Peking over the past five hundred years. In time this area became poorer and less productive than the south, and needed constant supplies. Thus in addition to the 15,000 courier stations that the state maintained in the eighteenth century for transmitting orders and information, there was a state-controlled transport network for transferring grain and goods. Its main artery was the Grand Canal, a successor to a canal first dug in Sui times (590-618) and again in operation today, running from north of the capital to Hangzhou in the south. In the late eighteenth century it handled over 400,000 tons of grain annually,

Under the Ming emperors (1368-1644) China enjoyed a period of relative peace and stability, but by the end of the 16th century corruption, bankruptcy and rebellion had paralysed the government. The emperor Wanli was among the most irresponsible of rulers, refusing to see his ministers or conduct affairs of state for years on end. He is pictured below seated on a royal barge returning from an expedition by river.

The Qianlong emperor (1736-95) holds court at the Summer Palace near Peking, built for him by European Jesuits. During his reign, the Qing empire expanded to 4.2 million square miles, and many Chinese look back to the period as a golden age of stability and prosperity. But the foundations of internal order were being undermined by the expense of wars of conquest abroad and by bribery and corruption, while the Western powers were already attempting to open up more of China's ports to overseas trade.

of which over a quarter of a million tons were shipped to Peking, employing more than 6000 grain ships and 75,000 boat crewmen.

The government's administrative resources were very thinly spread. The number of county magistrates never increased proportionately with the population: it remained at about 1500 for the whole of China from Tang times (618-906) for a thousand years. As the population grew, and grew unevenly, a single magistrate, who might have ruled over 5000 households in the twelfth century, could have had fifty times that number under his authority in the eighteenth.

To control one of China's counties (*xian*), even in Qing times, the magistrate would have at most half a dozen subordinate officials, a few clerks and some hundreds of 'runners', who acted as police, tax-collectors, jailers, gatekeepers and administerers of beatings and judicial torture. All were underpaid or unpaid, and local government was conducted within a complicated framework of customary fees and payments ('squeeze', as it was called by nineteenth-century foreign residents), or simple bribery, without which nothing got done. Local government survived by interfering very little, and did hardly more than collect taxes, organize labour services and maintain a basic level of law and order.

An eighteenth-century Jesuit missionary, Father D'Entrecolles, gave a graphic description of the administration of one particular city, Jingdezhen in the south-east, which had grown up round the imperial potteries:

The sight with which one is greeted on entering through one of the gorges consists of volumes of smoke and flame rising in different places, so as to define all the outlines of the town; approaching at nightfall, the scene reminds one of a burning city in flames, or of a huge furnace with vent-holes. It is surprising that such a populous place, full of such riches, and with an indefinite number of boats coming and going every day, and which has no walls that can be closed at night, should nevertheless be governed by a single mandarin, without the least disorder. It must be allowed that the policing is admirable; each street has one or more chiefs, according to its length, each chief has ten subordinates, every one of whom is responsible for ten houses. They must keep order, under pain of the bastinado, which is here administered liberally. The streets have barricades, which are closed at night, and opened by the watchman only to those who have the password. The mandarin of the place makes frequent rounds. . . Strangers are hardly permitted to sleep there; they must either spend the night in their boats or lodge with acquaintances, who become responsible for their conduct.*

With such a system of local government and self-regulation by local communities China was likened by scholars to a body that could continue to function even if the head were chopped off. In times of palace revolution or change of dynasty the machinery of administration could carry on at a very low level of routine efficiency more or less indefinitely even without central direction. But though the system was relatively efficient within its self-imposed limits, it also created great tensions in the countryside, because the officials and the gentry who controlled the villages mulcted it financially – the officials by corruption and the gentry by tax-evasion – so that they and the state could in the end be satisfied only by extracting more from the small farmers. And because the rural populace had not been sufficiently educated to eradicate their prejudice against starvation, they had a tendency to rebel, and from time to time to give their allegiance to anti-bureaucratic movements or to uprisings seeking a change of dynasty.

Popular disaffection was volatile and a source of constant apprehension to the magistrates. In the nineteenth century one of them tried to pin the matter down:

The bandits of Guangxi quickly gather into bands, then suddenly they disperse. At one moment they submit to the authority of the government, and at another moment they become outlaws again. Good people and even soldiers may turn into bandits. According to my humble estimate, two bandits in every ten are roused by their hatred towards officials, three in every ten are driven to extremity by hunger and cold, and four in every ten are forced to join a band of robbers which has captured them or driven them from their home villages. No more than one in ten has intentionally become a bandit.*

Some rebels could be as committed as the bureaucracy to a united China under the rule of an emperor with the Mandate of Heaven. When the current emperor had departed from 'The Way' – the true path of a good ruler who governed in accordance with Heaven's will – it was up to loyal subjects to replace him. Success in ousting him was evidence that Heaven had transferred its mandate. There was a popular saying, 'A man who steals a melon is a thief; a man who steals a kingdom is a king.'

Rulers of China have more than once emerged from among the ranks of popular insurgents: like the first emperor of the Han Dynasty, the first ruler of the Ming Dynasty was a rebel. Once in power, they and their successors were tamed and mellowed by the eternal verities and age-old scepticism of their civil servants and their courts. 'One can conquer an empire from the saddle,' the officials would tell the new emperor, 'but one cannot rule it from the saddle'.

Some rebellious movements had a religious basis. Peasants whose allegiance had been unsettled by floods, droughts and famines often interpreted these disasters as signs of a forthcoming cosmic cataclysm. Some rebels expected merely a new dynasty; others looked for a new world in which there would be no more suffering, everyone would have plenty to eat, and there would be no labour to be done in the fields. Popular religions, frowned on by the Confucian officials, often predicted such events. During a comparatively small uprising in 1813 the Eight Trigrams sect, who were expecting the end of the world, attacked the Forbidden City, the imperial

After the Opium War of 1840-2, the Qing Dynasty was shaken by a succession of internal disturbances and uprisings. The Taiping Rebellion, which broke out in 1850, was the most threatening; its leaders succeeded in establishing a separate state centred on Nanjing, which lasted for ten years. Twenty million people were killed before it was crushed. In the painting above, Chinese troops loyal to the Qing Dynasty put the rebels to flight.

A Japanese print illustrates in lurid colours the sinking of a Chinese ship during the Battle of the Yalu River, in the Sino-Japanese War of 1894, which broke out over rival territorial claims in Korea. China suffered humiliating losses on land and sea, and was forced to sign a treaty acknowledging Korea's independence. Later Korea was annexed by Japan.

palace in Peking, and planned to kill the emperor as he returned from hunting.* A number of them got inside the palace walls and ran about with knives, killing anyone they could see, before they were defeated by the eunuchs and by the crown prince, who shot at them with a sporting gun.

The leaders of the Eight Trigrams had designated each other King of Heaven, King of Earth and King of Men, in accordance with the traditional Chinese sense of the place of man in between these two extremes. They carried banners marked 'Entrusted by Heaven to Prepare the Way', strikingly like those carried by the fictional rebels in the great Ming popular novel, *The Water Margin*, (one of Mao Zedong's favourite books), 'Carry Out the Way on Behalf of Heaven'. Like the *Water Margin* heroes they saw themselves as loyal in a world where the emperor had gone astray. When Mao Zedong pronounced that 'to rebel is justified' he was thus not saying something new to the Chinese.

The most formidable of all popular rebellions was the Taiping Heavenly Kingdom, a movement that took some elements from Christianity and established a state within China. The movement's leader claimed to be a younger brother of Jesus Christ. It controlled some of the richest and most important parts of the empire, starting round Guangzhou and holding the city of Nanjing from 1853 to 1864. The presence of Christian elements in the beliefs of the Taiping rebels is evidence that European influence had already penetrated south China.

Although Macartney and his successors had failed as ambassadors, the British had won by superior military force, in the Opium War (1840-2) and at the Treaty of Nanjing (1842), what the emperors would not concede to diplomacy: the opening to British traders of ports other than Guangzhou. The effect of the treaty on Guangzhou was devastating. Two thirds of its export trade in tea vanished between 1845 and 1858. The unemployed boatmen and carriers in its hinterland were among the main recruits for the Taiping rebel armies.* Meanwhile Shanghai's tea trade increased thirteen-fold, beginning to transform this small and sleepy port into China's greatest city.

With the Taipings and other rebels still threatening them, the Qing government became involved in other confrontations with the Western powers in 1856, and in 1860 an Anglo-French expedition of seventeen thousand troops with more than a hundred ships routed the Chinese forces. The emperor fled to Jehol in the north, where Macartney had once been received. In the course of the hostilities the Chinese seized and executed some twenty soldiers from the party of the chief British negotiator, who were under a flag of truce. Lord Elgin, in command of the British forces, ordered in retaliation that the Summer Palace should be burned.

The Russians were meanwhile moving into the periphery of the Qing empire in Central Asia and Manchuria. Each such encroachment brought more deeply home to the Chinese the need to 'learn the superior technology of the barbarians in order to control them'. In the 1860s a movement began that was known as 'Self-Strengthening'. A new department was set up in the

Qing administration to deal with foreign affairs and to co-ordinate efforts to acquire foreign knowledge. It began half-heartedly to develop shipyards and arsenals, and to introduce modern military training to deal with the new threats.

But another challenge now arose, unexpectedly close at hand. Chinese and Japanese confrontation in Korea led to war. On the morning of 17 September 1894 a Japanese navy steamed towards the Chinese fleet off the Yalu River to settle the dispute. The Chinese had two modern battleships, each equipped with four twelve-inch Krupp guns, as well as other vessels on paper superior to their opponents, and they had British and German advisers. Until now they had generally considered Japan a nation of inferiors. However the Japanese ships turned out to be faster, and far more ably commanded. Sweeping twice across the Chinese line, by the late afternoon of a single day the Japanese had sunk five of the Chinese ships. The rest limped home to Weihaiwei, where they were dispatched by Japanese torpedo boats in February of the following year. The Chinese admiral committed suicide. In the land war the Chinese army fared even worse. This double defeat shocked the court into reform.

The young emperor Guangxu co-operated with several radical thinkers and in 1898 began what is called the 'Hundred Days' Reform'. 'More than forty reforming edicts were issued, and they dealt with almost every conceivable subject: setting up modern schools and remaking the examination system; revising the laws. . .; promoting agriculture, medicine, mining, commerce, inventions and study abroad; and modernizing the army, navy, police and postal systems.'* Earlier measures had built round existing institutions. This was a far more radical change than anything hitherto attempted. But the real power in Peking lay with the empress dowager, Cixi. She adamantly opposed all reform. The emperor had come to the throne as an infant, and she still dominated him. Now she staged a coup d'état and the emperor was imprisoned within the palace.

The attempt to deal with the empire's crisis after the coup d'état passed increasingly into the hands of xenophobic mobs incited by secret societies. The West called them 'Boxers' because of the public displays of Chinese boxing that they used to recruit members. Some of them believed that they could render themselves magically invulnerable to bullets. Bands of Boxers killed Chinese Christians and burned missionary establishments. The Western powers called on the government to suppress them, but the empress dowager, having deflected their xenophobia away from the Manchus, supported the Boxers. They finally besieged the foreign legation quarters in Peking and Tianjin (Tientsin), intent on killing all inside. In June 1900 the Western powers landed a powerful force and raised the sieges. Once again the Qing empire was humiliated, and had foreign armies on its soil. The emperor died mysteriously in 1908, one day before the dowager empress herself.

Increasingly the Chinese spoke of a double calamity that threatened them: 'loss of the state and extinction of the race' (*wangguo miezhong*).*

A cartoon in a French journal shows figures representing Britain, Germany, Russia, France and Japan poised to carve up the 'cake' of China. By 1898, the year this cartoon was published, 13 of China's 18 provinces had been declared foreign 'spheres of influence'. Chinese hatred of foreigners led to a popular uprising, the Boxer Rebellion, in 1900.

大清當今慈禧端佑康頤昭豫莊誠壽恭欽獻崇熙聖母皇太后

The empress dowager Cixi was the power behind the throne from 1861 till her death in 1908. An
intensely conservative and xenophobic woman, she blocked all plans for reform. Three years after
she died revolution broke out and the last of the Qing emperors, a boy of six, was forced to abdicate.

Anti-dynastic agitation now took on a new momentum. Followers of the Western-educated Sun Yat-sen (1866-1925) grew more influential, and a series of abortive uprisings took place in the south. Finally, in 1911, a military rising in Wuchang succeeded and spread. The stongest military commander, Yuan Shikai, was watching his chances. The Manchu court tried to persuade him to crush the rebellion; instead he used the opportunity to force the Manchus themselves to abdicate. Sun Yat-sen, who was the provisional president, in exchange for a truce with his military rival, ceded him the presidency of the new Republic of China.

The Chinese look back to 1911 as the date of the first successful revolution against the imperial regime. At the time, however, the year was an anti-climax. The imperial dynasty had abdicated. Tibet and Mongolia had asserted their independence. But in China itself the old order continued much as before. In one small village in Shandong, when a boy tried to make the elders cut their pigtails (originally imposed by the Manchus as a sign of submission), they refused, saying, 'We are men of Qing.' It was not long before Yuan Shikai tried to have himself made emperor rather than president.

But the Japanese had already set out to overthrow him because of his resistance to their increasingly insistent demands. When the European powers became embroiled in the First World War, Yuan Shikai told the American minister, 'The Japanese intend to use this war to take control of China.'* A Japanese switch to the German side could have been disastrous for the Allies, particularly for the British with their empire in the East. The Allied powers bought off this threat by promising to endow Japan with Germany's territories in China after the war. Japan meanwhile presented Yuan Shikai with a series of demands amounting to a Japanese protectorate over China. When Yuan resisted, they engineered his downfall. He died soon afterwards. In 1919 the Versailles Peace Congress fulfilled the earlier commitment and ceded the German territories in Shandong to Japan. This act precipitated the so-called 'May the 4th Movement' which marks the beginning of a phenomenon of great subsequent significance: self-conscious Chinese nationalism.

Yuan's generals could not agree on a successor after his death. They fought to defeat each other and gain control of the country. For nearly a decade there was 'warlord' rule. Not until 1927 did a new potential overlord of all China emerge in Chiang Kai-shek. In the political alignments of the 1920s, Chiang was seen as a man of the left. He came to power at the head of Sun Yat-sen's Nationalist Party, the Guomindang (Kuomintang). His war against the rival generals might not have succeeded but for material aid and weapons from the Soviet Union, and but for the advice of professional revolutionaries sent to China by the Comintern. The Soviet Union was eager to cause diversions on the fringes of the European empires in the Far East as a way of taking pressure off itself. The small Chinese Communist Party was ordered to join the Guomindang. Sun Yat-sen's optimistic programme was exceptionally broad and not in open conflict with the still nebulous goals of the Russian

Sun Yat-sen, photographed in 1915 with his wife, Song Qingling (Sung Ch'ing-ling), was the founder of the Guomindang (Kuomintang), the Chinese Nationalist Party, and the provisional president of the Republic of China when it was first founded.

Chiang Kai-shek succeeded Sun Yat-sen as leader of the Guomindang and brought some unity to China in the late 1920s after a decade of civil war.

Communist Party. The Chinese communists hoped to take advantage of the Guomindang's size and prestige. The Guomindang meanwhile tolerated them as the price of Russian support. Eventually one was bound to attack the other. Chiang struck first. Having used the communists in the conquest of the north in 1926 he turned on them in the following year, and in a swift series of raids and murders in Shanghai eliminated most of them.

Some of the survivors fled to rural hideouts from which they continued to threaten Chiang. For a time they held part of the province of Jiangxi, where the political commissar of the Red Army was Mao, then believed by his opponents to be a 'fanatical young man of thirty-five suffering from an incurable disease'.* In 1934, driven from the south, they made the famous 'Long March' to Yan'an (Yenan), a remote and poor area in north-west China. By 1936 Mao Zedong had emerged as their unquestioned leader and persuasive spokesman.

Mao was born in 1893 in Shaoshan, Hunan. He grew up in a rich peasant family but left the land in search of education, and became a teacher. He was among the founders of the Chinese Communist Party in 1921, though at the time he was not considered a particularly important member, and he was one of those who took to the hills in 1927: in the inaccessible border region between Jiangxi and Hunan he began to build an army by allying himself with two bandit chiefs and seeking to re-educate their men. He believed from the start that any human being could be remoulded into revolutionary material.

Mao studied the writings of Marx, Lenin and Stalin, and wrote painstaking theoretical and polemical works of his own. But his career was made not in the industrial cities where communism taught that revolutions began, but in the countryside, where traditional popular rebellions had

Communist troops evacuated their bases in Jiangxi Province in 1934 to march to Yan'an in Shaanxi Province in the north. The Long March, as it became known, is commemorated in this painting entitled 'Red Army over Snowy Mountain'.

started. He was never a member of the Westernized university elite: he knew no foreign languages and had no direct knowledge of the world outside China. But he had more knowledge of China's popular culture than many of his contemporaries and more sympathy with it. He understood organization and the uses of coercion and terror. He also knew how to discipline his troops to live with the peasants rather than, in the traditional manner, to live off them, and in Yan'an he was able to create a firm base with a largely self-supporting army.

Chiang Kai-shek once said, 'Communists are heart disease, Japanese are only skin disease.' But the skin now began to cause him more trouble. Since the beginning of the century one of the most important sources of contention between China and Japan had been Manchuria, the land from which the Qing emperors had originated, now growing into a rich industrial area. After 1919 the Japanese established an armed presence there. In 1932 they created a Manchurian state, ruled by the Qing ex-emperor Puyi, and from this base occupied much of north China. Chiang was urged to fight the Japanese by his rivals, but he calculated that he could not dislodge them, and lost much prestige by biding his time. In 1937 Japan unleashed a huge army, and within a year occupied most of north and east China.

The Nationalist government withdrew far inland to Sichuan (Szechuan), where, unable to defeat the Japanese, it continued to defy them. More than two million Chinese soldiers were killed or wounded on the battle fronts in central China. The government survived, gaining support from the West after Japan's entry into the Second World War; but corruption, ill-treatment of recruits, malnutrition among the soldiers and administrative chaos were the overwhelming impressions of the foreign community in Chongqing (Chungking), the wartime capital.

Mao Zedong's communists spent the war in Yan'an. Many Chinese students and some influential foreigners made their way there, and their vivid accounts of the austerity and self-discipline apparent in the communist army did much to increase Mao's reputation. During the eight years of war the communists extended their power over the strategic north-west of China. When the war ended unexpectedly in 1945 with the dropping of the first atomic bombs, the Nationalists were unable to restore their prewar control. Chiang Kai-shek made disastrous military mistakes. In a series of dramatic and well-organized campaigns Mao and his generals occupied the north-east, then swept into central China, and in 1949 defeated the exhausted and divided Nationalists, who retreated to Taiwan.

In the first years after his victory Mao followed Russian models closely. By 1958 the Communist government seemed to have accomplished much. Progress was being made with education; a subsistence level of nourishment was being restored in the countryside; and in the capital a Chinese state planning apparatus was at work, based on Russian experience and under Russian tutelage. It had produced one quite successful Five Year Plan in 1953 and was preparing another. Perhaps Mao was dissatisfied: there was not much of a role for him among the statisticians and economists. And there

The young Mao Zedong (Mao Tse-tung) addresses a meeting in 1938 in the city of Yan'an in Shaanxi Province where the Communist Party consolidated its power. After the defeat of Japan in 1945 Yan'an became the communist headquarters in the Civil War against the Nationalist government.

During the Cultural Revolution, many young people from the cities were sent to the countryside to work on the land.

were growing disagreements with Russia. The new leader, Khrushchev, was cautious about international relations; Mao's 'adventurist' ideas alarmed him. He was also two years younger than Mao, yet claimed the same seniority as Stalin, whom Mao had criticized yet respected.

In 1958, defying Russia, Mao launched a new economic policy. A continuation of the Russian-style plan at the expense of the peasants' living standards would have required the building of a massive industrial base before anything resembling communization could be attempted. Mao did not want to wait. He was not impressed by the results of such policies in Russia. And he felt his power and importance slowly slipping away into the hands of his colleagues and his central planners. Decentralized investment in agriculture itself and in rural light industry could allow the peasants to generate their own spending-power, a route to rural prosperity then being advocated by many economists, which has since become orthodox policy in China. But Mao's attempt to impose it rapidly in 1958 – the 'Great Leap Forward' – was a catastrophe, and this is what is most remembered today.

In the three years that followed the Great Leap, in addition to the direct effects of government policies, a terrible drought caused the worst disaster in the Chinese countryside since the famine of 1879. The death toll was of the same order as that suffered by China in the war with Japan: it has been admitted that some twenty million people perished.* In 1958 the peasants were given orders by officials and Party members equipped with slogans and precepts out of manuals of intensive cultivation, which, having proved successful in different conditions elsewhere, were introduced by fiat in the Chinese countryside. They supplanted the peasants' ancient and time-tested methods.

The slogans of the 'cadres' (as officials, managers and Party members are collectively called) show pathetic evidence of bureaucracy painfully trying to explain things to supposedly less sophisticated minds. Rice was to be planted close: the slogan might be a 'a sky full of stars'; the rows were to be set together in pairs: 'a pair of dragons setting out to sea'; each row closely spaced: 'ants starting to move'.* The peasants, already deprived of their individual land, were forced to work in collective in fields they did not know or personally care for. The results were catastrophic: plants failed to survive, or grew tall and spindly but bore little grain. Meanwhile propaganda had led the peasants to believe that hunger was a thing of the past. They were ordered into collective eating halls, where the watchword might be, 'Eat until the skin of your belly is tight.'* The seedcorn for future harvests was consumed. Some peasants melted down their family cooking pots to feed miniature steel furnaces they had been encouraged to build in their back yards, producing mostly useless scrap metal which clogged up the transport system. Equally disastrous policies were introduced in heavy industry. This was the era of wild slogans such as 'Overtake Britain in Fifteen Years'*, and bitter disillusionment. The policies of the 'Leap' were abandoned in 1959; but starvation and suffering continued.

Mao Zedong at once signalled a counter-attack on the experts and officials who now criticized him, by comparing himself to the emperor who first unified China, Qin Shihuangdi. In 1958 he made a particularly pointed reference to the first Qin emperor: 'Qin Shihuangdi did not amount to much. He buried only 460 scholars. We buried 46,000 of them.'* In July 1959, looking back on the disasters of the Great Leap, he made a speech half confessing his mistakes and half defying his colleagues to topple him, invoking the memories of the same man. Admitting, 'I am absolutely no good at construction and do not understand industrial planning,' he minimized his faults. 'The rightists say: "What made the first Qin emperor fall? Because he built the Great Wall." . . . Gentlemen . . . the divine continent is not going to sink and the sky is not going to fall . . . It is merely that for a period vegetables and hairclips have been in short supply . . . Everybody has his shortcomings. Even Confucius.'*

His opponents had been quoting against him an ancient saying, 'He who first made clay images of human beings to bury with the dead should have no posterity.' The phrase came from the Confucian tradition, which had always made the welfare of the people the main aim of the ruler. Confucius believed that the custom of burying pottery figures in a ruler's tomb had led to human sacrifice. The last phrase of the dialogue from which the quotation is taken

asks, 'What shall be thought of him who causes his people to die of hunger?'
Far from creating a new society Mao seemed, even to himself then, to have
committed the worst of crimes in the tradition of Chinese government. And
he had suffered a strangely traditional penalty: though he had married four
times, he was literally without posterity. One son had been killed in the
Korean war; the other was mad and would never marry.

*At a demonstration in Beijing's
Tiananmen Square in 1966, soon
after the beginning of the Cultural
Revolution, thousands of young
Chinese brandish the Little Red
Book of Mao's sayings and scream
slogans in his honour.*

Members of the Party whose policies are today the accepted orthodoxy in Beijing undertook to repair as much of the damage as possible. Liu Shaoqi in particular presided over the gradual reconstruction of the economy, the restoration of peasant agriculture and the return to regular education and administration. Just as the steady policies of the Five Year Plan had posed a threat to Mao, so too did those of the 1960s. But now the pattern of Mao's attempted response changed. In the 1950s he had used the Party and the organs of coercion to force people to adopt his policies: now he sought to use the people, and particularly the young, against the government and Party he felt had hemmed him in. This was the genesis of the Cultural Revolution, the better remembered of Mao's two great gambles: better remembered at least in part because intellectuals and high officials, rather than anonymous peasants, were its chief victims.

Mao Zedong started the Cultural Revolution in 1966, as an attack on bureaucracy and on the separation of intellectuals and cadres from the hardships of peasant work, and also as a means of deposing rivals like Liu Shaoqi. In place after place, the actors in local disputes and struggles put on the uniforms of Red Guard groups and fought their battles: battles which, while understood by the participants, were baffling to outsiders – even to other Chinese – who did not understand the local patterns of loyalty and inherited feuds. The Cultural Revolution rapidly became a reign of terror. Children who had earlier been encouraged to respect their elders and their teachers, and villagers who, after the first settling of scores in the 1950s had been restricted in the main to 'correcting the errors' of their earlier 'expropriators', were now required to denounce, strike, maim and in many cases kill their opponents for displaying traces of 'elitist' skill and knowledge (so surgeons would be sent to work cabbage patches); or of reverence for traditional culture (so books were burned); or of love of ancient art (sculpture and architecture from the past were smashed); or artistic talent (thus many of China's leading artists and writers were silenced, exiled to the countryside, had their works burned or were murdered); or of foreign influence (a writer who had read Western literature could be killed for that crime).

The Cultural Revolution did not accomplish what Mao himself had planned, and it created one of the most dangerous of all the legacies of his rule: a generation of young people whose confidence in any code of belief had been destroyed, and who had also lost their chances of education. Though many Red Guards have since attempted painfully to educate themselves as adult students in night classes, there is a 'missing generation' in the professions and sciences in China: the most competent specialists seem often to be either those well into middle age or else the extremely young, trained after Mao's death. Young people who a few years earlier would have been devoting all their attention to their studies found themselves during the Cultural Revolution destroying their classrooms, torturing or murdering their teachers, and engaging in widespread rape and sexual brutality. One former Red Guard tells of a deadly-serious night attack on a rival faction's dormitory:

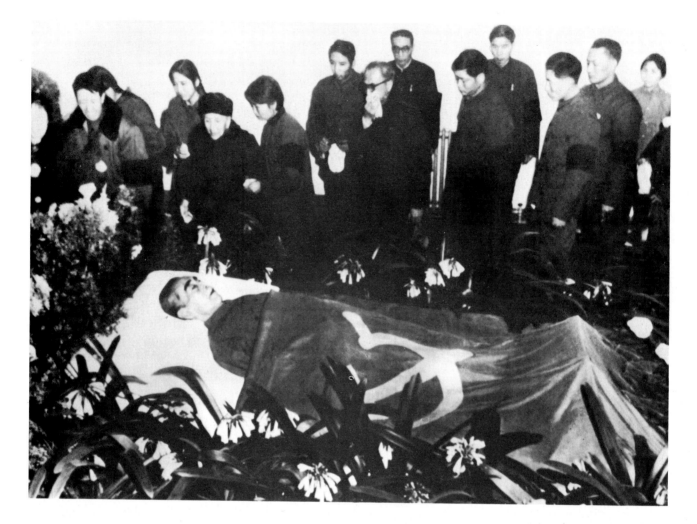

At the sight of girls, Boss [one of the Red Guards] became more excited than if he had seen opium. Telling us to wait a moment, he tiptoed onto a bed where a girl lay in a most enchanting position, and with all his might brought his foot down on her breast. '*Ai yo!*' The girl awoke, clutching the quilted cover and rolled onto the floor in pain. '*Ai yo!*'. . 'Save me!' It was pitiful. Still holding the cover, she crawled into a corner and bent over, her head touching the floor. Perhaps she would never recover from this injury.*

Many of her contemporaries died monstrous deaths. At the turning point of the Cultural Revolution the army was called in to stop it.

The Cultural Revolution was an outburst of hysterical fanaticism: it required the suppression of rival forms of belief, whereas in usual times the Chinese have tolerated the alternative creeds they have encountered. It was also Utopian, and was expected to produce a new kind of human being. The 'Little Red Book of Mao Zedong', which the Red Guards waved frantically at mass meetings, served both as a magic amulet and as a token of 'belonging'. In many of these characteristics the Cultural Revolution resembled the religiously-based popular uprisings of imperial times. But unlike them it was deliberately instigated from the capital; it was promoted,

Mourners pay their last respects to Prime Minister Zhou Enlai (Chou En-lai) who died on 8 January 1976. In contrast to Mao Zedong, Zhou had been educated in Paris and was at home in the world of international diplomacy. He became a symbol for many Chinese of resistance to the excesses of the Cultural Revolution.

like the Nazi excesses, by mass-communications; and its adherents were not hungry peasants but in the main young urban students, often the children of the most privileged groups in China. When their frenzy of devotion and violence was over, many decided that their idealism had been manipulated. They had lost their youth for nothing; they had lost hope for the future and trust in their leaders, or in nearly all of them.

Of the few leaders who still retained widespread respect, the most important was Zhou Enlai (Chou En-lai). Zhou, never an open adversary of Mao, nevertheless for a long time attempted to advocate different solutions to China's problems, and was seen by his admirers as a human symbol of resistance to the excesses of the Cultural Revolution. He had learned in 1972 that he had cancer, and in his remaining years he sought to arrange for a succession to Mao that would return power to the group in the Party that had earlier opposed the Great Leap. But around Mao were people who believed in the apocalyptic aspect of revolution and who saw their interests as inextricably bound up with such beliefs. As Mao became more feeble the so-called 'Gang of Four', which included Mao's wife Jiang Qing, sought to use the ageing Chairman's prestige to defeat Zhou's protégés and to ensure their own succession. For a few months after Zhou Enlai's death in January 1976 they strengthened their grip on China. But on 4–5 April 1976 their

Workers from a Beijing factory file past the body of Mao Zedong who died in September 1976. His prodigious reputation had survived the disasters of the Great Leap Forward and the Cultural Revolution and until his death he remained the object of a quasi-religious cult which still makes it difficult to assess his achievements clearly.

opponents amassed enormous crowds in the main ceremonial centre of Beijing, Tiananmen Square, to mourn for Zhou, and thus implicitly to protest against the regime.

When Mao Zedong himself died in early September 1976 his widow was soon arrested, together with her followers. A pause followed in China, first of amazement, then of relief. But the power struggle soon continued. Mao's designated successor, Hua Guofeng, managed to become chairman of the Party, but was gradually made to vacate his place at the top, though he was not disgraced. By devolving economic responsibility to groups often as small as the family, by greater trust in free markets, and by importing technical skills from abroad, the new leadership, under Deng Xiaoping (Teng Hsiao-p'ing), began to seek solutions to the economic and social problems that had been growing in severity for twenty years.

What sense are the Chinese to make of their two contrasting kinds of memory: that of the glorious past, visible in the splendours of the imperial palace in the capital and in the massive strength of the 'Great Wall' at Shanhaiguan on the Yellow Sea; and the other kind of memory, of famine, anarchy and murder, in their own and their families' remembered experience? They will not be the first Chinese to face such a contrast. Many generations over the past two thousand years have seen their country devastated by rebellions, civil wars and foreign invaders. The treasures and the formalities of the great civilization concentrated in the emperor's palace were always at most a matter of rumour for small farmers tilling recalcitrant soil in a harsh climate, threatened by drought and flood, with government tax collectors eating from one side of their grain bowl and landowners and money lenders from the other. But now that an optimistic, world-transforming creed is professed by the leadership of China, the contrast between what is officially supposed to be remembered and what is actually remembered is more striking than ever before.

History in China is like an old man's memory. The distant past is often more vivid than the present, and its stories are polished, exaggerated and distorted by many tellings. The Chinese have always looked to their ancestors for their sense of direction and of duty in life. They have had no epics and few creation stories, only history, full of moral examples to be drawn on and evaluated afresh in every generation. For history to the Chinese is not an objective account of the past. It is an endless morality tale in which the characters must be explicit villains and heroes, their virtues and vices made constantly relevant to the present day's concerns.

Now that Mao's successors are forced to find a way forward out of the material difficulties and the spiritual void created by the Great Leap and the Cultural Revolution they need to define their relationship not merely to the ideas of Marx, Lenin and Mao Zedong, but also to China's past, and to the two dominant inheritances of Chinese civilization: that of Confucius, the benevolent sage, who expected men to be led by gentleness; and that of Qin Shihuangdi, the great but ruthless unifier, who created a temporary, universal peace by universal terror.

Massive defensive walls, built at various times in north China, were linked into a unified system of defence against northern invaders by the emperor who united China, Qin Shihuangdi. Strengthened and elaborated by successive dynasties, and at other times allowed to decay, they have become known collectively as 'The Great Wall'. This picture shows a much-visited section of seventeenth-century wall in the mountains north of Beijing.

BELIEVING

信仰

HEAVEN EARTH AND MARX

A lorry hurtling on the wrong side of the road towards a heavily loaded bicycle is a familiar sight on the roads of China. Perhaps it is overtaking a handcart, while the cyclist with his wife and child aboard is passing a three-horse wagon heaped with coal. Any non-Chinese traveller, with or without a religion, may find himself praying at such a moment, if only so that he can close his eyes. When he opens them and sees that disaster has been avoided he is likely to be left wondering at the Chinese sense of balance.

The quality that enables the cyclist to swerve gracefully, faced with death from two directions, is more than a metaphor for the Chinese ideal of balance in all of life: in health, in the affairs of state, even in the workings of the universe; and nowhere is balance more important than in matters of belief. There have traditionally been three beliefs or 'teachings' in China: Confucianism, Daoism and Buddhism. But there is a fourth, more fundamental than any of them: that the differences between the other three do not really matter. 'San jiao fa yi', the Chinese used to say: 'the three teachings flow into one'.

The Chinese are very practical. Ritual observances have worldly purposes: health, good relationships and prosperity. The principal sanctuary in the Temple of Heaven in Peking, where the Emperor left offerings on behalf of the people, is called 'Sanctuary of Prayer for a Bumper Harvest'. If one teaching offers benefits, three may bring more. Three teachings are in any case safer than one.

So at a traditional funeral, in a strict Confucian family, ceremonies might have been said both by Daoist monks and by Buddhist priests; and even as the dead man's family were preparing to worship him as an ancestor, they might have been going through rituals to influence the reincarnation of his soul in a different body.* Christians, to whom one belief excludes another, have often been scandalized by this open-mindedness. If the Chinese could welcome Jesuits to their court and yet not abandon their previous teachings, could they really ever be 'converted'? But for the Chinese there was no conflict between Christianity and what they believed. The Jesuits were interested in God. The Chinese were interested in man. The Jesuits talked about rewards in the hereafter. The Chinese thought about results here and now. The Jesuits were interested in sin. The Chinese were concerned about crime. They did not even have a separate word for 'sin'.

The sacred mountain of Taishan in Shandong Province.

'There is no man in the sky judging misdemeanours,' the thinker Zhu Xi had said in the twelfth century, and he was in a tradition already more than fifteen hundred years old.

In the earliest recorded Chinese beliefs, the world was thought of as without beginning, without creation or creator. It was man who had shaped it. Mythical cultural heroes, portrayed as early 'emperors', had invented fire, writing and irrigation. Their stories merged almost imperceptibly into those of the historical rulers of China. When, about the third or fourth century AD, a creation story did develop, it probably came from the outer edges of the empire, or was imported. In this myth Pan Gu, the first being, was born from the egg of chaos, and as he grew he separated heaven and earth. From his body when he died came the sacred mountains and the waters. His eyes became the sun and the moon, his hair and beard the stars, and the hair on his body the vegetable world. In some versions of the myth Pan Gu was himself the first man: thus it was man who created the relationship between heaven and earth. In other versions the origins of the human race are more modestly ascribed to the fleas on Pan Gu's body.

Already in the sixth century BC a man was saying to his contemporaries, 'We know so little about how to live in this life that there is no point in worrying about what may happen to us after death. First let us learn to live in the right way with other men and then let whatever happens next take care of itself.' These (roughly translated) were the words of the great sage of China, whom the West calls Confucius and the Chinese call Kong Qiu. It was the Jesuit missionaries of the seventeenth century who called him Confucius, because of an elaborate Chinese form 'Kong Fuzi' (Master Kong); and the oddly Latinate name has stuck in most Western books about China since.

Confucius was born, allegedly, at Qufu in Shandong Province in the state of Lu, in about 551 BC, and he died in 479 BC. He lived at the end of a troubled age called the 'Spring and Autumn' period, in which the states of the old Zhou empire were fighting for supremacy, and the resulting chaos led many thinkers to search for fundamental principles of social order and harmony. The period is named after a famous history of the state of Lu which Confucius is said to have composed, which records the events of each year by seasons.

He was a scholar who wandered about from court to court attempting to find employment and to convince rulers of the right way to govern. Not surprisingly perhaps, he proposed that they should employ scholars and institute the study of the classics in a thoroughly scholarly way. More surprisingly, he convinced them: not his immediate contemporaries (he died a disappointed man), but generations of Chinese rulers since.

He has had a greater influence on China than any other human being. Yet almost nothing is known about him as a man. The Confucius who has had the influence is not the Kong Qiu who actually lived, but the imaginary perfect teacher round whom his disciples have woven their mythology of ideals. His character thus has to be imagined from what his disciples have said were his sayings. These are made more obscure, for the West, by being

Confucius lived about 500 years before Christ in the area of modern Shandong Province.

(Left)
A Ming Dynasty painting, 'The Three Teachings', shows the founders of Confucianism, Buddhism and Daoism. The tall, dark figure of Confucius stands in the middle; and the Sakyamuni Buddha is shown, deep in meditation, on his left; and Lao Zi (Lao-tze), the semi-mythical founder of Daoism, is on his right.

In a painting from the 'Classic of Filial Piety', a son kneels submissively in front of his parents seated on a dais. Confucianism encouraged strict social hierarchy and submission to authority. Social order began at home with unquestioning obedience to one's parents and to all seniors within the family. Obedience to the ruler was also expected to be unquestioning.

called for some reason his 'Analects'; and as nobody knows what an analect is without looking it up in a dictionary, he has been made to seem almost like some nuclear physicist of the moral world, inaccessible to all except the specialist. Yet nothing could be simpler than what he had to say.

The central teaching of Confucius was that nothing is more important to man than man. He himself refused to have anything to do with four kinds of thing: what was violent, what was disorderly, what was strange and what had to do with the supernatural. 'One should revere the ghosts and gods,' he once said, 'but still keep them distant.' His disciples say that he took part in sacrifices as if the gods were present. Ritual and music were the best influences on a man's character. Ritual formed him and kept him in order; music united him to other men and brought him joy.

Confucianism has always fitted naturally into the ancient Chinese pattern of close family ties and absolute rule in which the father governed like an emperor and the emperor was supposed to care for his subjects like a father, while those below obeyed both. This system of belief, through which China was for so long governed, exalts mainly those virtues that fit a static and ideally gentle world, where every family has its place beneath the ruler, every individual has his place within the family, and force and administration are kept to a minimum.

There are five Confucian virtues: humanity or benevolence (*ren*), righteousness (*yi*), propriety (*li*), wisdom (*zhi*) and trustworthiness (*xin*). And there are also 'five Confucian relationships', of which only one is between equals: that of friend to friend. The others are all hierarchical: between father and son; between ruler and ruled; between husband and wife; and between elder brother and younger brother. They are the virtues and relationships of a society where all are kept in order by those closest to them and where there is, ideally, little for the state or the police to do. Confucius did not believe that the nobility needed to be under any laws; they could govern their conduct entirely by rules of propriety. The Chinese term for Confucian, which is *ru*, meant originally 'weakling'. It was the gentleness, refinement and calmness of the scholarly life that was admired in Confucianism, plus a certain scepticism about everything, or about everything except keeping the right relationships with other people.

The right relationships depended on more than a mere mechanical performance of duties; they required 'filial submission' (*xiao*), 'loyalty' (*zhong*), and the complementary virtue to loyalty: 'decency' or 'reciprocity' (*shu*), the duty of the emperor to rule justly and to take note of the advice of his subjects. Critics of Confucianism could argue that loyalty was inculcated more strongly – that decency was voluntary but loyalty was compulsory – because the scholar-officials depended for their livelihood on the emperor, not the people. But scholars often risked punishment or death for pointing out to their emperors that they were failing to do their duty to the people. Confucianism was not merely authoritarian; it was not a doctrine of arbitrary rule. Outward order could only be a reflection of internal self-discipline, particularly in those placed in authority. The ruler must be good or society would decay, while he himself could lose the support of his people and thus the Mandate of Heaven and his throne, if he neglected the five virtues.

The idea of a good ruler was not, for the Confucians, an unattainable ideal. What was good was held to be latent within man and was expected to come out unless it was overclouded by errors. Hence sessions of public criticism such as those that were encouraged in the Cultural Revolution, which have often seemed to the West mere mental violence and have certainly contained that, are not new to China. They fit a permanently optimistic view of human nature – a kind of revivalism without grace – that the Chinese have held for a long time. It is said that in the bathing tub of Tang, the first sovereign of the Shang Dynasty (c.1523-c.1028 BC), was written the sentence, 'Renew yourself every day.' And the twelfth-century philosopher Zhu Xi, who fused Buddhist ideas with traditional Confucianism, described the effect of moral criticism as 'wiping the dust from the face of an old mirror so that it shall be once more bright'.

The relationship between friend and friend, the only equal one of the five, has been of unusual importance in China: Confucian scholars, writing poems, have often addressed other scholars in deeply affectionate terms and maintained close relationships, based on having studied together, to the end of their lives. One of the strangest things of all about the Cultural Revolution (to jump two and a half millennia, since the Chinese habitually do the same) is that friends and even members of the same family could in certain circumstances betray each other for a creed. For a crime they had been required to report each other for centuries; for a creed, never, unless they discovered a neighbour who believed in some rebellious cause that might endanger the state. In order to achieve the betrayal of friend by friend, the Chinese leaders had to attack the historical figure who represented the opposite principle, and who stood for hierarchy, order and relationships unshakeable by any difference of mere belief. Hence the slogan which amazed the West in the late stages of the Cultural Revolution, 'Criticize Lin Biao and Confucius.' Could one imagine a slogan like 'Criticize Richard Nixon and Aristotle' being carried on placards through the streets of Washington in 1973? China's is a very ancient culture, and two and a half thousand years after his death one man could still represent an entire way of thinking and living: one that has lasted through the Cultural Revolution in many ways and is still part of the texture of Chinese life today.

One school among the followers of Confucius, led by Meng Zi (Mencius), stressed even further his view that the nature of man was originally good and that goodness could always be restored by the right kind of moral teaching and criticism. But other more pessimistic Confucians, led by Xun Zi, believed that ritual was needed to discipline human nature, which was intrinsically antisocial. An even darker view was held by the group known as the Legalists. This pessimistic and authoritarian school of practical rulers and philosophers went further than Xun Zi, and argued that only a stern system of rewards and punishments could keep mankind in order. Although not considered one of 'the three teachings' by the Chinese, Legalism once competed with Daoism and Confucianism as a philosophy of life and has never ceased to play a part in Chinese ideas of statecraft. The Legalists insisted that there must be no exceptions to their rules: and they opposed the aristocratic privileges inherent in Confucianism. One of them, Shang Yang, was chief minister of Qin in about 360 BC, and gave a harsh, Legalist discipline to the state that in the following century was to unify China. The duke of Qin, whose name was Xiao,

. . . cherished the idea of rolling up the empire like a mat, of lifting up the whole world in his arms and of tying up the four seas in a sack; moreover he had the intention of swallowing up the eight wild countries. At this time the Lord of Shang was his chief minister . . . In the interior [Shang] Yang made cruel use of the punishments of sword and saw, and abroad he was deeply steeped in killing by means of the war-axe. Whoever measured land with paces more than six feet long was punished, and whoever threw ashes on the street incurred corporal punishment . . . One day he sentenced more than seven hundred men, on the brink of the Wei River, so that the water of the Wei became entirely red and the sound of crying and weeping stirred up heaven and earth.*

Lao Zi, pictured in a 16th-century painting, is the legendary founder of Daoism; he is supposed to have been a contemporary of Confucius.

After the foundation and rapid fall of the Qin Dynasty (221-207 BC) Legalist and Confucian ideas were merged to some extent in the Han Dynasty which succeeded it (206 BC-AD 220). Since then there has always been both a Legalist and a Confucian element in Chinese political belief and in the practice of Chinese government.

Daoism was consciously opposed to Confucianism and also to Legalism. The Chinese word 'Dao' means simply 'The Way', and in the pure and philosophical form of Daoism this is the Way of Nature. For its main sacred text Daoism looks back to the *Daodejing* (*Tao Te Ching*). The title means 'The Way and Its Power'; it is attributed to Lao Zi (Lao-tze), a legendary sage of about the same time as Confucius, though it was probably written by an unknown author in the fourth century BC. A second sacred text is the book of parables of Zhuang Zi, which expresses Daoist ideas allegorically. The essential doctrine of these two texts is that man should understand himself as part of nature and should see change as the way of everything in the universe. Man, with his cycle of growth, decay and death, is no different from any other thing in nature: from a stick, an animal, a cloud. So he should not insist on human order and hierarchy or cling to any particular form, even to the form of his own body, which must dissolve. Only in this way can he gain life, either by enduring longer in the world or by attaining physical immortality.

For a Daoist, immortality is not impossible. There are two parts of the soul, one heavenly, the other earthly. The heavenly element tends upwards; breathing techniques and sexual exercises are intended to lighten the soul so that it will dissolve into the universe, where it will endure. In the highest form of philosophical Daoism the health of the body has been sought in simple, balanced diet and in exercise. Daoists, and also Buddhists, have developed the famous *taijiquan* shadow-boxing exercises that groups of people, old and young, can be seen practising in the early mornings in the parks of China today.

Some early Daoists favoured the hermit life. But by the fourth century AD the need to retire to a wilderness had given way to an acceptance of normal social life and to the idea that detachment could be found anywhere, as a Daoist poet of that century, Tao Qian, declared:

> I have built my hut beside a busy road
> But I can hear no clatter from passing carts and horses.
> Do you want to know how?
> When the mind is detached, where you are is remote also.
> Picking chrysanthemums by the east hedge
> I can see the hills to the south a long way away:
> It is sunset and the air over the mountains is beautiful;
> Birds are flying in flocks back to their nests.
> This tastes real.
> I would like to talk about it, but there are no words.*

That poem comes from a collection called *Drinking Wine*. Drinking, except in strict moderation, is not a Confucian trait, and is frowned on also by

Master Kuang, an 86-year-old Daoist priest, practises sword play in the grounds of a secluded mountainside temple. Sword play is not just a traditional form of physical exercise; it also plays an important part in Daoist rituals.

Buddhists who, to sharpen the conscious mind, are tea-drinkers. Wine is associated with Daoism because it helps man to lose what is specifically human about him, and to give release to nature.

Daoist mystics and poets have valued freedom from time, from care and from entanglement with bureaucracies and power. Daoism has thus contributed to Chinese thought an anarchistic strand, which has questioned the established Confucian organization myths that justified central power in the hands of one emperor and the dragooning of men into imperial works, such as wall-building and irrigation.

Perhaps Daoists were natural failers of examinations and interviews. For whatever reasons, someone who was in favour at court might embrace the official, or officious, beliefs of a Confucian; someone who was 'out' was more likely to become a Daoist. The transformation could be made in the course of a day, the official putting away his Confucianism like a briefcase on returning home, and reaching for his Daoism as he might for a fishing rod. Fishing, with the contemplation of the changing element of water that it involves, was in fact an accepted gesture of withdrawal from imperial office, and a symbolic occupation for an official who had been banished or was unemployed, which could also be interpreted as a hint that he should be recalled. The practice is ancient. Jiang Taigong, who advised the founders of the Zhou Dynasty, was famous for fishing his way to office. King Wen of Zhou needed a sage to help him win the empire. He saw Jiang waiting for fish to come to his line, which had no hook, in the belief that the fish would come to him of their own volition when they were ready. Wen hired him; and Wen's son Wu, using Jiang's strategy of waiting before going into battle, overthrew the Shang Dynasty. The idea of *wuwei* – sometimes translated as 'non-action' – was a central tenet of Daoism and has been important in most Chinese books on military strategy also. *Wuwei* means not so much inactivity as doing nothing out of harmony with the flow of things. It can be the code of a swordsman as much as of a fisherman.

An elderly Daoist such as High Priest Kuang of Laoshan, aged about 86 (as far as he knows), can still perform amazing feats of agility with the sword. These are not mere exercises to keep fit, though they have that function also. The characteristic circling movements of sword exercises and *taijiquan* shadow-boxing are modelled on observation of the fighting tactics of animals, particularly of birds and of panthers. Circling movements put man in tune with the movement of the stars and with the natural cycle of water as it rises in clouds and falls in rain.

In traditional China, while the Confucian officials stressed the peaceful pursuit of culture, Daoist tradition emphasized fighting and the martial arts. In Daoism battle was seen as an element of all life, against mortal enemies and also against immortals within and outside the body. Wooden weapons play a prominent part in Daoist rituals. And Daoists or their predecessors have written the main military treatises of China. Zhang Liang, the general who helped the first Han ruler to conquer the empire, was an early advocate of the breathing techniques characteristic of Daoism, and many Daoist high priests have been named Zhang and have claimed descent from him. Sun Zi's *Art of War* in the fourth century BC already recommends a characteristically Daoist approach: working with nature by dexterity and balance rather than by brute force, outwitting the enemy, winning by bluff without a battle, and 'the strategy of the empty city': a reference to the story of a general who deceived the enemy into thinking an undefended city contained a huge army by leaving its gates wide open and playing the lute idly on the city walls. Mao Zedong drew on the military ideas of some of these ancient treatises to formulate the strategy of his armies.

Daoism was also associated with alchemy and magic, and it was these aspects of it that attracted the emperor who unified China, Qin Shihuangdi. Several attempts were made to assassinate him, and he was terrified of death. In his last years he spent much of his time moving secretly from one palace to another and attempting to secure the elixir of life. Alchemy, though some philosophical Chinese later engaged in it for purposes of contemplation, was at one time a practical way of seeking the elixir, by the transmutation of base matter into gold. Gold was associated with immortality because of its durability and constancy under changing conditions: the word 'alchemy' derives via Arabic from the Chinese word for gold, *jin*. Since the ingredients used for preparing elixirs included arsenic and mercury, they sometimes had the opposite effect to the one intended: more than one Chinese emperor died of 'elixir poisoning'.

On one occasion Qin Shihuangdi financed an expedition by a plausible shaman called Xu Fu who proposed to find the islands of the immortals. The old fraud (if such he was: perhaps he believed in it too) assured the emperor that the islands were somewhere east of the coast of Shandong and that he could there find the elixir of life. The emperor, not forgetting his policy of expansion in his quest for immortality, provided Xu Fu with a shipload of

young girls and boys to people the island for the Qin Dynasty; and the shaman and his crew, richly provided for the expedition, presumably enjoyed a delightful life somewhere beyond the ocean, if they survived. When they failed to return, and further expeditions found neither them nor the islands, the magicians round the emperor told him that the difficulties were all due to a large fish which was thwarting his plans just off the east coast of China. Qin Shihuangdi sent a number of skilled archers to stalk the beaches with crossbows. Eventually a fish of exceptional size was transfixed. Unfortunately the magicians must have made a minor error in their divinations, perhaps leaving out a 'not' somewhere, since the emperor shortly afterwards died.

Daoism is still a flourishing religion in Taiwan and elsewhere among the overseas Chinese. A few scattered Daoist monasteries still survive in mainland China, and the beliefs of its monks or priests appear to be an amalgam of philosophical and magical Daoism. In the early 1980s the eighty-six-year-old Daoist Kuang on the holy mountain of Laoshan explained his religion as something 'completely Chinese'. The *Daodejing* is mainly concerned with breathing techniques; though, as he added in an afterthought, it also contains 'ordinary stuff' about ruling the world.

One of the early members of his particular sect had been spiritual adviser to Genghis Khan, and had made the sound suggestion that he should stop killing people. Unfortunately the consultation appears to have taken place late in the emperor's career. Other notable predecessors had become immortals and left their mark in the neighbourhood. One, 'Magician Li', had a ravine nearby named after a teaching method he hit on for a particularly flamboyant disciple. The man was a very wealthy landlord and a good musician. He used to play every day outside his front door, and kept deliberately breaking the strings in the middle of the notes and then tying them together before the notes had ended. The spectators used to applaud. Magician Li proposed that he should leave home and learn to control his breath instead. The man had two wives and children and they tried to stop him, but when he took a stick to them they let him go. Li threw nine coins into a ravine on the volcano, which was full of thistles, and made the landlord look for them; it took him three years to find eight. Li taught him breath-control meanwhile, and then showed him the ninth coin which, with his highly developed spiritual powers, he could see. The man stayed on as a disciple. The place is called 'Grope-for-Money Ravine' to this day. 'But there are plenty of such stories,' added the Daoist. 'It would be a waste of time to tell more.'

Speaking formally in front of his monks he stated some of the central tenets of Daoist belief:

Lao Zi was a wise man with great intelligence. He used to say, 'Discover how Nature acts by observing the Way of Nature.' He observed how yin and yang in the universe match each other. Birth is due to the intercourse between man and woman. The combination of yin and yang is life. The deep-breathing exercise (*qigong*) is used to co-ordinate yin and yang. You will enjoy long life without old age if you keep practising this exercise. You need to sit in meditation. Out of the depth of extreme tranquillity comes activity. When you are full of energy, your 'cinnabar centre' [a nerve-centre two inches below the navel] will produce heat. With your hand you can cure sickness. Those with very high perfection can bake pancakes on the abdomen by the heat produced from the cinnabar centre, or can boil water on a leg. We should absorb the natural essence of the universe, and store our own energy. So you cannot get married. In the past, nobody talked about this, particularly to outsiders. The more energy you have, the more vigorous you will become, and gradually you will be able to renew your youth. The main purpose of a Daoist is to become an immortal. My teacher, whose nickname was 'Long Leg Yi Ye', achieved spiritual perfection during the Republican period. He could walk four hundred li [over a hundred miles] a day. After his tomb was dug up, they found nothing in it but one of his shoes. Everyone thought that he had died of diarrhoea. People had laughed and said, 'How can a Daoist die of diarrhoea? It's a disgrace to Daoism.' But on the same day as his shoe was found in the tomb he was seen in a different city, alive. He did not die at all in fact, because he had already attained spiritual perfection. I have achieved quite a high level of perfection, but now my standard has dropped. I am in charge of administrative work. Because I have to do the administration my spiritual level is bound to get worse.

The parting shot about administration is completely Daoist; no Confucian or even Buddhist would be likely to speak so slightingly of the task of the bureaucrat.

It was not until the second century AD that Daoists, contrary to their original nature, organized themselves into a formal religion and set up a priesthood. They did this in response to the challenge of Buddhism, China's first great organized religion, which came from India probably about a hundred years before it was recognized by the court in the first century AD, and spread rapidly in the wars and disasters that followed the fall of the Han

Dynasty in 220. Under the Tang Dynasty Daoism and Buddhism alternated in favour at court; but gradually most of China became Buddhist in that period, and by the eighth century there were a third of a million monks in China. As Confucianism revived towards the end of the Tang and in the Song Dynasty, the influence of organized Buddhism declined, but 'neo-Confucianism' was deeply influenced by Buddhist ideas.

Perhaps the fundamental doctrine of Buddhism is that all life involves suffering, and that the only way to avoid suffering in the end is to escape from life and from an otherwise endless cycle of reincarnations. Suffering is due to desire. So one must rid oneself of desire, even if this means ridding oneself of life altogether.

The expectation of happiness in the world is an illusion; so is the idea of a separate individual existence. It is these two illusions which cause both suffering and wrongdoing. People seek their own personal individual advantage; they hope and they fear; and they cling to insubstantial elements of an unreal world. By these means they bring suffering on themselves, mainly through doing evil to others.

For in the world there is a great self-regulating mechanism of rewards and punishments, by which evil deeds return ultimately on those who do them, and by which virtue is correspondingly rewarded. This is true both in everyday life and also between lives, as each creature is continually reincarnated after death in a higher or lower form of existence, depending on

In a 16th-century painting illustrating a Daoist poem, a scholar asleep in his thatched cottage dreams that he is an immortal, floating over the mountains.

the virtues or vices of its last life, until in the end escape is found from the cycle of illusion in non-being, the ultimate aim of all existence.

Today the differences between the three ancient teachings may be recognizable in the style of speech as well as in appearance of those who represent them now. A professor at a college of Confucian studies may answer a question with a list of pros and cons, set out in five well-balanced pairs; a Daoist monk's words will flow unpredictably and unrestrainedly; Buddhists' sentences tend to be severe and unadorned like the shaven heads of their monks, as in this account of his religion by Master Ju Zan, head of the Buddhist Association of China:

The founder of Buddhism was Sakyamuni. When he became a monk he realized not only that human beings suffer from birth, age, illness and death, but that the whole universe is impermanent, and everything is subject to extinction and change. If people do not understand the law of change within the universe, they do evil things, which means doing harm to others and benefiting oneself at the expense of others. Those who do evil things will get retribution and they will suffer. To avoid suffering means mainly to be kind to others. Good will be rewarded with good. If everyone behaved according to this principle, human beings in the world would enjoy peace: there would be no fighting, and nobody would try to cheat or outwit anyone else.

Buddhists do not believe in the existence of God, nor do they believe that destiny is decided by God. Buddhists believe that destiny is controlled by men themselves. When Buddhism was brought to China, it conformed to Chinese traditional thought. The Chinese do not believe in God. Although some people in ancient times believed in destiny, the Confucians believed that destiny was controlled by men. You could call China the second home of Buddhism, because the two cultural traditions agree with each other. Confucians recommend five virtues, which are the normal ideas of ordinary people. These five virtues conform to the five commandments advocated by the Buddhists: 'Thou shalt not kill, Thou shalt not steal, Thou shalt not be obscene, Thou shalt not tell lies and Thou shalt not drink alcohol.'

In those sects of Buddhism closest to its Indian origins enlightenment and non-being can be reached only by slow, incremental steps, first through the practice of virtues and secondly through monasticism, which is the highest form of human life and the necessary preparation for what lies beyond. But China has always transformed the beliefs that it has imported, and some forms of Chinese Buddhism have stressed the value of virtue for its own sake, as in Confucianism, while others again, as in Daoism, have looked for a kind of enlightenment that comes without preparation.

Chan Buddhism is a fusion of native Daoist and other Chinese beliefs with those imported from India. The word 'chan', which in Japanese is 'zen', is an adaptation of the Sanskrit dhyana, meaning meditation. The Indian Buddhist idea that it was necessary to be a monk before becoming enlightened conflicted with the Chinese concern with family life and the engendering of descendants. In Chan Buddhism monks could marry, and in any case there was no need to be a monk in order to be 'enlightened'. The original Buddhists believed in enlightenment by slow and careful steps. For Daoists it was possible to be in accord with nature in the here and now, and carefulness was quite likely to be a hindrance to enlightenment. In Chan Buddhism and even more clearly in Japanese Zen, freedom from hope, from fear and from the illusion of separate individual existence can come suddenly, without

A 12th-century painting shows disciples of Buddha giving alms to beggars. Buddhism arrived from India around the time of Christ. With its hope of individual salvation, it attracted many people in the times of trouble and foreign invasion that recurred frequently over the next thousand years.

The Fayuan Si in Beijing is an old Buddhist monastery. Since the end of the Cultural Revolution the practice of religion has been officially tolerated by the state, and a few monasteries such as the Fayuan Si train novice monks today.

warning, sometimes through a blow on the head, sometimes through a short riddle or *gongan* (*kōan* in Japanese), generally one that encapsulates the absurdity of life. This freedom can also be suddenly lost.

Partly because of their belief in clarity, emptiness and simplicity, the Zen Buddhists in Japan kept the original austere tastes of Tang and early Song architecture in China, and their temples, generally without colour and ornament, have done much to influence the entire architecture of Japan. In China Chan Buddhist temples show a delight in red and gold colours and in intricate decoration. Buddhists of all persuasions in China seem to like surfaces made busy with a multiplicity of human figures. It was considered virtuous by the Buddhists to multiply holy images and to copy out sacred writings; the first instances of printing, which is a Chinese invention, were Buddhist sacred texts. It is a remarkable sight to see a so-called 'Thousand Buddha Cave' with something like that number of separate, almost identical images of the Buddha, each one of which has had its face individually hacked away by some axe or bludgeon. It is sometimes said by modern guides that Daoists and Buddhists desecrated each other's sculpture; others blame Red Guards. In fact, much of the vandalism may have been the work of iconoclastic rebels or even of the antique trade. This has traditionally been in the hands of Moslems.

The faiths of the Near East and the West have been tolerated by the Chinese in enclaves. Moslems, for example, have been allowed their own mosques, and there have been flourishing Moslem communities in China since the Middle Ages. Christianity, despite scattered contacts, has made little impact on the beliefs of the Chinese, though it had some surprisingly early adherents. There are Christian monuments in China dating back to the eighth century. A monk of the Nestorian persuasion from eastern China, Rabban Bar Sauma, visited Rome and Paris in 1287-8 and celebrated mass in front of the pope to demonstrate that Nestorians were as Christian as anyone in Rome. Both faiths, Islam and Christianity, had the drawback of requiring belief in a personal creator, always a harder idea for the Chinese to grasp than that of an unbroken line of family relationships stretching back into the remote past. One convert in the nineteenth century is said to have complained to his missionary: 'I have read the whole Bible, and nowhere does it tell us God's surname.'

After many years of such misunderstandings one missionary summed up his experience by saying that in China the educated believe nothing and the uneducated believe everything. The kernel of truth in this remark is that popular religion in China has been very different in character from the sophisticated and sceptical tolerance of the literary elite; and where the three beliefs, and many more, have 'flowed into one' at a popular level they have tended to produce an amalgam – sometimes known as 'popular Daoism', sometimes as 'popular Buddhism' – of both these teachings with the worship of a whole pantheon of gods and lesser spirits – 'immortals', spirits of the woods, spirits of particular lakes and mountains, and beings difficult to define but translated resolutely by the Chinese as 'fairies'.

The richness of the mixture is evident in the most famous of Chinese popular religious tracts, *The Book of Rewards and Punishments,* which dates originally from the fourth century AD, and includes elements of magical Daoism, and of Buddhist doctrines of judgement, together with a great deal else besides, in its definition of a thoroughly wicked man:

Popular religions existed in all parts of China, often based on local myths and legends and borrowing elements from Daoism and Buddhism. Hundreds of gods and demons populated the spiritual world of many of the Chinese. One of the best known popular deities, the 'Great Spiritual Chaser of Demons', is portrayed in this print, dated 1873.

He leaps over wells and hearths; over food and men. Destroys young children and unborn infants. Does many secret and perverse things. Sings and dances on the last day of the month or year; shouts in anger on the first of the month or in the morning; weeps, spits or behaves indecently towards the north; hums and mutters before the hearth; uses the hearth fire for burning incense. Prepares food with dirty firewood; goes abroad at night exposed and naked. Inflicts punishment during the 'eight periods'; spits at shooting stars; points at the rainbow, at the sun, moon and stars in an irreverent manner; stares at the sun and moon. Fires brushwood and hunts in the spring; curses towards the north; and kills tortoises and snakes needlessly . . . For such crimes as these the Minister of Life administers punishment according to the nature of the offence – curtailing life by twelve years or a hundred days. This done, death ensues.

The Bodhisattva Avelokitesvaria, originally a male Buddhist deity, became the popular female goddess of mercy, Guanyin, represented in the blanc-de-chine figure above. In the 10th-century painting from the Dunhuang caves shown opposite, the family of the painting's donor worship Guanyin.

The Chinese authorities have frequently dreaded the irrationality and fanaticism of popular religious sects, which have often been associated with disturbances, and sometimes with rebellions. For instance in the spring of 3 BC, after a great drought, there was an outburst of religious fervour in which the devotees of the great goddess of Chinese popular religion, the Mother Ruler of the West, became convinced that the world was coming to an end. *The History of the Former Han Dynasty* records that they 'frightened each other . . . became very excited and ran about, each holding a stalk or straw of hemp which they carried and passed on to others saying, "I am transporting the wand." . . . They met on the . . . lanes . . . singing and dancing and sacrificing to the Mother Ruler of the West; . . . they galloped fast, and made themselves post-messengers to transmit and transport the wands.' At night they lit beacon fires on the housetops, waiting for the end of the world, beating drums, calling out, 'exciting and frightening one another', and expecting 'persons with vertical slanting eyes' to visit the earth. When none came by the autumn, 'the frenzy stopped'.*

How deep was the felt need for some feminine archetype by contrast with the official spiritual hierarchy of male ancestors, emperors and 'ministers' of the afterlife, can only be a matter for speculation. But the worship of the Mother Ruler did not die out in the centuries that followed. She it was who presided over the Western Paradise of the Daoists. She was also popularly associated with the feminine deity who instructed the Daoist 'Yellow Emperor' in sexual lore. When Buddhism came in from India she became identified with Guanyin, goddess of mercy, originally a male deity in Indian Buddhism, and turned by the Chinese into the figure of a mother generally shown holding a small child. The Mother Ruler was also thought to be the deity who reigned in the popular Buddhist 'Pure Land', a place without suffering and without wrongdoing to which all her children would be welcomed. One popular Buddhist text says, 'The Eternal Mother weeps as she thinks of her children. She has sent them many messages and letters to return home and stop devoting themselves solely to avarice in the sea of bitterness, to return to the Pure Land, to come back to Ling Shan, so that mother and children can meet again and sit together on the golden lotus'.*

The Pure Land seems to have had associations, for its devotees, with the 'ancestral village' which is so important to all Chinese, with the Buddhist nirvana in which the cycle of deaths and reincarnations would be at an end, and perhaps also with the idea of returning to a life before birth, for one scripture in this tradition says that, 'When he ascends to the eternal realm the child sees his dear mother. When he enters the mother's womb . . . he eternally returns to peace and security.' It was a sect of her followers, the Eight Trigrams, who, believing that a cosmic cycle was about to come to an end, broke into the Forbidden City in 1813 and tried to take over the empire. Other groups of believers in the Mother Ruler, known as 'White Lotus' sects, caused massive disturbances at various times in the Ming and Qing Dynasties, particularly in the 1790s, when a White Lotus rising involved millions of rebels and tied down huge armies before it was suppressed.

Old women make the arduous climb up the 6293 steps that lead to the summit of the sacred mountain of Taishan, setting off in the evening in order to arrive six or eight hours later, at dawn.

By contrast with the cult of the Mother Ruler of the West, another element of popular belief, the belief in sacred mountains, became integrated in the orthodox system of imperial ritual. There have been sacred mountains in China from the earliest recorded times. Taishan is sacred several times over. Rising about five thousand feet above sea level, rugged and irregular in silhouette and lightly wooded with pines, it is the centre of a multitude of ancient cults, some still alive today. A young man and his wife may still leave a stone on Taishan as an offering to promote their chances of having a male child. Nearly every branch in the trees and shrubs near the summit is laden with them. In the early 1980s a sophisticated young interpreter could cheerfully say that only a year earlier he had put a stone in a tree and that he and his wife had just had a baby boy.

Since religion and prosperity are partners in China, it is natural that the province of Shandong should have been a favourite holiday resort of the rich over the past hundred years, as well as full of sacred places. On the coast the air is pleasant, cool in summer yet not so wet as the subtropical south. Inland, the mountains enable one to be nearer heaven than elsewhere; the same features provide holidaymakers with spectacular views. The view from Taishan itself is magnificent, with ridge after ridge of bare rocky peaks, like the spines of some prehistoric monster, arching along the back of the Shandong peninsula.

It is impossible to say whether religion or the view is what attracts so many Chinese to the top of the mountain today, but among those who visit Taishan are old women, who are unlikely to have abandoned all ancient beliefs, and some still climb laboriously through the night up the 6293 granite steps that lead to its summit to see the sun rise over the surrounding mountains, the special object of a pilgrimage to Taishan.

Some of the greatest emperors, including Qin Shihuangdi, made the journey to the summit, attended by an immense retinue, to sacrifice to Heaven and to present the trophies of their campaigns and the evidence of their virtuous rule to Heaven at the nearest point to it in China. Taishan recalls some of the most fundamental beliefs of China: reverence for Heaven; the sense of the importance of the family; the idea that the right rituals can bring about prosperity; and the deep belief in balance and duality and in the twin forces in nature, yin and yang.

In ancient China a mountain could be a god, an actual being. Taishan, one of the five Daoist holy mountains at the compass points and in the centre of China, presided over the east. Therefore it was the mountain of the sun, and particularly symbolized the bright male force (yang) that makes the sap rise in the trees and that generates all new life. But the shadowy female force (yin) is also represented by the same mountain. Since Chinese beliefs are not mutually exclusive Taishan could be not only the home of a god and of a goddess, the 'Jade Emperor' and his daughter the 'Princess of the Coloured Clouds', but also a god itself. The cults of the mountain thus doubly concerned the central need of every Chinese family: a child – above all a male – to continue its existence after death in the memory of a line of descendants.

The tradition of 'ancestor worship' has long been a matter of ritual observances and family feasts rather than of literal belief for many Chinese. But it is rooted in an ancient idea that the spirits of the dead would continue to haunt their families' land. Observances were held for both male and female forbears, but those for males were more important because the family line was carried through the male side, and the family has always been the central bond in Chinese life.

On Taishan some people still burn special paper 'money' for their ancestors, especially at the Qing Ming festival in spring, traditionally the best day for such sacrifices. The money was thought to be needed for bribing officials in the underworld. The Chinese have always pictured the afterlife as rather like this life, and have therefore generally expected it to be staffed by bureaucrats. One Chinese, trying to explain the idea of gods in the early 1980s, defined them as 'civil servants in the sky'.

In traditional China the afterlife was expected to be lived a little below ground, in the region of the so-called 'Yellow Springs'; and in the mid-twentieth century, according to the historian of Chinese science and civilization Joseph Needham, some miners were still afraid that their shallow tunnels might debouch into the country of the dead. Because of this literal-minded view of the life of the dead, tomb-makers have been at least as important as architects in China, and have been thought to be doing something similar. The ancient carvers who cut the low reliefs in the Han Dynasty tombs at Mixian outside Zhengzhou were furnishing an entire house for the dead. In its stables they showed animals, together with chariots; though for moving under the earth or across the clouds of heaven they had skis, or something like them, instead of wheels; and in its kitchen they carved food, and had every possible piece of equipment for cooking delicious meals.

Food was the main form of offering left for ancestors, whether long dead or newly dead. Their descendants would make particularly lavish offerings to them at Qing Ming, though at a family feast afterwards they might eat the sacrifices themselves. In the Record of Rites (*Liji*), a famous ceremonial book of early China, there is an account of the funeral ritual practised in the Zhou Dynasty (1027-256 BC):

When one died, they went upon the housetop, and called out his name in a prolonged note, saying, 'Come back . . .' After this they filled the mouth (of the dead) with uncooked rice, and (set forth as offerings to him) packets of flesh. They looked up to heaven . . . and buried (the body) in the earth. The body and the animal soul go downwards; and the intelligent spirit is on high. In all these matters the earliest practice is followed.*

Besides his concubines and tomb-builders, thousands of carved figures of soldiers were buried with the first Qin emperor. They represent a survival of an earlier practice of burying real food and real attendants with a dead ruler, though Confucius believed that burying pottery figures was the earlier institution. The saving to be made by leaving sculpture rather than live attendants with the corpse must have made a considerable appeal to the managers of royal households when the practice came in during the first millennium BC. It may also have had its attractions for the attendants.

In present-day China even such residual practices as leaving food for the dead are officially discouraged. Although since the late 1970s organized religions have again been tolerated, Marxism-Leninism defines all religion as superstition, and the Party seeks to educate the people in 'science' instead. In the cities, though not in the countryside, cremation has largely replaced burial. As the Party secretary in the crematorium at Nanjing explained, burial was far less satisfactory in the Party's opinion, since it used up land for graves and wood for coffins, and both were key factors in the Four Modernizations (of industry, agriculture, defence and science-and-technology). Furthermore cremation enabled the dead man's workmates and relations to receive, in his view, a helpful lesson in science at an impressionable time.

But ancient attitudes do not vanish easily. Wands of the kind that were put in the hands of corpses in traditional Buddhist funeral ceremonies have been known to be thrust into coffins at the last minute before cremation today. And status after death, among the most ancient and the most consistent preoccupations of the Chinese, clearly still matters. A courtyard near Beijing is set aside for the ashes of prominent Party leaders, arranged in hierarchical order. Great significance was attached to the announcement, in June 1983, that other Party leaders were to be commemorated in the mausoleum in Tiananmen Square previously reserved for Mao Zedong alone. Even the common crematorium at Nanjing includes a huge four-floor repository in which the correct floor for each individual's ashes is selected by a central committee in the town, according to merit during lifetime. This is no doubt judged on strict egalitarian and atheistic principles. But the shop downstairs sells caskets, priced according to size, with elaborate carvings on the inside of the more expensive ones; and these still feature the traditional Chinese symbol of immortality, the stork.

The Chinese have so far been tolerant of many apparent contradictions in their beliefs; and they have previously been successful in transforming the creeds that have been exported to them. Will Marxism be the next belief of China to 'flow into one' with the others? Will the Chinese create, as they did with Buddhism, a kind of Chan Marxism?

In this century Russian Marxist theoreticians have sometimes been shocked, just as some Christian missionaries were, at the apparent pliability of Chinese belief. The Chinese could declare their allegiance to a revolution of urban workers that ought to be attainable, according to the Marxist textbooks, only after a long delay for industrialization, and could set about creating it immediately, and with an army of peasants. But to the Chinese, why not? There is no point in too much concern about theoretical conflicts with Karl Marx, who was after all a German. As a European he is unlikely to have understood China; for the Chinese tend to feel intuitively that China is not quite like the rest of the world, or rather that the rest of the world is not quite like China.

In any fusion of Marxism with Chinese belief it would be unsafe to predict that Marxism will come out unaltered. Some of the reservations the Chinese may all along have made in accepting Marxism may be seen in an extract from an imaginary conversation between Marx and Confucius, written before Marxism became the official ideology of China by Guo Moruo (1892-1979), a personal friend of Mao Zedong and a poet, translator and polymath who was president of the Chinese Academy of Sciences. In a temple, Confucius and his disciples are discovered eating a very Chinese dish, cold pig's head. A red-faced, bearded gentleman in a suit, who comes in on a litter borne by four young businessmen, turns out to be the theoretician of the class struggle himself. One has the impression that even for a foreigner he seems a little eccentric to the Chinese. He expounds his views vigorously:

This 1979 poster has a Marxist slogan, 'Science is a productive force'.

'Because I developed a materialist doctrine,' said Marx, 'most people take me for a kind of animal or at least someone who only understands eating and drinking, but has no ideals. The truth is that I have a very high, very distant ideal world . . . Actually, I am afraid that I may be the idealist with the highest ideals history ever produced. For one thing, my ideal world postulates that myriads of people live harmoniously as if they were a single person, and that they develop their talents in freedom and equality; that all men will be able to do their best without hope for reward; that everyone gets what he needs to live without suffering from the misery of hunger and cold: such would be the communist society of which it is said, "From each according to his ability, to each according to his needs." Wouldn't it be heaven on earth if this society became reality?'

'It certainly would,' Confucius exclaimed. For in spite of all his dignity, he was so enthusiastic, he could not help clapping his hands. 'This ideal society of yours and my world of Great Equality accord completely, without our having expressly agreed on it beforehand. Let me have your permission to recite a section from an old essay of mine,' (and he recited the entire section on the age of 'Great Equality' as it is written in the ritual classic).

His voice was solemn as he quoted his favourite essay, and . . . he nodded his head to the rhythm of his words so that one might have thought he was hypnotizing himself. But Marx had become utterly silent and did not look as if he could see anything of consequence in this part of Confucius's work.

'Treat with the reverence due to age the elders in your own family,' said Confucius, 'so that the elders in the families of others shall be similarly treated; treat with the kindness due to youth the young in your own family, so that the young in the families of others shall be similarly treated. Treat with love the women in your own family, so that the women in the families of others shall be similarly treated. And thus, I love your wife.'

When Marx heard these words, he shouted out loud with indignation. 'What? Herr Kong Number Two! I only advocate the socialization of the means of production. But you seem to advocate that of women. Your system of thought is even more dangerous than mine! I don't have the courage to provoke you further.' And with that, he hastily called out to the four respectable businessmen who carried his sedan chair, fleeing head over heels as if he had lost a battle. He must have been afraid that his wife – far away in distant Europe – was going to be socialized by Confucius then and there.

After the master and his three disciples had seen the large sedan chair disappear behind the western outer gate . . . Confucius laughed amusedly and said,' I was only joking and having fun when I said those things.' All of them laughed loudly. Then they sat back down at the table and continued chewing away at their cold pig's head.*

Marx is laughed at; Confucius, with his lighter style, is laughed with; and significantly this friend of Mao makes Marx lose the argument, or at least lose his dignity. The Chineseness of Chinese communism is not to be underestimated; Marx is more remote in his foreignness than Confucius across the gap of millennia.

Woodcuts displaying communist ideas became a popular art form in the areas occupied by the communists during the 1930s and 40s. In the two examples above peasants denounce their landlord (left) and soldiers on a farm are shown helping the peasants with the harvest (right).

The Chinese version of Marxism is at least as much a form of nationalism as it is of socialism. Before the twentieth century, the Chinese had no separate word for 'nationalism'. In many contexts 'the world' was synonymous with the Chinese empire itself. So outsiders were not rivals. But the dominance of the Western powers in the nineteenth century created the beginnings of a Chinese nationalism and gave it models to imitate. The dramatic date of the birth of a nationalist movement in China is 4 May 1919, when the German territory in Shandong was ceded to Japan. It was reinforced by the Japanese invasion in the 1930s and 1940s. Fused with Marxism, nationalism has formed a new and potent creed. It was Mao Zedong above all who joined the two. He owed his victories as much to his success in symbolizing Chinese resistance to the Japanese as to any of his socialist theories. The official system of belief of modern China, which he instituted, is called 'Marxism-Leninism-Mao Zedong Thought'.

One believer in such thought is Mr Zhao Kuisheng, a Party member since the war with Japan, who for some thirty years has been leader of Zhuji Production Brigade at Yantai in Shandong, a post which gives him responsibility for the prosperity and discipline of some two thousand five hundred people. He is also the secretary-general of the brigade's Communist Party branch. It is hard to assess how idealistic most Chinese managers at the brigade level are; and in a country of a thousand million people, with some thirty million members of the Communist Party, no one man's or Party member's beliefs can be said to be 'typical'. Mr Zhao's views have been formed by his experience. But that experience has a certain archetypal quality; in fact, his life is almost a model example of the Party's version of the recent past. Just as the vision of the settler's family in its covered wagon formed the standard heroic picture of the American west in the nineteenth century, so in its own context the picture of pre-revolutionary conditions and 'liberation' that Mr Zhao gives constitutes the model self-portrait of the cadres of the People's Republic of China.

Mr Zhao's brief, staccato sentences are characteristically Chinese:

My grandfather and grandmother had to go begging. When my grandfather and grandmother came to Yantai they brought my little aunt with them. Because they couldn't afford to feed her, on the way they gave her to another family. We don't know where she is. I am sixty-one years old. I never saw my aunt. When my grandfather and grandmother came to this village they thought they might become rich. But it was the same as before. 'All crows are black'; evil people are all the same everywhere. The poor people were exploited in the village. In the old society, especially when the Japanese were here, there were four hundred families living on begging. I am rather thin, I don't have much strength. What could I do? I sometimes dug up edible wild herbs, kept some to eat, and took others to the market to sell. With the money I would buy some flour. In the old society there were twenty-eight landlords and wealthy peasants in the village. There was one landlord who had business in town. He wore silk and satins and didn't do any work. He had four or five wives. During the summer they went by rickshaw to Yantai and enjoyed themselves. The landlord was always in the front, his wives followed behind. They went to the best restaurants in Yantai and ate the best food.

When I was sixteen I asked someone to help me find a job in an ironworks. Working with iron used to be called 'earning a living with black claws'. People doing this kind of job were despised.

While I was working in the Dalian Manufactory I joined the Yi Guan Dao Secret Society. You pay two yuan and you have to kowtow and burn joss sticks. They tell you to do good deeds, not to kill and murder; there are some good points. But still there is a lot of superstition in it. With the gods' blessing and protection, you will become rich; the gods will protect you. I was in the Yi Guan Dao for one or two years, but the gods didn't protect me. I was still poor. I then lost interest in it. If someone was interested in it today, I would be against it.

When I joined the revolution, I didn't really know why. At that time there was no such thing as communism in my head. I joined the revolution because the poor people's life was very hard in those days. We got land. Our aim had been fulfilled. Later, after the Party taught us Marxism-Leninism, my understanding gradually progressed. Our great leader Chairman Mao integrated the truth of Marxism-Leninism with the concrete situation of China. After the socialist revolution the life of our people became better step by step. That is why I am full of energy in revolutionary work. Our target is revolution not only in China but also in the world. In a communist society material life is rich. You can't say you can have everything you want, but almost. When we achieve communism the people will not have evil trends and noxious influences. There will be no stealing and robbing, because there will be enough material goods.

There are two goals we want to achieve in socialist modernization. The first is to build a highly-developed socialist material world. The second is to build up the socialist spiritual world. I think the spiritual world is more important than the material world. To modernize our country we need to seek unity in the whole population. When we talk about the spiritual side this means politics. We must educate the people, tell them why we must build the Four Modernizations. When people have a high spirit they create more wealth. If the nation is rich, the people are strong. That's why we must firmly grasp the spiritual world.

I am a Party member; I have been educated by the Party for a long time. But some of the masses, especially the commune members of our brigade, know nothing about the theory of Marxism-Leninism. They only know Chairman Mao. It was Chairman Mao who led them to stand up. The landlords and the capitalists were overthrown. The life of the commune members in our production team has got better and better. The masses believe that only under the leadership of the Party can the life of the people become better. The masses believing in the Communist Party is the same as their believing in Marxism-Leninism.

Much of the previous experience of China in matters of belief is recognizable in this statement. People believe 'because their life is getting better'. Beliefs that do not make one better-off will be dropped. The 'masses' are thought of as naturally unreflective and in need of educated guidance from those above. Those higher up are not to be questioned. If they were not correct, they would not be higher up.

A strong element in the beliefs of local leaders like Mr Zhao, and still more, apparently, in the beliefs of his commune members, is the part played by the single great leader. The Chinese have always looked to a ruler endowed with a supreme rightness and goodness to symbolize the unity of the state and the coherence and ultimate moral rightness of obedience. It was not difficult to envisage Mao Zedong in this traditional role, and the comparative unity of the country in the mid-twentieth century owed not a little to the 'fit' between his character and the ancient imperial role in Chinese society.

Then came the Cultural Revolution. Sacrifices were made in the 'Terrible Ten Years' and crimes were committed through what are recognized today as 'errors'. It is sometimes argued that the 'crimes' were those of the 'Gang of Four' and that at worst only the 'errors' were Mao Zedong's. Mao has not been repudiated, and extremely complex argument is required to exonerate him from the main responsibility for a period that everyone now execrates, including many who at the time merely enjoyed the excitement and release of attacking their seniors. Some who were swept into it saw a simple idealistic meaning in Mao's call for the destruction of everything old. For example, speaking in 1982, Liang Jiashan, a Red Guard during the Cultural Revolution, and now Mr Zhao's second-in-command as deputy secretary-general of Zhuji Production Brigade, recalled the 1960s in this way:

In our village we knocked down statues of gods; ancestor tablets and things like that were burned. The main aim was to educate people to hand in and burn feudal paintings, books and religious objects. Some people refused and did not agree. Then the angry masses would put a paper hat on them and a board on their shoulders and parade them in the streets as 'Capitalist-Roaders'. We were made to attack old revolutionary cadres and all leaders, even at team and brigade level. We all had absolute loyalty to Chairman Mao. We felt he was the saviour. We never thought anything could go wrong if we followed him. We believed it was for the good of the country. Mr Zhao the brigade leader did not suffer much because he was quite ill then. But he was taken to a meeting with hat and board. Then he left to go to hospital in another city. There were big-character posters attacking him. Ten years of the Cultural Revolution didn't improve anything and the economy was sabotaged. The social order was destroyed. Many revolutionary cadres were killed or persecuted during the Cultural Revolution. The good tradition of the party was severely damaged. All these things made us realize the Cultural Revolution was a total disaster.

Land, work and responsibility in China have been allocated in a succession of different ways since 1949, and the people have been required to believe, each time, in the rightness of the new Party Line. Today therefore Chinese leaders face a problem of belief. People who have experienced the 'Ten Terrible Years' of the Cultural Revolution, and have then learned that it was a gigantic and criminal mistake, may find it hard to believe in anything. In public, China's leaders still speak of the future as a single upward march of much the same kind as in the recent past. Mr Hu Yaobang, for example, then chairman and now secretary-general of the Communist Party of China, speaking on the sixtieth anniversary of the founding of the Party, said:

The road before us is still long and tortuous. It is like climbing Mount Taishan; when we have reached the Half-Way Gate to Heaven, we find that the three [sets of] Eighteen Bends lie ahead of us, demanding heroic efforts. But once at the South Gate to Heaven, we shall be in a

呼毛主席关于派军队支持革命左派的伟大号召！
《铁血队》死保联动反动透顶！

Red Guards parade an official accused by them of counter-revolutionary activities through the streets of Beijing. The tall cap, worn as a mark of public shame, labels him a 'political pickpocket'.

position to appreciate the great Tang Dynasty poet Du Fu's well-known lines, 'Viewed from the topmost summit, all mountains around are dwarfed.' The hardships that once towered like 'mountains' will then look small and we will be able to negotiate the obstacles on the way to the 'topmost summit' more or less easily.

But after the many adjustments of belief that have been required of the people since 1949 the leaders must fear that scepticism, previously the preserve of the educated bureaucracy, could become universal; and, above all, scepticism about socialism. Such a possibility is particularly evident in the generation of young people displaced from the cities to the countryside in the Cultural Revolution, most of whom had their schooling interrupted, and who have since found it hard to return to the cities or get regular employment.

The Cultural Revolution destroyed so much that the leaders seem willing to tolerate, in the short term at least, almost any surviving element of morality and religious teaching to restore some level of ethical order and

During the Cultural Revolution, Red Guards roamed the country attacking anything that represented authority, culture, religion or old traditions.

some belief in a meaning in life. There is a mild revival of organized Buddhism and other established religions, including Christianity, under the somewhat ostentatious tolerance of the government. Monks are useful for showing the new waves of foreign tourists round temples. And the Communists' initial persecution of religions and of certain minority peoples was not good for China's 'image' abroad. Toleration helps with foreign policy: Buddhism with Japan, Islam with the Near East, Christianity with America and Europe. Daoism, by contrast, has no significant number of foreign adherents, and in any case has seldom been on particularly good terms for long with any government. The authorities' support for Daoism is not quite as prominent today as their support for other religions.

In the long term the aim of building a 'socialist spiritual culture' will almost certainly entail the rooting out of such religious belief as is tolerated for the present. Even today, a Communist Party member who still believes in a religion – a Moslem, for example – will be subjected by his colleagues to long and passionate argument aimed at deconversion.

In this period the Chinese state has also been promoting civic virtue along traditional lines, in a movement that might almost be called Marxist Confucianism. Again the leadership may see this as an intermediate stage in the creation of the Chinese 'socialist spiritual culture'. It would be serving a useful purpose for the government if it steered the people between a 'crisis of belief' following the Terrible Ten Years and the kind of 'spiritual void' that, according to the Chinese authorities, exists today in the West.

After autumn 1981 all grades of primary schools were required to teach 'ideology and conduct', spelled out in terms of 'The Five Stresses and The Four Points of Beauty'. The Five Stesses were on decorum, manners, hygiene, discipline and morals. The Four Points of Beauty were: making the mind beautiful by ideology, personal morality and Party loyalty; making

In 1976, peasants from a commune in Fujian Province read wall posters denouncing the 'Gang of Four', arrested in the autumn of that year.

63

Members of the Young Pioneers, the semi-military official youth organization for all children between the ages of 7 and 15, parade in ranks during a visit to the Revolutionary Martyrs' Memorial at Yantai in Shandong Province. The salute, with one hand held above the head, symbolizes putting the Party and the country before self.

language beautiful (not being rude to people); making behaviour beautiful (helping old people or working for the collective); and making the environment beautiful by personal hygiene and sanitation.

In April 1982 a 'Socialist Ethics and Courtesy Month' was held, extending to adults the ideals of good behaviour previously enjoined on children. The neat lists of virtues and stresses, and the tendency to number them in fives, though minor details, are typical of the ancient Chinese ethical tradition. There are special teachers in most schools in charge of moral education. A chart on the wall of the school may show the number of good deeds each child has done: for instance in 1982 a board in the Zhuji brigade primary school proclaimed that in the previous year 2900 good deeds had been done by its pupils. School outings from Zhuji often go to the nearby Yantai Revolutionary Martyrs' Memorial, where new members may be admitted to the Pioneers, the junior version of the Young Communist League; with its uniform of red scarf, worn knotted loosely at the neck, it appears almost like a Boy Scout movement, until the ranks spring to attention, adopt zealously scowling expressions and sing revolutionary anthems in throaty unison.

The Boy Scout movement has perhaps a closer parallel in the 'Learn from Lei Feng' groups. The Chinese, having long treated Confucius as an ideal teacher, still seem to find it natural to model themselves on ideal examples. Lei Feng was a soldier who devoted his life to serving the people and died young. Children are taught how he helped old women across the street and did other good deeds that would have deeply pleased Baden Powell. Going off after school, six or seven at a time, they polish old people's windows and clean their houses for them, just as Lei Feng would have done.

Stories about moral heroes are part of the main content of radio and television programmes in China: local broadcasting is in fact often mainly about good deeds done by people in the vicinity. Radio and television are conscious instruments of propaganda for the Party, and are controlled by the authorities; from one point of view broadcasting is merely a traditional but more rapid means whereby the power of the centre can be diffused to the peripheries of Chinese society.

But since the spread of individual radio and television sets in the late 1970s – a change that could have profound consequences for the beliefs of China – they are listened to and watched mainly in families rather than in large communal groups, and, irrespective of any particular messages they may have transmitted, their increasingly widespread use must have had the effect, in China as elsewhere, of reinforcing the physical closeness and shared experience of each individual family.

Television and radio also both encourage and symbolize a new prosperity. In cinemas and on television, films are shown that celebrate the higher standards of living that individual enterprise in the free markets can achieve, and which explicitly encourage the efforts of individual families to enrich themselves and so to enrich their country, by working harder on their private plots and by marketing their surplus products vigorously. But if the mass media contain such messages of hope for prosperity, they must also encourage longings for the fruits of prosperity, in particular for the radio and television sets through which the messages themselves are disseminated.

As recently as the 1970s a Chinese bride and her family expected the husband to provide her with 'the Four Wheels': one each in the sewing machine and the watch, and two in the bicycle. On the conjugal shopping lists of the 1980s they have become less significant than a camera, a radio, hi-fi equipment and a television, as press cartoons scathingly suggest.*

Though people in all countries, when they see prosperity in films and television, make allowances for their own position, and continue to feel more envy of the slightly richer family next door than of the vastly richer families shown on the screen, such pictures cannot but have some long-term effect in shaping the expectations and beliefs of the Chinese people. To what extent will there be a 'convergence' between those in China who have grown up with television and young people in other countries throughout the world? And to what extent will this, if it happens, be merely a phase, a swing of the pendulum, to be reversed by a change of mind or a change of faces at the top of China's power-structure?

The 'revolution of rising expectations' that the leaders need in order to persuade people to work harder could produce more dissatisfaction than prosperity. The policies they have followed recently – free markets and family responsibility in agriculture – have initially proved widely popular, and have permitted an increase in prosperity in many areas; but they must be concerned about foreign influence, about advertising, and about the presence of overseas Chinese 'capitalists', of foreigners engaged in joint ventures in China, and even of the millions of tourists.

Today, at the summit of Taishan, where the greatest emperors of China once climbed with their retinue to sacrifice to Heaven, there is a television transmitter. As it reaches up to mediate between Heaven and Earth and to speak to man in between, Mr Zhao Kuisheng of Zhuji looks towards the future, thinking of the forces at work in the minds of the commune members – the 'masses' as he thinks of them – in his brigade:

Though life has improved, some of the commune members are still not satisfied. Some of them, especially the young newly-married couples, set up rather nice homes: they have radios, washing machines, television sets, shutter windows, double glazing, sofas, all these things. They build new houses. They are still not satisfied. They are looking for an even higher standard of living. They want the things in the house to be even more luxurious. Now there are quite a few commune members who, when they have the money, go on holiday to other places, sightseeing. This is what the commune members are thinking of at the moment: they want to have a prosperous life, the opportunity to go sightseeing, to look around, and to be happy.

Mr Zhao, like the middle-level officials in villages in the Chinese countryside everywhere in the 1980s, walks home to his wife and children every night past rows of other houses with families gathered inside: some laughing and talking, some playing cards (not for money of course; no gambling in China), some cooking or eating their meals, and many, an increasing number, watching the flickering light of television and making out of its collective messages their own individual meanings.

MARRYING

WIVES AND CONCUBINES

In some parts of China it was customary for a bride to curse her new in-laws and her husband-to-be for three days before the wedding. There was an established genre of cursing songs, passed on between the girls of the villages and elaborated on by each new bride as she came near her wedding day. In them she would vilify the family to which she was going as 'dead' or 'worthless'; she might compare herself to her sisters, whom she envied for continuing in the warmth of her own family, and sometimes she might abuse her own father and mother for allowing her to be estranged to another, distant family. But it was above all her future mother-in-law who bore the brunt of the curses.*

Western men make jokes about their mothers-in-law. In China the mother-in-law jokes are told by women. Women were subordinated to men in traditional China; but they were subordinated more immediately to other, older women.

A Chinese woman in traditional society 'married into a family' in a far more literal sense than in the West. So long as she remained unmarried she was not an adult, no matter what her age. When she married her links with her own blood-relations were broken, and would be restored only if she were repudiated by her husband; but in that case her family was not bound to take her back. If her husband died she would remain in his household; and if her children were still minors, she might become the household head.

The Chinese family developed in a settled agrarian society. Village life and agricultural needs formed it. Children were needed to till the land as their parents grew old, and to provide labour from their own late childhood on. Boys were valued much more highly than girls; they were stronger, as child labour, and they were a permanent investment, whereas to bring up a daughter was to nourish a wasting asset, since almost all daughters married into other families. As children, young girls might enjoy close and affectionate ties with their parents, but hanging over them was always the certainty of separation. They were no more than guests, in a way, in their own homes. In the words of a poem written by Fu Xuan in the third century:

19th-century Chinese watercolour.

A young Chinese woman was persuaded to unbandage her foot for the benefit of photographer John Thomson who visited China in the 1870s.

How sad it is to be a woman!
Nothing on earth is held so cheap.
Boys stand leaning at the door
Like gods fallen out of heaven.
Their hearts brave the Four Oceans,
The wind and dust of a thousand miles.
No one is glad when a girl is born;
By her the family sets no store.*

Girls were sometimes drowned at birth, a practice which has not entirely died out. Others were sold, as babies, to be brought up as household servants. For those who remained at home, especially in north and central China, footbinding was almost mandatory if the girl were later to be marriageable.

Footbinding took place between the ages of five and seven, and the process of bending back the foot so that the bones of the instep were completely broken was agonizing. Historically, the practice was associated with a court craze for small feet in the Tang Dynasty (618–906), when dancers would bind their feet in order to take exceptionally light steps, appearing to hover like lotuses suspended above the surface of a pool. A famous dance called 'The Golden Lotus' has given its name to the entire strange practice. In the Song Dynasty (960–1279), by which time the custom had spread from the court to society as a whole, footbound women could not have danced; they had to hobble in slippers. A fashionable-sized foot was only three inches long. The customary explanation of this strange custom – for which there may have been less conscious reasons also – is that footbinding stopped the wives and concubines of the rich from straying, and that it was imitated by the poor even though they had no concubines. Most Chinese families, except the poor in the south, came to require footbound brides for their sons.

Marriage was not primarily a union of a man and a woman; it was a union between two families which proclaimed their related social standing. Every lineage and every family had its 'marriage strategy', depending on its ambitions. A man might marry his daughter to a promising young colleague or subordinate, with an eye to future security. Sometimes two lineages would cross-marry, generation after generation. A poor man usually had to pay a bride-price for a wife, whereas in rich families it was customary for the bride's family to provide a dowry.

Marriage between two people of the same surname, even if they were not related, was considered incestuous. Marriage within the same village was also rare. Many people, especially in the south, lived in clan villages where everybody had the same surname. Thus girls would usually be obliged to leave everything familiar behind them, not only their home but also their native village, when they were married.

Marriage was far too serious a business to be left to a young man and woman. All marriages were arranged, for a fee, through a neutral third party, often an elderly woman with connections in the surrounding villages, or a travelling tradesman. It was quite usual for the bride and groom not to

have met before the wedding. In imperial China the bride might be only fourteen and the husband sixteen.

Unless the husband had lost his parents, the bride did not move immediately into an independent establishment. She normally joined the husband's parents' household, where she was subject to their control to the same degree of submission as if she had been their own child.

The family was hierarchical, and those who were inferior were expected at all times to defer to, obey and serve those who were superior. A member of an older generation was always superior to a member of a younger generation; within the same generation an older brother was superior to a younger; and men were superior to women. The first and last principles conflicted in the relationship of mother and son. Generally, outside the home the son was superior; at home sons deferred to their mothers. A man did not need to be concerned about his relationship to his mother-in-law, since, in a different family, she played almost no part in his life.

Confucian ideas, which permeated much of society, protected and promoted the enduring family ruled by its senior male and looking back to his progenitors in ancestor-worship. Ancestors were buried on or near the land they had farmed, and their graves were a constant reminder of the duty owed to the dead as well as of the trust in which land was held for descendants. Ancestor-worship stressed the same hierarchy as that of the

A group portrait of the women of a rich Manchu family makes a formidable gathering. Manchu women did not bind their feet.

A 19th-century painting shows the women of a rich Chinese family playing music.

family: senior males took precedence in rituals over both younger men and all women, and on death became guardian gods of the family. Women generally had a lesser role in worship, and when they died they were deified in the role of wife and mother rather than as individuals in their own right.

Popular morality tales placed a heavy emphasis on the observance of absolute service to superiors; state law backed this up by providing the death penalty (by decapitation) for any son who struck his mother or father, even if the blow caused no injury.* A wife or concubine who conspired against her husband could suffer the severest penalty of all, the death by slow slicing.* A wife who failed to bear a son or who suffered from persistent ill-health could be divorced, and in such matters the husband's first duty would be to his family, not his wife. The ancient *Record of Rites (Liji)* said, 'If [the son] very much approves of his wife, and his parents do not like her, he should divorce her; if he does not approve of his wife, and his parents say "She serves us well," he should behave to her in all respects as a husband – without fail even to the end of her life.'*

But whereas in theory the wife was meant to be completely submissive to

A woodcut of 1937 by Yang Nawei depicts the misery of the family of an absent soldier, conscripted into the army.

her husband, to his parents and to some extent to her own sons, personalities played a powerful role in establishing what sort of relationship in fact emerged. In practice a woman could often come to rule a family, especially if she first dominated her son and then, on her husband's death, became the widowed mother of the head of a house. Even while her husband was alive the wife had great responsibilities in most families, not only in running the household and the servants if there were any, but in controlling the budget. No wife could achieve her full power until her mother-in-law was dead. But as the dowager 'matriarch', she held the purse strings and was supreme ruler of all business in the small world of the home. If part of the house was to be let, she did the negotiation: the head of the house, son or husband, merely introduced the would-be tenant to her. She also settled, or had great influence on, the marriages of daughters and sons. She decided on the upbringing of children, including grandsons, grandnieces and grand-nephews if their parents had died or were absent. If there were no male heirs and the adoption of a son became vital to the continuity of the family, she regulated it. Children were taught to obey her, answer her summons immediately and never dispute her decisions; she ordained how they should be punished if they misbehaved.

From childhood to later life a woman was thus under the authority of one matriarch or the other, first of her own mother, then of her mother-in-law. Her father-in-law by contrast would have virtually no direct dealings with her; a new wife would be told to avoid him and also her brothers-in-law.

'When you go to your husband's home, do not behave well', counselled a Han Dynasty mother, 'for whatever you do will be wrong in any case.' Quarrels, brutality and beatings were often the result of the relationship between mother- and daughter-in-law. The main strength a woman had on arrival in the new household was her personal force, generally evinced by her tongue. 'If a Chinese woman has a violent temper,' wrote one foreigner in the nineteenth century, 'if she is able at a moment's notice to raise a tornado and keep it blowing at the rate of 100 miles an hour . . . then the most termagant of mothers-in-law hesitates to attack one who has no fear of men or demons.' Alternatively she could refuse to speak at all under any provocation, preserving a powerful and radiating silence.

Much of the terrorization by the mother-in-law of her daughter-in-law may have arisen out of the older woman's jealousy of a younger rival for the affection of her son. Relationships between mother and son were generally relaxed and friendly, particularly before the son's marriage. The mother would have gained power and position through giving birth to her son, and might well have tried to establish his love for her before his marriage introduced a new and dangerous element to the family. The son could show affection for his mother without fear of scorn, and often found in her a sympathetic ear when relations with his father or perhaps with his wife were difficult.

Publicly the relationship between husband and wife was one of indifference, with neither openly even mentioning the existence of the other. The young couple would owe their coming together to their parents; they might have little liking for each other; and they would be encouraged to speak and work together as little as possible. In private the relationship was often a tense battle on the wife's part to win affection and respect from her husband; until her sons grew up this was her only hope of future security and power. As time went by the relationship might become more friendly.

Sisters had warm and intense but short-lived relationships with each other; at marriage they parted, often never to see each other again. Sisters also tended to have affectionate relationships with their brothers until a brother married, and after her own marriage a sister would often retain the relationship with her brother and rely on it for companionship if her married life were difficult, and for financial support or helpful introductions for her children.

It has long been common for Chinese men to complain that the falling out of brothers is caused by the incompatibility of their wives. The various wives of brothers did often quarrel among themselves, and in large families the women were often divided into factions, with the mother-in-law

deliberately stirring up one daughter-in-law against another. However, even if this were not the case, it was less shameful to blame the wives than to admit that one of the five Confucian relationships, that between an elder brother and younger brother, had broken down. In practice it often did, under the pressure of a code which required submission by the younger brother while the family remained intact, but which made all brothers equal in inheritance. Though all property was inherited through the male line it was shared out among all the family's sons equally, so that a younger brother could be said to gain by causing the break-up of the family. It is indicative of the frequency with which families did fall apart in imperial China that the agrarian landscape was until 1949 like a patchwork quilt, many fields being of minute proportions owing to the constant dividing and subdividing of estates.

In any dispute between husband and wife the assumption of the husband's authority over the wife automatically gave him the benefit of the doubt. In the Tang and Song Dynasties divorce by mutual consent because of incompatibility seems to have been common: it was accepted that two people could not be expected to stay together if they were 'like a cat and a rat living in the same hole'. In more recent centuries the husband had the right unilaterally to set aside his wife for any of the 'seven reasons for divorce', mostly offences against his authority or failure to produce an heir, while the wife was protected only by the 'three reasons for not repudiating a wife': she could not be sent away if she had mourned her husband's parents' death for three years, if her husband's family had become rich after their marriage, or if she had no family to take her in. In practice divorce was rare. The poor could not afford to marry a second time, as they usually had to pay for a bride, and a rich man did not need to discard his wife when he took another women as a concubine. Besides, divorce was a disgrace.

A wife who was threatened by repudiation could respond with the threat of suicide. This was indeed the weapon of last resort to which Chinese wives did and still do have recourse when driven beyond endurance. It may have offered the satisfaction of knowing that an oppressive mother-in-law would be obliged to follow the coffin, that all the neighbours would know of her cruelty and would be mocking her, and that the entire family, whom the wife might hate, would be embroiled in legal investigations and proceedings. If a wife did commit suicide, her family could sue the husband's family, and, though by no means all families could afford to go to law, fear of a lawsuit could never be discounted, while even without one the prospect of an investigation by the local authorities, involving much trouble and expense and possibly judicial torture, gave a woman a certain measure of protection. In one area where the traditional marriage system had declined in the twentieth century, it was noted that the suicide rate for young married women had fallen. The suicide rate among mothers-in-law had correspondingly increased.*

Concubines were not protected by the 'three reasons' against divorce, but even they could not be discarded without considerable negotiations with their original family. A concubine was a serious member of the household in

An illustration to a 17th-century edition of the popular prose romance, The Water Margin, *shows Gold Lotus feeding poison to her husband Wu Da while he is asleep. An old matchmaker, who is acting as an intermediary between Gold Lotus and her lover, looks on.*

淫婦藥鴆武大郎

traditional China, normally a permanent member of it, at least while the husband lived. She was brought into the household with a view to bearing children, usually after the first wife had proved barren or had failed to produce a son. She was not a member of a harem, but an assistant wife who would help entertain guests, and thus had to be socially part of the family. She often shared in much the same sort of household duties as the wife, and might call her 'Elder Sister'. She was, however, usually either hired, like a superior servant, or bought.

Concubinage was confined to the rich, the vast mass of the Chinese people being monogamous through necessity. A concubine often introduced tension into a household: sexual jealousy for the wife, factions and favouritism among the servants. She was usually much younger than her husband: it was normal for a man to put off acquiring a concubine until his wife was about forty. She thus tended to upset the regular relations between generations in the family, both male and female. The guides to household economy, frequently published from the Song Dynasty onwards, recommend elaborate precautions to isolate concubines from possible lovers, and warn particularly against visiting Buddhist monks and masseurs. Concubines could cause conflicts between father and son, since a son might be attracted by a paternal concubine. The Empress Wu in the Tang Dynasty was the concubine both of a father and of his son. The plot of the *Jin Ping Mei*, a famous satirical erotic novel of the Ming Dynasty, includes a passionate love affair between the antihero's concubine, Gold Lotus, and his son-in-law, Young Chen.

The imperial family had a very large establishment of concubines, arranged in a hierarchy and holding high official rank. If the empress died without male children, or had never had any, the son of one of the high-ranking concubines would be the heir to the throne. The children of concubines in all ranks of society were treated, legally, as equal in status and rights to children of the chief wife. In practice the standing of the concubine's original family made a lot of difference. Occasionally, on the early death of the wife, a concubine would become the new chief wife and matriarch, especially if she were the mother of the only surviving son. Like Empress Wu, Empress Dowager Cixi of the Qing Dynasty had once been an imperial concubine.

It was a high honour to be chosen as an imperial concubine, eagerly sought after in the highest social ranks. Elsewhere the normal origin of concubines was either from among the daughters of tenant farmers or of merchants engaged in doing business with a rich man or high official, who were often glad to see a daughter enter his household, or from the ranks of prostitutes or entertainers. So-called 'sing-song girls' from the entertainment industry would often have originated in poor families, and would have been, in effect, sold to the training establishments. They were taught to sing, play music, carry on light but entertaining conversation and read and write, unusual accomplishments for a woman in traditional China. They were sent to entertain the wealthy at banquets, where no family women would be present, but for the most part did not give sexual favours. These had to be paid for at very high prices, and an accomplished girl held out; she would accept only concubinage. That was the ultimate aim of her career and education. Part of the price went to the house to which she belonged, part was retained by the girl herself, who also had her elaborate and expensive wardrobe, the jewellery she had obtained as presents and some money of her own as well. The husband would have had to buy out her contract and pay off any debts she still had. She thus entered her new home as a person of some standing, and usually as the favourite of an elderly husband, though she was nonetheless under the authority of the matriarch. She was not always resented. Since marriages were arranged, love did not necessarily follow, and the wife might have found sexual relations with her husband an unpleasant duty; she might thus well not mind another woman taking them over and leaving the running of the household in her own hands.

In the decades before the communist regime, the custom of taking concubines had become a little out of fashion. But in provincial small-town society it still flourished, and some generals of the warlord age were notorious for the numbers in their households. One, Zhang Zongchang, possessed some forty concubines of different nationalities, several of them White Russian refugees. Because he allegedly did not know how much money he possessed, how many troops he commanded or how many concubines he had, he was sometimes referred to as General 'Three Don't Knows' (*San Buzhi*).

China was a society with considerable social mobility, and elite values were shared by many peasants and minority peoples, particularly as their indigenous cultures decayed; but they were not universal.* For instance not only concubinage, but also strict hierarchical relationships within the family and the practice of marrying the bride into the husband's family were to be found much more regularly among the Han Chinese elite and those families that aspired to join it than among the poor and the national minorities. There were many poor men who could not afford to pay for a bride and had to marry into a somewhat richer family, moving into the bride's house and giving the children either her family's surname or alternate surnames. Even though such marriages spared the bride the pain of separation from her family they were generally dreaded because it was usually assumed that no worthwhile man would agree to this arrangement.

Very poor families might have had to sell their daughters as babies as an alternative to drowning them, either as servants or to be brought up as child-brides for the infant son of another family. Such girls, though again spared the pain of a later separation on marriage, often greatly resented their parents. It was found in one area that their rate of divorce was higher than average, while they also tended to have fewer children. Both these differences have been explained by the difficulty of adjusting to a sexual relationship with someone with whom they had grown up virtually as sister to brother.*

Among peasant women the mother might work in the fields along with her unmarried daughters and daughters-in-law. Poor women were often engaged in some small business after their marriage: as dressmakers in the cities, as midwives and sometimes in the south as household servants. In the south and among many non-Han peoples peasant women would not be footbound. Two of the crops of the south – silk and tea – were the province of women, and the tending of the mulberry trees and the cultivation and picking of the tea demanded the active labour of women able to walk naturally. The large population in the south who lived on the rivers and along the coast, engaged either in transport, fishing, or both, never bound the women's feet, and in fact the women ran the boats, rowed, sailed, cooked and looked after small children tethered by a cord to the foot of the mast, while the men worked ashore. Northern women and the rich in the south used a contemptuous name for these southerners: 'bigfooted women' (*dajiao guniang*). But sensitive richer girls could envy peasants whose own lives seemed in this respect immeasurably preferable to their own.*

There is evidence that there was greater sexual freedom in some areas of the countryside than the Confucian code implied. Disapproving reports from Confucian scholar-officials in the nineteenth century complain of this,* and documentary writings such as those of Shen Congwen in the early twentieth century allude to it. Shen was, like Mao Zedong, a native of Hunan and was a leader of the 'May 4th' literary group based on the movement of that name that marked the birth of Chinese nationalism in 1919. It was among the main beliefs of this group that a writer should use the language of everyday speech and should write about the common people. Shen described the world of the boat people of the Yuan River, one little touched by Confucian official morality. This excerpt is from a book written as a series of letters to his wife:

It was 7.40 by my watch, yet not very light . . . As they prepared to cast off, men who had spent the night ashore came back in relays to help those who had slept on board . . . The boatmen who had slept in the stilt-houses, snug in a woman's quilt, came marching down through the boulders to their boats. Many women . . . draped clothes over their shoulders to lean out a window . . . It was obvious that their lovemaking last night had already cost each of them some tears and resentment.

On a boat not far from ours I heard a boatman yell hoarsely . . . 'Niu Bao, Niu Bao, you dog-shit. Stop screwing that woman, will you?' Only then did the man in the stilt-house appear to wake with a start from his sweet dreams and jump out from the woman's arms in the warm quilt. Padding naked to the window he called back, 'What are you yelling for, Songsong? It's still early.'*

And so the story goes on, with cursing, swearing and casual lovemaking, described with a certain distanced dignity by Shen Congwen. His vision gives a sense of how shallow were the roots of Confucian morality among at least some of the common people, though no one can tell how many.

In general such liberties as were created for women after 1949 were an

In a Western-style gown donned for the occasion, a bride waits her turn to be photographed with her groom.

inheritance from the freedoms enjoyed by the peasant women of old China; peasant models, social and economic, were at the root of this as of many of the other practices ordained by the new regime. But these freedoms did not extend to sexual relations. In the 1930s there had been much talk in the Communist Party of destroying the nuclear family. Mao Zedong was not a puritan in his personal life, and in his earlier writings he praised the non-conformist sexual customs of the peasantry of his native Hunan. But when he came to power no such freedoms were to be permitted for the people. This was in the old imperial tradition: the 'masses' were there to work, and the nuclear family was to be the central unit of revolutionary production. When Mao did attack the nuclear family in the Great Leap Forward of 1958, it was not in order to offer more sexual freedom to the people of China, but in certain cases less: some men and women were made to live in separate barracks, their family houses destroyed. It was also normal for husbands and wives with specialist training to find themselves posted to different parts of the country, able to see each other for only a few days a year, at national holidays. In this respect the Communist Party has spread to society as a whole not the liberties of peasants but some of the traditional restraints of the literate elite, whose code was deeply affected by the expectation that an official would be required to spend many years of his life in provinces other than his native one, often without his family. Scholar-officials, though they were not denied sexual freedom by their code, were encouraged to think of sex as physically debilitating and of desire as a distraction from the proper concerns of a gentleman.

The first communist Marriage Law in 1950 contained a considerable emphasis on duty: Article 8 stated, 'Husband and wife are in duty bound to love, respect, assist and look after each other, to live in harmony, to engage in productive work, to care for the children and to strive jointly for the welfare of the family and for the building up of the new society.' Article 13 added that, 'Parents have the duty to rear and educate their children; the children have the duty to support and assist their parents.' The first provision has been somewhat modified in favour of a more contractual relationship in the 1981 Marriage Law; the second provision has been retained. The fact that in China children are legally and financially responsible for their parents gives an added edge to the preference for sons over daughters: women in general earn less than men in China, and still nearly always marry into their husband's family.

In some respects however the 1950 Marriage Law did proclaim a new liberty. It announced, 'The feudal marriage system based on arbitrary and compulsory arrangements and the supremacy of men over women, and in disregard of the children, is abolished.' The young were now free to choose their partners, to marry 'for love' as many of them put it, though others continued to defer to their parents' wishes. Women also became free to divorce their husbands in 1950. Many did, and many more attempted to. It was partly because of this that there was considerable resistance from men to the Marriage Law when it was first promulgated. It was widely known as the

Elaborate styles and curls, which were considered unthinkably frivolous during the Cultural Revolution, were back in fashion in the early 1980s.

Divorce Law. Peasant men occasionally killed women sent to their village to expound it. Divorce meant the division of property, and in the countryside this could mean economic instability or ruin. Especially after 1953, when the Communist Party decided there was too much marital instability, women applying for divorce would be talked out of the idea rather than granted what they demanded; and this is still frequently the case.

The legal equality between women and men created in 1949 was not always an unmixed blessing. The same rights and the same duties were granted and expected of women as of men; but in practice this might mean that women would be expected to undertake the same duties as men in addition to their traditional household work rather than instead of it.

The Marriage Law was intended to weaken the extended family and to coincide with land reform, in the course of which 'lineage land' or 'clan land', held in common by large families, was to be confiscated and redistributed. The Communist Party wanted to break clan ties because the clan was considered an impediment to efficient production and also a focus of potential resistance to the power of the state.

The hierarchical nature of the traditional family had been criticized by the Communist Party from the beginning, and in the Cultural Revolution this criticism rose to a crescendo. Red Guards were encouraged to attack their parents. Chinese mothers whose children were born about 1949 felt they had had the worst of two worlds: subjected to parents and their mothers-in-law in their youth, and now brutally subordinated to their sons and daughters in their middle age.

Since the death of Mao the family has been given an increasingly positive role, especially in the economic sphere. Often it is the main contracting

A young couple cannot conceal their delight as they carry a new television set home.

work-group under the Responsibility System.* There is also less official hostility than there was to ancient customs; anything attacked in the Cultural Revolution cannot be considered entirely harmful today. That is perhaps why a traditional wedding, complete with its ancient customs, could still take place in 1982 in a village such as Maoping in Zhejiang Province.*

The young man and the girl in this instance had decided that they wanted to marry, but they felt they could not do so without the consent of the girl's mother. So they engaged a matchmaker to secure it and to arrange all the practical details of the wedding. The matchmaker, who was the manager of the brigade factory where the girl worked, went to ask the girl's mother for her permission. The mother refused, saying that her daughter was too young (the legal age is now twenty: she was still nineteen). But her main objection was that her family was short of labour and that she needed her daughter to help her at home. During the course of the next year the girl's father died and the boy endeared himself to her mother by helping in the family's fields. The mother began to give him small treats, such as eggs. Eventually she consented, under the matchmaker's repeated urging, and an auspicious date for the marriage was fixed.

The girl was to provide all the household goods, from furniture and bedding down to the toothbrushes. The bridegroom bought her a bicycle and sewing machine, a watch, and a hundred yuan-worth of clothes. The mother hinted to the matchmaker that many of her relations would require presents. In the end it was decided that the groom should provide five hundred steamed buns, forty *jin* (twenty kilograms) of meat to be shared among the relations, ten tins of moon-cakes (a traditional Chinese festival food), some sugar and one carton of cigarettes. Another round of presents was then required for the wedding feast, which the groom, by now somewhat apprehensive at the extent of the expenditure, also had to buy. A civil ceremony was held in the nearby town; then, several days later, the traditional ceremony took place in the village. Much of the food eaten in the marriage feast, such as round balls of sweetened rice, sugar cane and fish, had symbolic significance. The first meant a life of unbroken harmony; sugar cane indicated a sweet future; and fish in Chinese is also a homonym for 'abundance'. Date soup was eaten because the Chinese characters for 'date' are pronounced in the same way as the characters for 'early [birth of a] son'.

In the past many peasants went into debt or were ruined in paying for their wedding. In this case, despite the government's constant exhortations to dispense with extravagances which the peasants can hardly afford, the wedding cost the groom about five years' income.

Besides high spending on weddings there are other ancient customs and attitudes which the Communist Party would like to eradicate but which are proving more recalcitrant. Much of the time of the women's committees in Chinese villages is taken up in urging sterilization or abortion on those who have had one child, and in trying to convince parents and, with greater difficulty, grandparents, that a girl baby is as good today as a boy. It is a constant struggle, by all accounts, and there still needs to be a clause in the

Chinese Marriage Law which states, 'Drowning babies and other acts of murdering girl babies are prohibited.' An article in the official *China Youth Daily* on 9 November 1982 reminded its readers of this clause and revealed the horrifying statistic that in some communes ratios of 6:4 were being reported between surviving baby boys and baby girls. The article ended by emphasizing the consequences, ironically, for the baby boys: it stated that if this practice were not checked immediately, in twenty years' time there would be a very severe social problem, as many of these young men would be without spouses.

It is not clear how far back into history the lower valuation of women's lives than men's can be traced. It has been argued that China may once have been inhabited by matriarchal peoples or at least by a society with egalitarian relationships between men and women. The ancient cosmology of yin and yang may reflect a sense of complementary equality between the sexes. Yin, which is associated with the feminine principle, means principally 'dark' or 'shadowed'; yang means primarily 'bright'; in an agricultural context these concepts need not imply inequality. However there are characters in Chinese which suggest ideas of femininity that are hard to reconcile with any supposed egalitarianism in the period when they evolved. Some that include the character for 'woman' mean 'evil', 'slave', 'anger', 'jealousy' or 'hatred', 'suspicion', 'avarice' and 'obstruction', 'evil spirit', 'demon' or 'witch' (with the meaning also of 'bewitching') 'fornication' or 'seduction', the last being built of the character 'woman' and another character meaning 'to flatter' or 'to fawn'. At some quite early date sensuality and sexual appetite appear to have been associated much more firmly with women than with men, at least among the literate elite. Even so a saying has survived from early times:

> For a man to take his pleasure
> Is a thing that may be condoned,
> That a girl should take her pleasure
> Cannot be condoned.*

Stories told of Confucius in the sixth century show considerable contempt for the opposite sex. 'We should not be too familiar with the lower orders or with women,' he is once recorded as saying. The earliest Chinese historical records contain many examples of the subordination of women and of contemptuous attitudes toward them. Sima Qian, the great historian of early China, who lived in the Han Dynasty, tells how a famous general, Sun Wu, was asked by the king of one of the Warring States to demonstrate his military theories. It was suggested that he should drill a hundred and eighty women. Sun Wu divided them into two companies, with the king's two favourite concubines as their leaders. He explained the rules of drill and asked them if they understood:

The women assured him that they did. With the roll of a drum he gave the order 'Turn right!' The women burst out laughing. Sun Wu tried again, and when the same thing happened he

Terracotta figures of women playing polo date from the Tang Dynasty (618-906) and show that women then enjoyed far greater freedom than in later times. From the next dynasty, the Song (960-1279), onwards, women's activities were largely restricted to the home.

prepared to execute both company leaders. The king, watching from his stand, [sent a messenger] saying, 'I can see you are an able general. But without these two concubines my food would lose all flavour. I beg you to spare them.'

In fact Sun Wu had them killed.*

The contrast between devotion to one's job and concern with the attractions of women was frequently drawn in Confucian ethical anecdotes, and in the histories of China written by Confucian scholars many examples are given of the trouble caused when the emperor became too fond of women and neglected his duty to his subjects, or when he promoted his concubines' relations at court.

The most celebrated concubine in Chinese history is probably Yang Guifei, who was loved by the Tang emperor Xuanzong. The An-Lushan Rebellion, the greatest disaster in the history of the Tang Dynasty, which allowed barbarians to establish new frontiers within sixty miles of the imperial capital at Chang'an (Xi'an), arose out of the factional struggles in which Yang Guifei's many relations, elevated by her patronage, embroiled the court. The fleeing emperor's bodyguards insisted on having Yang Guifei handed over to them and strangled her. An earlier pair of lovers, often compared with them, were the emperor Han Wudi (141-86 BC) and his favourite concubine Li Furen. It was in his reign that the practice which the story of Yang Guifei exemplified began: influential groups formed factions to control the government by supplying the emperor with a member of their family as a concubine, and would rise to power and official positions as she rose in the emperor's favour.

Han Wudi was allegedly introduced to Li Furen by her brother, Li Yannian, an actor castrated for a crime, who was also an imperial favourite. The emperors of the Former Han Dynasty (206 BC-AD 9) were notably bisexual, and gave the Chinese language a name for homosexuality, 'the cut sleeve' (*duanxiu*), because one emperor, rather than disturb his sleeping favourite who was lying on the imperial gown, cut off its sleeve when he had to attend a meeting.* Both literature and history in China reveal a widespread acceptance of homosexuality and bisexuality until the early part of the twentieth century. Today, it may be treated as a serious crime, and in certain circumstances can, or could recently, be punished by death.*

In the Han Dynasty and also the Tang (618-906), women seem to have been more emancipated than in later periods. The Tang was the last great dynasty before footbinding became the rule; and in contrast to the immobilized women of the Song Dynasty (960-1279), almost like potted plants, Tang women rode horses, hunted, played polo and took part in politics. The influence of Daoism may have been significant: Daoists generally valued women much more highly than did Confucians and allowed them to enter their monasteries. Daoism also accorded a high value to the sexual fulfilment of women and to sexual life in general. Numerous books detailing Daoist sexual practices were ascribed to one of the Daoists' most revered mythical figures, the Yellow Emperor, and to his instructress the Dark Girl or the Plain Girl. The scholar who has most deeply studied this subject in the West, Robert Van Gulik, writes that the Plain Girl is sometimes identified with the Mother Goddess who presided over the Daoist Western Paradise, the famous Mother Ruler of the West.*

The Daoists saw the great source of life-nourishing force for men – yin – in the sexual fulfilment of women while a man remained unfulfilled. Thus the Han scholar Bian Rang writes of the central figure of a scene of love, 'He retires to a spacious tower, cooled by the breeze, and there practises the important methods of the Yellow Emperor,' and the commentary observes, 'The Yellow Emperor learned the Art of the Bedchambers from the Dark Girl. It consists of suppressing emissions, absorbing the woman's fluid and making the semen return to strengthen the brain, thereby to obtain longevity.'* In the words of Robert van Gulik:

Such books . . . taught how a man could live long and happily by maintaining harmonious sexual relations with his women, and obtain healthy offspring from them. At the same time Daoist students of the art of prolonging life used these books as guides for their sexual disciplines . . . The polygamic family system contributed to this principle being maintained throughout the centuries . . . [A] householder could satisfy the sexual needs of his wives and concubines without injuring his health and potency. Thus in Chinese literature on sex the following two basic facts are stressed again and again. First, a man's semen is his most precious possession, the source not only of his health but of his very life; every emission of semen will diminish this vital force, unless compensated by the acquiring of an equivalent amount of yin essence from the woman. Second, the man should give the woman complete satisfaction every time he cohabits with her, but he should allow himself to reach orgasm only on certain specified occasions. The above basic thoughts explain fully the ancient Chinese attitude to all phenomena of sex, as expressed in both old and later writing on this subject.*

A famous court poet of the Han Dynasty, Sima Xiangru, was capable of combining tenderness and eroticism with a sense that such matters are ultimately concerned with the man's physical well-being. Once, he says, in winter, he passed a large, beautiful and apparently deserted house – perhaps an idealized way of describing the residence of a courtesan – and found inside

. . . a lovely girl alone in her room, reclining on a couch . . . She prepared excellent wine and took out a lute. I struck the strings and played the tunes 'Dark Orchid' and 'White Snow'. The girl then sang the song:

> All alone in the bedroom, it seems unbearably lonely,
> Thinking of a handsome man, my feelings pain me.
> Why did this charming person hesitate to come?
> Time runs out fast, the flower will wither –
> I entrust my body to you, for eternal love . . .

The sun was setting in the west, and darkness filled the room with its shadows. There was a cold breeze outside, and the snow came down in floating flakes. But the bedroom was quiet and close, one did not hear a single sound . . . She then shed her upper robe and took off her undergarment revealing her white body, with thin bones and soft flesh. When then we made love with each other her body was soft and moist like ointment. Thereafter the blood in my veins had settled, and my heart had become steadied in my bosom.*

In a copy of a Tang Dynasty scroll painting the emperor Xuanzong (712-756) watches as his favourite, Yang Guifei, mounts a horse with the help of her handmaidens. As a result of her influence, and that of her relations promoted through her patronage, the emperor took disastrous political decisions which led to his own dethronement, her death, and the near downfall of the Tang Dynasty.

Besides such quasi-medical eroticism the Chinese also have a rich literature of more romantic love. Collections of folksongs and classical poetry are as full of themes of love as those of any other civilization, and Chinese poets were particularly prone to regard the single enduring love of one person for another as one of the highest values in life. The image of a pair of mandarin ducks, who mate for life, is a very common one in literature. An even more romantic image that occurs sometimes in poetry is that of two lovers as a pair of birds, each with one wing only, who can never fly until the one finds the other.

The greatest of classical Chinese novels of love, *The Red Chamber Dream* (which has also been translated as *The Story of the Stone*) by Cao Xueqin, is the book that many adolescent girls read in China even today, or follow in strip cartoons in magazines. It is a spacious novel, set in the bustling life of a rich Chinese family of the eighteenth century. A boy, Jia Baoyu, is born with a piece of magic jade in his mouth. The central thread of the novel is the story of his unconsummated love for one of his girl cousins, the orphan Lin Daiyu; the love of his serving maid Aroma is a more physical though subordinate thread at the start of the story. Daiyu was sickly, frail and excessively sensitive; Baoyu was rich and handsome. She was not considered a good match for him; another cousin was chosen as his wife. Baoyu was deceived by his family into believing that he was marrying Daiyu, for the bride remained heavily veiled until after the marriage ceremony. While everyone was attending the wedding, Daiyu was alone, dying of consumption. Baoyu married the girl chosen for him, but one day he disappeared, never to return. To the Western reader the hero may seem passive, somewhat spoilt and petulant. He has traditionally been the ideal of young Chinese girls. This is explained by his sensitivity (he would become ill if Daiyu was unhappy); his talent (he wrote poetry); his non-conformism (he did not want to study and become an official); and the faithfulness of his love.

The book that most young Chinese boys read, by contrast, which gives an utterly different picture of relationships between men and women, is *The Water Margin*, a swashbuckling novel written down and edited in the Ming Dynasty (1368-1644), but based on earlier oral traditions. It relates the adventures of a band of robbers and rebels in the troubled period at the end of the Song Dynasty, when the Mongols were ravaging north China. The rebels display their virility by avoiding or even by attacking women, who appear either as temptations to be resisted, dangerous because they weaken a man's military resolve, or as shrewish and aggressive, scolding and complaining, to a point where even a brigand hero is reduced to powerlessness. Gold Lotus, for example, wife of Wu Da, rails at him and his brother thus: 'I'm a real man in woman's clothes, a solid woman who can lift up men with her hands and horses with her forearms, not one of those old turtles whose heads you can't jolt out. Since I was married to Wu Da not an ant has dared to enter this house.'*

Representations of powerful women are not uncommon in Chinese popular culture, and are especially frequent in opera. The story of Mulan, a

heroine of the fifth or sixth century, is one of the most popular of all operas. Her father was old and infirm and her brother was young; when her family had to supply a soldier to fight against the barbarians she went to war instead of them and became a general. Returning home victorious, she changed back into her woman's clothes, to the amazement of her soldiers. A less obvious example of a dominant Chinese woman on the stage is to be seen in the opera brought by the local girls' opera troupe to the village of Maoping in Zhejiang Province in October 1982. The woman is shown powerfully resisting the pleadings of her small and apparently dominated scholar-husband. All goes badly for him until he brings into play his ultimate armament – the nuclear deterrent of the nuclear family – her mother-in-law. Then she capitulates.

Little can be said in generalizations about the relationships between the sexes in any society. Female subordination was no doubt a real and miserable aspect of Chinese traditional life, stretching back into the distant past, if not necessarily to the earliest times. It is not to minimize or deny this to point out the mysterious imbalance in the opposite direction which Chinese literature, folklore and opera often vividly portray, the power of women over men.

Particularly in an older woman, this might be exerted mainly through an intricate knowledge of codes of propriety and a capacity to impose embarrassment and shame on those who resisted her. A notable description of such power in action occurs in *The Red Chamber Dream*. The hero Baoyu was his grandmother's favourite. He had been beaten almost to death by his father Jia Zheng. She heard of what had been done to him:

'There was a cry of "Her Old Ladyship!" from one of the maids, interrupted by a quavering voice outside the window.

'"Kill me first! You may as well kill both of us while you are about it!"' Jia Zheng hurried out to meet her, 'as much distressed by his mother's words as . . . alarmed by her arrival'. She accused him of having always been an unfilial son. 'Wounded in his most sensitive spot, Jia Zheng fell on his knees before her. The voice in which he replied to her was broken with tears:

'"How can I bear it, Mother, if you speak to me like that? What I did to the boy I did for the honour of the family."

'Grandmother Jia spat contemptuously. "A single harsh word from me and you start whining that you can't bear it. How do you think Baoyu could bear your cruel rod? And you say you've been punishing him for the honour of the family, but you just tell me this: did your own father ever punish you in such a way? – I think not . . . Call my carriage. Your Mistress and I and Baoyu are going back to Nanjing. We shall be leaving immediately."' She continued in this vein until Jia Zheng's kowtows 'were . . . describing the whole quarter-circle from perpendicular to ground. But the old lady walked on inside, ignoring him.'*

Despite all that has been said about the theoretical submission of women to men, in the words of one historian of China, 'Anyone who has had long and varied dealings with Chinese will have noticed that submissive and docile women do not seem to emerge very regularly.'

MEDIATING

CARING AND CONTROL

The main festival of the Chinese year is concerned with the family and the agricultural cycle. It occurs about the end of January, at a time when farming activity is at its lowest, and in the past it could last a fortnight. Today most people will get about four days off work. In the past it was a time of clan and family celebration, a time for healing rifts and quarrels and for feasting. All debts had to be settled before the holiday; none could be collected while the festival lasted.

Even though clan loyalties are no longer as important as they were, Chinese families still try to be together at New Year. In every home that can afford it, a huge meal will be prepared, to be eaten as midnight strikes. Red streamers, lanterns and firecrackers abound. Babies born in the preceding year are passed from hand to hand. Husbands and wives, sometimes apart for months at a time at different ends of the country, meet again; in the matter-of-fact Chinese style the birth control authorities are instructed to be 'especially vigilant and vigorous' in their propaganda at New Year.

Preparation for the festival involves sweeping floors, polishing furniture, repapering windows and doing repairs about the house. Barbers and hairdressers ply a brisk trade; traditionally no knives or cutting implements may be used on New Year's day. For the cook this means that the meat dumplings – *jiaozi* and *baozi* – must be made beforehand, and it is said that on the preceding day any home where one cannot hear the sound of the meat chopper must be a very poor one.

Urban families make their country cousins especially welcome at this time. They may be bringing fresh poultry and vegetables and inspecting the new television sets and cassette-recorders that some time soon they hope to be able to afford. Another factor serves to unite the Chinese on that day: at New Year they all become one year older. Chinese celebrate birthdays like everyone else, but traditionally they count their age from the number of New Years they have passed.

The Chinese have needed to keep close to their families. 'In that great sea', it was said of the old empire, 'a lone man drowned'. China has always been huge, and most people who have been uprooted from family and village have quickly died. Equally, the family has needed every pair of hands, and has had to work as a single unit to tend the land, which can never be neglected, and to succour the old and the young. The village may also have

A weighty statue of the ancient Chinese goddess of mercy, Guanyin, here represented by a mother cradling a child, has been placed by the authorities in the grounds of a state hydroelectric station at Mangshan on the Yellow River.

In another illustration to the 12th-century 'Classic of Filial Piety' children pay their respects to their father. The family has traditionally been the most important social and economic unit in China. In return for unquestioning loyalty and submission within the family, each member could hope for assistance and support from his kinsmen throughout his life.

needed to work as one in the frequent times of crisis such as flood and drought, which have never ceased to threaten this most fertile, most densely populated of lands.

Religion and philosophy in China have put family first and community a close second, ahead of any such aims in life as individual happiness or freedom. The state has added its influence on the same side, supporting the family with its laws, modelling itself on a stern father in its dealings with its subjects, and for two thousand years seeking intermittently to enforce systems of collective responsibility on groups of ten families, so that if one committed a crime, all suffered.

The Chinese live in a tight mesh of relationships and obligations in which each person is both supported and under surveillance, not only in times of trouble but also when not in trouble: tied down, as it may seem to a Westerner, more closely than Gulliver was by Lilliputian threads of obligation, each one slender, but together unbreakable. The threads can get tangled: obligations to family and obligations to the state can conflict; family feuds can cut across the demands of neighbourliness; and to people who have a strong sense of duty such conflicting obligations can cause pain. Family obligations will usually in the end prevail; for the family is still the strongest force shaping each person to fit into the role required by society, defined now as in the past by the idea of 'order' or 'propriety'.

The conception of order in traditional China was a Confucian idea, based on the fundamental belief that the nature of man was good, and only needed cleansing or purification to be restored: it was a moral order, which ruled the relationships of Heaven and Earth, sovereign and subject, parent and child. Human relationships were to be regulated by codes of honour, moral conduct, respectful behaviour and courtesy. The Chinese word *li*, by which these codes were collectively known, meant originally 'rites', and came to signify all behaviour in accordance with the requirements of the moral order. The fact that life was based on this concept is perhaps one of the chief reasons why the Chinese have been able to live in large family groups or modern collectives, apparently with less friction than other peoples. They have needed to do so to survive.

Most of the old and retired, for instance, look to the family for their main or only support. When the Communist Party came to power in 1949 it initially proposed to replace the family with government institutions to provide for those in need. In the countryside it proclaimed 'The Five Guarantees' – of food, clothing, housing, medical care and burial – for those who could not afford them, and it set up 'Mutual Aid Teams' to execute the proposal. Care for the elderly was largely removed from the family's responsibilities. In the Great Leap Forward in 1958 the Party went further: the traditional family was represented as a source of 'feudal' ideas and influence, a potential threat to the socialist state. During the formation of the People's Communes care of the elderly, child-rearing and domestic activities like cookery and laundry were all communalized. These experiments proved inefficient and expensive. The policies were reversed. Mao Zedong summed up his chastened later views in the statement, 'The family is still of use. . . It will disappear only after maybe a thousand years, or several hundred years at least'.

However the attacks made at the time on the ancient concept of 'filial submission' had weakened the tradition of respect and family support for the aged. Stories of neglected old people wandering the streets, of maltreatment and suicides, were common. The Communist Party began to run campaigns exhorting young people to care for their parents, and the Confucian legacy was called on for slogans adapted to the times: 'To grow old is to gain respect'; 'To support one's parents is a virtue which should be highly promoted.'

The government's own assessment at the time was that, 'If the system of state care for the aged is adopted it will plunge the nation into deep financial troubles and cause serious interference with the development of socialist reconstruction.' So the prime responsibility for the welfare of the aged was returned to the family. Pensions today are paid only to those who have worked in heavy industries run by the state or in a few other rich work-units. Then they are generous: up to 70% of previous wages. The minimum pensionable age was 55 for women and 60 for men in the early 1980s; life-expectancy, according to official statistics, was then 69.5 for women and 66.9 for men.

One man who a generation earlier had already outlived average life expectancy for China was the country's expert on such statistics, Ma Yinchu. In 1957, at the age of 76, he had published a paper recommending family planning. For this he had been disgraced and punished. Mao Zedong was against birth control: he thought it was a capitalist idea foisted on the Chinese to keep them weak internationally, and he persecuted those Chinese who advocated it. Later, he had doubts about his policies. Ma Yinchu survived his persecutor, and was rehabilitated in 1979, at the age of 98. Mao meanwhile had presided before he died over something like a fifty per cent increase in the population.

The 'one-child family' is now official Party policy, and both the Constitution and the 1981 Marriage Law oblige couples to practise family planning. The attempt to promote the one-child family is an example of the Chinese system of persuasive government in action. Those families who sign a certificate saying they will have only one child get privileges both for the child and for themselves, for example free or subsidized education and health care for the child and up to six months' maternity leave. These privileges are withdrawn if they have two children, and increasingly severe penalties follow for every further child. Pressure for abortion can be intense, even if the pregnancy is advanced. The policy has achieved less success in the countryside than in the towns, where lack of housing in any case encourages small families, and the authorities can keep a close watch on everyone. In the country, the Responsibility System, which gives individual families an incentive to increase their earnings by tilling family fields intensively, encouraging farmers to have at least one son, and thus on average to want to have at least two children, conflicts with the one-child policy. The Chinese in any case love children.

The care of children in their earliest years is warm, and the discipline is easy. As an example, infants wear trousers that are not sewn up at the back so that they can relieve themselves at any time in the open air without anxiety. Small children are hardly ever left alone: they are almost always being held by a mother or a grandmother or being carried by a father, an elder brother or a neighbour. They may sleep beside one or other of their parents when they are small, a country custom that the housing shortage maintains in many cities. It is rare to see a child crying in public.

Between the ages of five and seven there is a change. In imperial China it

(Right)
In a boisterous scene from a Song Dynasty painting, 'A Hundred Children at Play', little boys wear false moustaches as they ape portly magistrates. Some children play in a miniature band while others perform juggling tricks or ride hobbyhorses.

was dramatic. Most girls were footbound at five, and at six or a little older boys were made to learn if they were rich, or made to work if they were poor. If the family were in difficulties during famine, children, especially girl children, could be sent away from home. One foreign traveller wrote in the nineteenth century, when Western methods of industrial production had been adopted in the Shanghai silk industry, of seeing, 'long lines of children, many not more than eight years old, standing twelve hours a day over boiling vats of cocoons with swollen red fingers, crying from the beating of the foreman.'

Corporal punishment was widely practised in traditional China. Today speaking kindly to the child and pointing out misdeeds is said to be the appropriate method of discipline; but most children, particularly in the countryside, seem to have been beaten at some time or other.

Children, like adults, are subjected to criticism and made to feel ashamed if they disturb the harmony of the family and the neighbourhood. And in the family they see adults acting on the whole as they themselves are required to act, for the world of Chinese adults is not, as often in the West, one with very different rules from those for children.

In the past education was a means of gaining entrance to the civil service and thus of bringing credit, influence and wealth to one's family. Only men could be civil servants; schools were for boys alone. Some girls were taught to read and write by their fathers, and occasionally a reformer like Yuan Mei, the eighteenth-century writer, would teach girls to sing and write poetry. He faced accusations of loose morals for doing so. 'A woman with education causes trouble,' was a proverb of the time. A future husband would normally be mainly concerned to know that his bride had good family connections and three-inch feet.

From the earliest times education consisted largely of rote-learning: reading, writing and memorizing the classics. Boys might be made to learn a passage of a thousand characters whose meaning was not at first explained. When they were judged to know all the words and able to repeat them they had to turn away from the book and repeat the text, first as it was written, then backwards. At every mistake the teacher, cane in hand, might deal them a blow. This was known as the *bei shu* (back to the book) system. The text would normally be of Confucian ethical content.

Both moral instruction and rote-learning still play a large part in Chinese education. School children are encouraged to display the same kind of co-operative behaviour that they have been used to in their family training. Aggression, individualism and competitiveness are discouraged. A primary school will put up public lists showing the good deeds done by different children, as well as their marks in class.

Primary schools take children from six or seven to twelve; they teach elementary mathematics, basic use of the abacus, and reading and writing, which inevitably involve a great deal of learning by rote. Since each character has to be memorized separately the mastery of reading and writing takes up far more of a child's time than the learning of an alphabet requires elsewhere in the world. The People's Republic now uses many simplified characters, which makes the task somewhat easier, but prevents mainland Chinese from understanding without further instruction what is written by overseas Chinese and books printed in the past.

The Party has a long-term policy to teach everyone in the country *putonghua* (the 'mandarin' dialect), even though in most areas of China it has to be learned almost as a second language. This will for the first time give a single pronunciation to every character all over China, and in principle make it possible to spell Chinese alphabetically, using the pinyin system of

romanization. But earlier attempts at using the alphabet instead of characters have encountered formidable difficulties: for example since all words are monosyllabic there can be as many as two hundred different words all capable of being written with the same few letters in pinyin. Meanwhile the spread of literacy and the use of one dialect in all schools, as well as on radio and television, contribute to the closer unification of the country, which has always been held together to a large extent by the single written language. The disadvantage is that, as with simplified characters, the down-grading of dialects will inevitably tend to alienate modern Chinese to some extent from their elders and to a great extent from the inherited oral culture of their region.

It is not until junior-middle school, which takes pupils from twelve to sixteen, that a first foreign language, English, is taught, and in most senior-middle schools, for sixteen-to-eighteen year olds, there is no other language available. Only in some 'key schools', which have been promoted

A primary school child enacts a short play to music for the entertainment of guests. In Chinese schools great emphasis is placed on the learning of appropriate behaviour in society.

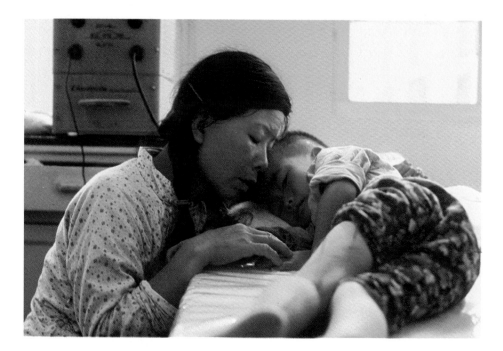

since 1981 for bright children, and which lead to elite higher institutions, can pupils study a second foreign language.

Literacy in China is about seventy-five per cent and has been growing. The Responsibility System may prevent, or slow, its growth in the country. Country children can help with feeding animals, drawing water, cleaning the house or growing vegetables. Ten per cent of primary school pupils and a quarter of junior-middle school children stay away from school, mainly to do this work, and only one child in three goes on to senior-middle school.

As the child grows up many of the responsibilities and much of the surveillance previously exercised by family and school become mainly the concern of the 'work-unit'. In the countryside the work-unit is usually a hamlet or village formally classified as a 'brigade' or a 'production team'. Family and neighbours work together, and with part-time labour already familiar to the child there is no sudden transition from school to work. In the city the pattern is more complex: family, street and work-place have separate existences. Even so, elements of village life remain. Blocks of flats and neighbourhood housing are often owned by work-units, and in theory contain only workers from that unit, though in practice inheritance by widows and unofficial trading of inconvenient housing between people in different units or different cities makes for some variety.

Every neighbourhood in the city has a formal 'neighbourhood committee', with fifteen to twenty-five local people, paid by the municipality, caring for and controlling its residents. There may also be committees in every street, block of flats or courtyard. Many Chinese live in old courtyard houses, once the houses of extended families that have been converted into separate dwellings. About a third of the members of a neighbourhood committee may be full-time. The local representative of the Public Security Bureau is automatically a member. The committee is required by the higher authorities to take on the supervision of birth control, cleanliness and peaceful relations between people in its neighbourhood, and to look after the welfare of those in need. Neighbourhood committees can constitute a formidable power, if only because so many of their members are retired people who can devote their full efforts to ensuring that order is maintained; while there is a preponderance of elderly women who may inherit some of the moral authority that 'matriarchs' had in extended Chinese families. If the committee wants to persuade a woman to abort a second child, it may visit her thirty or forty times to argue the case.

Those for whose welfare the committee is formally responsible include the elderly without pensions, the chronically sick who are confined to bed, the blind or handicapped and those of the mentally ill who are not in mental hospitals. In the models held up to committees by the state they are intended to promote small-scale enterprises in their territory, such as electrical components workshops to be staffed by school-leavers, factories to employ disabled workers or neighbourhood service stations to be organized by retired people to wash and mend clothes. Such projects are intended to generate money for welfare support. How much of this activity goes on in any one case depends on the enthusiasm of particular committees.

Local mediation committees and neighbourhood committees tend to have overlapping membership. They also usually have a core of retired people or full-time committee members; but they can sometimes be set up ad-hoc from a group of people who work in the same factory or live in the same area as those involved in a dispute. Their members are in either case likely to have little or no legal knowledge. Nevertheless a mediation committee has extensive powers over personal and domestic matters. It is empowered to criticize and 'instil self-criticism'. It can demand a written apology promising a change of attitude; it can grant pardon for misdemeanours, organize the return of stolen goods and inflict punishment up to a limited number of days of labour. It can also hand over offenders to the Public Security Bureau, who can award three to five years in a labour camp without a trial. Besides these powers, the committees are charged with a wide range of responsibilities on the borderlines of local government, including the prevention of fires, measures in case of drought and the protection of forestry.

Like the neighbourhood committees, the mediation committees have inherited tasks once carried out by educated landowners, village elders or heads of minor divisions of local government. Local landowners would see to it that villages disciplined their own offenders. Matters would be kept within the community, not only out of a feeling of shared shame at the public appearance of any crime, but also because once the formal authority of the magistrate was involved, there would be trouble and cost for all within reach, with interrogation, judicial torture and possibly imprisonment of neighbours and witnesses.

A poster exhorts people to 'practise birth control for the sake of the revolution'. The one-child family has been vigorously promoted by the government since the end of the 1970s.

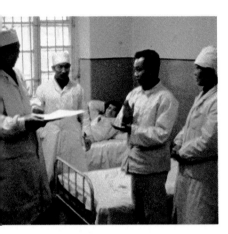

A patient in a mental hospital tells the psychiatrists on their rounds about the progress of his own plans for China, 'My Four Modernizations'.

In traditional China there was sharp division between 'order' for those who conformed and 'law' for anyone classified as criminal. The former was persuasive, tolerant and often compromising, the latter was cruel and harsh. It has often been observed that when two or more Chinese are engaged in angry dispute in the streets of a town, furious abuse, obscene curses, even menacing gestures may be exchanged, but never blows. Actual violence would alter the whole position, and in a very dangerous way for the parties involved. Under the imperial regime, the exceptional individual who did strike was at once classed a criminal. The idea that a fist fight could be ignored by the police if it was no more than a private row between adversaries was not acceptable in China. Violence in restraint of violence was a formidable part of the means of maintenance of law and order in traditional society and it was very severe. There was a proverb: 'In death, avoid hell. In life, avoid the law courts.'

When the Communist Party came to power Mao Zedong wanted to prevent the growth of a powerful legal system which could constitute a threat to the power of the Party, and he preferred traditional methods of settling disputes to a formal system of courts with codified laws. He placed great weight on the role of mediation committees. Deng Xiaoping was already critical of this approach in the 1950s, and in the early 1980s he moved China towards a partial formalization of the law, while leaving mediation committees with considerable powers. They still deal with the majority of disputes and minor infractions of law and order in China, working by discussion and persuasion.

But not all disorders are capable of being dealt with by the forces of mediation in China; and not all who infringe the codes of propriety are brought into harmony with the social order by discussion alone. Madness has usually been a condition that the Chinese system of codes and proprieties could not deal with. 'Mental patients constitute a very helpless class of people in China,' wrote Lord Macartney, a descendant of George III's ambassador, in the 1920s. 'If caught upon the streets doing anything wrong they are arrested and thrown into prison as criminals. If they are harmless and wander in the streets, they are mocked and laughed at and often stoned. Their families usually treat them as strangers and confine them to a dark room . . . their closest relatives usually disown them.' The traditional peasant belief was that mental disorders and many other diseases were the result of possession by evil spirits. This led to avoidance and horror of the mentally ill among the common people.

However the Chinese literate elite had a rational and comprehensive classification of insanity at a remarkably early date. A psychiatric textbook, *Standards for Diagnosis and Treatment*, written in the Ming Dynasty (1368-1644) by a physician, Wang Xizhong, says:

One kind of patient is sometimes violent, sometimes stupid, singing and laughing or sad and weeping . . . This is the first kind of insanity, and those with frustrated ambition are liable to be so affected. The second kind is mania. The patient is garrulous and boisterous, raving, stubborn and violent. He abuses everyone indiscriminately, friends, relations and strangers.

He may even climb to any eminence near at hand, take off his clothes and run away . . . The third kind is 'fits'. The patient becomes dizzy and cannot recognize people. He falls to the ground, having convulsions and suffering from jerks over which he has no control.

Mental hospitals date from the arrival of Western medical practice in China in the late nineteenth century. Asylums were built in Peking, Suzhou, Nanjing and Shanghai. By 1949 there were about six thousand psychiatric beds in China. When the Communist Party took over, it brought in the Pavlovian explanation of mental disorder, compulsorily imposed in Russia under Stalin. Insanity was said to be brought about by an 'imbalance of the excitatory and inhibitory functions of the nervous system', and to be curable by varying the conditioned reflexes of those concerned. In the Cultural Revolution even such minimal reasoning as this was discouraged; medical schools were closed down, training was stopped and psychiatric theory and treatment were labelled 'bourgeois' or 'revisionist'. On madness as on other matters the policies of the Cultural Revolution have since been reversed: there are about two hundred psychiatric hospitals or clinics in China today, with some four thousand practising psychiatrists.

Besides using drugs, acupuncture and other chemical and medical therapies Chinese mental hospitals also rely on discussion and persuasion. The patient, like any other deviant, is seen as in need of reincorporation into the normal order of society, and the main means by which the Chinese seek to achieve this, in any area, is a change of attitude on the part of the person classified as a deviant. Patients are encouraged to see themselves as society sees them. One inmate of the asylum at Harbin, a northern industrial city, explained his condition in this way:

The causes of my illness are tiredness, anger, anxiety and shock. When I first came here, I wouldn't admit that I was ill; now I do admit it. In the past, I was good-natured and docile; when I became ill, I even beat up my father, smashed the doors and windows . . . six times I smashed them. They were puzzled that the good-natured and docile man had changed so much, but later they realized that I was ill.

In some forms of insanity it seems almost as if the workings of the social and political system itself are dramatized in the mind of the sufferer. One patient in the same institution recites great quantities of poetry. His room-mates snigger at him, but only a hundred years ago this was a main requirement for success in the examinations that led to an official career. Another patient appears to be responding to more recent political pressures. Asked how he is, he says, 'I hope my Four Modernizations will be realized soon.' '*Your* Four Modernizations?' says the doctor. 'Yes, my Four Modernizations.' As if at a mass-meeting, he goes on: 'I want to see meals feastized; clothes woollenized; housing towerized; transport motorized . . .' Then, shouting more loudly, 'Meals state-banquetized; clothes westernized; the whole country mansionized; transport limousinized!'

Improvement appears to be measured by a willingness not merely to abandon but to reverse such subjectivity. The patient is expected to describe himself in external terms, much as he might be described by professionals responsible in an institution for his 'case'.

Much the same is true in the penal system, where, in addition to being closely guarded and required to do forced labour, prisoners are subjected to intensive criticism directed towards changing their 'attitude'. In some prisons, such as the model jail at Harbin, this aspect of the system is particularly prominent.

Harbin Jail has been described in a Chinese picture magazine as a 'special school'* where although 'the inmates are put under strict control and armed surveillance,' nevertheless 'within the high walls of the prison are neatly arranged workshops and spotless prison houses with a spacious courtyard dotted with lovely flowers.' Harbin is a rich industrial city in Manchuria, much of it built by the Russians and the Japanese, and its institutions cannot be seen as typical of China. But the concern with 'change of attitude' in its prison, though perhaps more marked than elsewhere, is not uncharacteristic.

One of the current inmates, a young murderer under suspended sentence, said that only in China would a criminal be treated 'as if he were ill'. The motto of the governor of Harbin is 'rescue, reform and educate'. The guards are particularly proud of one of their successes: it was in this jail that the last emperor of China's 'attitude' was changed after several years of imprisonment.

When the system of mediation is looked at in detail, it is on such 'changes of attitude' in those who are seen as deviant that everything generally turns. In many countries, if a judge believed a man had tried to have his wife sewn up during a Caesarean section in order to suffocate his own child, on discovering that it was to be a girl rather than a boy, the case would be reported to the police and dealt with by the courts. For some Chinese it may be viewed differently, as something to be dealt with by a mediation committee. In 1982 one such supposed case was referred to a committee in Nanjing by a district judge, Chen Li, to whose attention it had come when the wife sued the husband for divorce. The application was refused because, as the judge said, he still detected signs of affection between the couple. The mediation committee saw it as its task to persuade the couple to drop the divorce proceedings. In order to do so, it went over the story of the breakdown of the marriage, in detail, on several occasions, sometimes with the two parties and their families separately and sometimes together. At a plenary hearing the civil court judge of the local district court sat side by side with the head of the neighbourhood mediation committee, who was a sixty-three-year-old woman. Representatives of the two young people's work-units were there, with the wife's mother and elder brother, and the husband's parents.

Gu Lingping, who was twenty-six at the time, was a store-keeper at a department store. Her estranged husband, Cai Xuanzhi, aged thirty-one, was a lathe operator. They had met in 1978 and decided to get married when they were apprentices in the same lathing factory, and after their marriage in April 1980 had lived reasonably happily until the birth of their first child. When, in the course of the Caesarean section, the husband discovered that

the baby was to be a girl and, according to the judge, asked for his wife to be sewn up, the doctors and the wife's relations prevented him from interfering.

After the child was delivered he hardly bothered to visit his wife in hospital. As Gu Lingping complained:

I had just had an operation; I couldn't get out of bed at all; so the doctor asked him to feed me with food. It is the family who ought to feed the patients, isn't that right? Though he fed me, it was not willingly and gladly. He fed me so quickly: it was one mouthful straight after the other. He even said to me: 'If the child is sick later on, don't get her cured.' This shows that he didn't want me to have this baby. That was his idea. To my mind, even if I have a lame or a blind baby, I have to do my best to cure it, let alone if my baby is born quite normal. He didn't want her at all. He had neither the child nor me in his heart. That was his attitude during those nine days. When I talked to him he always gave me an angry stare. He lost his temper easily. If I had done anything wrong at the hospital it would have been right to criticize me. But he oughtn't to have treated me like that during a time of confinement, let alone when I had done nothing wrong.

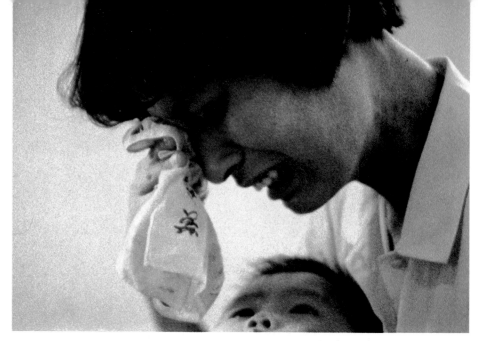

She turned on her husband and addressed him directly:

You were not like that while we were making friends before our marriage. The affection
between us ought to have been much better than before. But you treated me much worse. It
was entirely because of the baby; because your ideal hadn't been realized, and nobody would
inherit your family name.

The day before I left the hospital I asked him to fetch me home by tricycle. Do you know
what he said? He said that the bicycle would be all right and that the tricycle was not necessary.
He had hurt my feelings completely. At my ward there were five patients. The husbands of
the other four stayed and looked after them every day. That was real comfort. He not only did
not give me any comfort, but he hurt my feelings. In these circumstances, I couldn't get on
with him any longer. But I restrained myself during those nine days. [She cried while she was
speaking.]

I remember that during my confinement, once, the baby cried. I said to him, 'You should
rock the cradle to make her stop crying.' He said he wouldn't. Then he rocked it so hard that
the baby was almost thrown out. The baby was so small and the cradle was so wide. If he kept
rocking like that, the baby would be bound to be thrown out, wouldn't she? Another time he
took the bedclothes away from the baby. He was hoping she would freeze. He hasn't this child
in his eyes. He hoped that I had the same heart as his, to kill the child in my confinement.

It was after this last attempt – or what she alleged was an attempt – to kill the
child that Gu Lingping took her daughter and went to live with her mother.
Her husband visited her there, saying he was bringing presents. She thought
he had come for a quite different reason, or so she said:

Once you snatched the child, and danced with joy before us and fought with us. My mother is
old but you dragged her from the third floor to the ground floor, didn't you? And after you
had snatched the child away, you said you would choke her with water. Was that your way of
coming to see the child? Now you have no right, you have no right to take the child in your
arms . . . Now we are living in the new society. Men and women share equal rights. Why
should my daughter and I suffer oppression from you? Have I done anything wrong? Have I
broken the law? Now even my life is not safe from you.

The husband's version of the same events was very different. He said he had
never wanted his wife to leave him and had consistently asked her to come
back to him. He had tried several times to see his daughter at his

mother-in-law's house, but his wife's family had always rejected him and refused to let him. His mother-in-law had misinterpreted his visits and seemed to think that he was trying to kidnap his daughter. On one occasion, when the mother-in-law barred the door, he pushed it open, he admitted, rather violently, and since she had been standing behind it, it knocked her down and she was injured. His wife had then accused him of trying to attack her mother. That was when she had sued him for divorce.

The mediation committee had already held many sessions of talks with Cai Xuanzhi during which, as they put it in a report, he had 'recognized that his previous feudalistic attitude was an error'. They had then set up meetings to convince everyone concerned that the husband's attitude to his wife had changed and was no longer 'feudal', and that he had never intended to injure his mother-in-law. He meanwhile had gone to visit her in hospital. But his wife still would not go back to him. He felt that he was being misunderstood and that everything he was doing to try to heal the quarrel was being ignored. By this time, the committee found that new points of contention had overlaid the original quarrel. There was trouble over the wife's bicycle, which the husband's sister had begun to use when she left home. The wife insisted that her husband or his sister should pay her rent for the bicycle or else buy it. They agreed, but then did not pay. Meanwhile the husband had become so angry that he deliberately delayed giving his wife the child's support money and food coupons. When his wife demanded the money he told her to go and get it from his work-unit. So the wife went back to court and made a second application for divorce. And so the story went on.

The committee brought about a reconciliation by asking each party to look at the course of events from a fresh point of view. They argued that Cai Xuanzhi's greatest error had been to underestimate his wife's feelings. And they appealed to her family to view his intentions more favourably. Both sides were asked to exercise restraint.

The parties to the dispute had already frequently referred to their restraint in relating their stories. For example Gu Lingping, in telling of her suffering, said, 'I cried in secret. To prevent my mother seeing me crying I wiped my tears immediately . . . When Cai Xuanzhi was furious and started cursing my mother, she restrained herself. She didn't quarrel with him. I cried extremely badly. He went on cursing. We kept quiet. We restrained ourselves in this way for a month.'

Restraint or forbearance (*rennai*) is an essential virtue which the closely knit Chinese family has traditionally required of its members. In a manual for householders written eight hundred years ago, dealing with everything from keeping out burglars to preventing family quarrels, a certain Yuan Cai suggested devices for attaining this virtue:

Dissipate anger as the occasion arises instead of hiding it in your chest. Do this by saying to yourself, 'He wasn't thinking, he doesn't know any better, he made a mistake, he is narrow in his outlook, how much harm can this really do?' If you keep the anger from entering your heart, then even if someone offends you ten times a day, neither your speech nor your behaviour will be affected. You will then see the magnitude of the benefits of forbearance.*

The Chinese habit of looking for devices to make compromises and resolutions by mediation, and also the habit of looking at something that has gone wrong from a new point of view in order to avoid anger or despair may perhaps be related to their capacity to accept more than one belief at the same time. The Chinese appear to have felt little need to reject alternative teachings or religions because they were, by Western standards, mutually contradictory: three or more approaches – Confucian, Daoist, Buddhist and today perhaps Marxist – could and can all be invoked according to occasion, like sentences in different languages that are never cross-translated. It is perhaps easier to give reality a slightly different 'twist' when one is not constrained to interpret it in a single way, than when a single definite judgement on everything is regarded as ultimately right.

The Chinese have a favourite term, *banfa*, meaning any stratagem for getting round an obstacle; and the chief skill of a mediator often lies in his capacity to think of a solution that will get people out of a conflict while saving everyone's 'face': avoiding a quarrel and achieving a reconciliation by making people see things differently, preferably in such a way that no one's dignity is lost.

In the case of Gu Lingping and Cai Xuanzhi, the chief mediator proposed a benevolent interpretation of the husband's actions, without any questioning of his motives. Cai's response was to admit that he had been wrong and to stress that he had been changed. When the chief mediator asked whether he had not been hoping for a second child, a son, he replied, 'I was before; but now that I have been educated by so many people I no longer have this idea.' It was then his mother's turn to confess to her faults: 'Whose responsibility is this? It's mine. I gave birth to him, but I haven't educated him well. I am to blame. I must go to his mother-in-law's home and apologize for my son's offence.'

'They cannot be reconciled simply through a few words,' Judge Chen Li said. There was indeed a sense of endlessness about the proceedings, and a feeling, perhaps, on the part of both husband and wife, that no solution was likely to be accepted by the committee as a final outcome except a reconciliation between them; that people would go on talking until they agreed not to have a divorce. The couple probably knew fairly well that if the committee meetings were ever going to end they were going to have to put up with each other: only if both sides had wanted a divorce and the committee could have seen no hope might they have been allowed to part. Eventually, they signed a document saying that they were reconciled.

Society and the family come before the individual; and the family must be maintained, whether husband and wife like each other or not. It is only in the last few decades that the Chinese have been expected to marry someone they liked, and, as an official said to one couple seeking a divorce, 'Since you chose to marry, why should you now want to part?' Beneath the Chinese family virtue of restraint or forbearance may lie a still deeper capacity for resignation and endurance.

(Right)
Young Chinese learn from their earliest days to live together without friction in closely-knit groups.

EATING

FRUGALITY AND FEASTING

'I consider that the mouth and stomach do more harm than good,' wrote Li Yu the poet (1611-80). 'It was a mistake for Heaven to endow us with them. They make life complicated and give rise to crime. Plants have no mouths or stomachs but nothing stops them growing. Rocks neither eat nor drink, but they last without any difficulty . . . We can only blame Heaven for the mistake it made in our case.' Li Yu may have written these lines with feeling. As the father of a family, the manager of a troupe of singing girls and possessor of several concubines, he had found himself in middle age with more than forty mouths to feed. 'Nevertheless,' he added only a few words later, 'while I have never had difficulty in describing the virtues of all kinds of foods, I have never been able to describe those shellfish we call crab or why I delight in them. The fact is I love them to distraction. My mouth relishes them, and I can never forget them . . . It is a weakness of mine and a strange phenomenon of the universe. Every year I save up money, waiting for crabs to come into season. My family all tease me about my obsession; they say crabs are my life. So I call my crab money the ransom money for my life.'*

Li Yu is eloquently displaying a characteristically Chinese double-sidedness in matters of food. On the one hand there is a frugality, which shows through in the disapproval, mock-serious though it may be, of the consequences of hunger and greed; and on the other there is a delight in food, above all in special foods linking man to the seasons and to the world of water, eaten so fresh the life is almost in them.

This ambivalence is already to be seen in Confucius. It is said of Confucius that, 'He did not eat rice which had been injured by heat or damp and turned sour, nor fish or flesh which was gone. He did not eat what was discoloured or what was of a bad flavour, nor anything that was ill-cooked, or was not in season. He did not eat meat which was not cut properly, nor what was served without its proper sauce . . . He did not partake of wine and dried meat bought in the market. He never used ginger when he ate.' However, at one point he himself said, 'With coarse (grain) to eat, with water to drink and my bended arm for a pillow, I have still joy in the midst of these things.' The chronicler adds, 'He did not eat much.'*

The dualism shows in another way; for there are always two stories to be told about eating in China. One is of delicious food discussed with relish among connoisseurs who may also be poets, since food has always been a

A detail from a painting attributed to the 12th-century emperor Huizong shows a group of scholars meeting in a garden to enjoy food and conversation.

subject for verse and prose in China. But there is also the second story: of hunger, suffering and even, as Li Yu says here, of crime, showing through from time to time to the outside world like bone through flesh, as in the pictures from *Tragic Scenes from the Great Famine of 1877 in Henan*, with its original caption, 'Living skeletons scrambling to cut flesh from those who have starved to death on the road.'* The ever-present possibility of famine lies behind the habits of frugality instilled in children, and behind the economy with which the Chinese use land, not for grazing, but for growing grain and vegetables.

'Grain' and 'vegetables' are the categories into which the Chinese divide all food. Grain (*fan*) is the basis of every normal meal, without which the Chinese do not feel properly fed. 'Vegetables' (*cai*) is the word they use for everything else, including meat and fish. Except at feasts, meat is used not as a main element in the dish, as in the West, but to flavour and complement the grain. At feasts the order is reversed. The *cai* becomes the main part of the meal, and the *fan* is eaten last as a final filler and hardly treated seriously. So essential at normal times is grain that *fan* is also the generic word for all food, as 'meat' once was in England.

The predominance of grain in the Chinese diet probably emerged in the course of the New Stone Age. Fish was previously much more important than it is today. Chinese civilization seems to have grown up to a considerable extent in river valleys. Banpo, near Xi'an, perhaps the most remarkable of the rediscovered villages of neolithic China, has revealed well-designed fish hooks and extraordinarily fine stylized paintings of fish, together with many instances of netting patterns, on pottery. At Banpo, fish was probably the staple food that could be relied on while experiments with agriculture were still being made.

The Chinese have evolved one particularly ingenious way of catching fish: using cormorants. The practice was described by a sixteenth-century European traveller, Galeote Pereira:

At the hour appointed to fish, all the barges are brought together in a circle, where the river is shallow, and the cormorants, tied together under the wings, are let leap down into the water, some under, some above, worth the looking upon. Each one as he hath filled his bag, goeth to his own barge and emptieth it, which done, he returneth to fish again. Thus having taken good store of fish, they set the cormorants at liberty, and do suffer them to fish for their own pleasure. There were in that city, where I was, twenty barges at the least of those aforesaid cormorants. I went almost every day to see them, yet I could never be thoroughly satisfied to see so strange a kind of fishing.*

To this day some of the fishermen on the Li River in Guangxi still live by this ancient trade, training the cormorant to come to its master's cry, tying a string round its neck to prevent it swallowing, then letting it loose in the water. The landscape in which they work is one of the most beautiful in China, with that contrast between near-vertical mountains and level lakes and rivers that has delighted Chinese painters for fifteen hundred years. As the slowly-poled boats move towards the fishing grounds at twilight a song can sometimes be heard in time to the rhythm of poling. Sometimes a boat

Cormorant fishermen on the Li River in Guanxi Province.

will pass another and a greeting will be hailed across the water. In the prow of every boat, tethered by one leg and with a tight string round its neck, is the cormorant. A dozen or more boats congregate at a bend in the river, and as darkness falls the fishermen light their lamps. Then, forming a ring in the river, they focus the lamps on a circle of water, which fills with swarming fish. Each fisherman releases his bird, and urges it on with differently pitched cries, to plunge under the water, grip a fish in its beak and return to the boat with it repeatedly. One cormorant can feed a fisherman and his family.

Meat is more important today than fish in the Chinese diet. Pork and poultry are the main kinds of meat eaten, except in the north, where mutton plays a larger role. Cattle are rare because there is no spare land for grazing, and oxen are too valuable as draught animals to be killed for food. The

Chinese, like most Asians, use few dairy products and find them difficult to digest. Bean-curd has much the same role as cheese in the West. Game, which was once plentiful throughout China, is now scarce, and almost non-existent in the north, which has been deforested for some three thousand years. But pigs, which can live by eating wastes, are kept by almost every household in the countryside.

Although the scarcity of meat in the Chinese diet is mainly due to poverty, there is also a long tradition of religious vegetarianism that still survives today. It came originally with Buddhism from India. The Buddhist principle was that all life was of equal value, or perhaps of equal valuelessness; our spirits move from one body to another, often of a different species, at death. Buddhists were thus enjoined to eat no meat; they might after all be eating their ancestors. Instead they made elaborate imitations of all kinds of meat and fish wholly out of vegetables, and still do. There was a delicate Buddhist ceremony, performed during the Southern Song Dynasty on the famous West Lake at Hangzhou, which consisted in buying water-turtles and shellfish, and throwing them back into the lake still living.* It is occasionally still done today.

The poet Li Yu, despite his devotion to crabs, seems to have had some vegetarian leanings:

There is a well-known saying, 'Meat eaters are contemptible.' The tiger is the stupidest of animals; it does not eat small children because it thinks children are brave, not realizing that they are not afraid of the tiger because they do not know what it is. It does not eat drunken people, thinking them aggressive, without realizing they are only drunk . . . Its mind is blocked and cannot function properly. Similarly meat eaters are muddle-headed because their minds' openings are blocked by the grease which meat produces.*

The vegetables Li Yu loved included bamboo:

The ways of preparing bamboo shoots are: for the vegetarians, cook with plain water; for others, with fat pork. Bamboo should not be mixed with anything highly aromatic, otherwise its delicate flavour will vanish . . . After it is cooked, the fat meat should be taken away, and some clear soup added. The only condiments to be used are vinegar and wine.

For good measure he added to the recipe a poem by his predecessor Su Dongpo, the greatest poet of the eleventh century, who loved bamboo not so much for its taste as for its distinction:

> I would rather eat a meal without meat
> Than live in a place with no bamboos.
> Without meat one may become thin:
> Without bamboos one becomes vulgar.

Of all vegetables, those that Li Yu loved most were mushrooms. He praised them in Daoist terms: 'The mushroom, having no roots, springs to life suddenly as if from the void. It is the spirit of wild nature: when one consumes it one imbibes the essence of nature.'

An ink rubbing from moulded tiles in a Han tomb records scenes from everyday life in the fertile region of Sichuan. The top half shows archers at a lakeside shooting wild geese in flight. In the bottom half men are harvesting and threshing grain.

Li Yu was a native of Zhejiang, in the east of China, one of the great regions of Chinese cooking. The Chinese like lists of five, and just as there are five Confucian virtues and five elements or 'phases' in nature,* so there are 'the five grains', 'the five strongly odoured foods', 'the five savoury substances' and 'the five great regions of cooking'. Chinese gourmets sometimes disagree on their exact boundaries, but all accept that the far south, the coastal provinces centering on Guangzhou (Canton), is one of the five, and probably the greatest. These lands are blessed not only with the warmest but also with the wettest climate in China; wild-life is abundant and everything grows, including double or triple crops of rice, the staple grain of all southern China. The Cantonese delight in fresh tastes, enjoyed in their own right. They use no sauces, apart from a few such as oyster sauce to give food a sharp seafood savour.

Northerners say that the Cantonese eat 'anything with four legs except tables, and anything that flies except aeroplanes'. Endowed with a variety of minority peoples, late to be included in the empire by the northern Chinese, still later to be integrated into their culture (if they yet are) and inheriting that curiosity about all foods that was once characteristic of China even in the north, the Cantonese still have, in their markets, an astonishing array of animals on sale for food, including dogs, cats, wild cats, pangolins (creatures looking like armadillos) and snakes. They are carrying on an ancient tradition recorded in a sixteenth-century book which mentions that animals eaten in that period included not only crabs and many shellfish, but rats, wolves, foxes, wild goats, bears, camels, wild boar, deer, tigers, moles, donkeys, horses, dogs, swans, ravens, magpies, swallows, peacocks, cranes, storks, owls and cormorants.*

The Chinese usually think of the Lower Yangtze basin, including Li Yu's native Zhejiang, inland to Anhui and up to Shandong or the Huai River, as a second great region, 'the east'. This is also a region of rice, but with wheat playing more of a supporting role than in the far south; of fish and of shellfish, especially in Fujian; of soups (three substantial soups at one meal); of oil, lard and sugar; of rice-wine and vinegar liberally used in cooking and eating. Like the south it is an area where freshness and simple tastes are highly prized. As Li Yu wrote of his favourite food:

This bowl, dating from about 4800 BC, but already showing what was to become a classical Chinese shape, is decorated with abstract designs based on the shape of fish.

To use crab in a soup is to spoil its texture, though it will still taste good. To hash it fine will destroy its real taste although its richness will remain. What is worst is to cut it up, marinade it and fry it. Many things are best when they are left alone. To try to improve the crab's taste by adding other ingredients is like trying to make the sun brighter by lighting a fire.*

The west of China, including Hunan, Sichuan and Yunnan, is the realm of hot spices. This is not because of Indian influence. Records from as early as 300 BC already mention that smartweed, Chinese pepper and sharp pungent herbs were characteristic of Hunan. Sichuan was nearly depopulated in the wars of the seventeenth century, when the Ming Dynasty fell to the Manchus, and the Hunan cooking style came in with new settlers from further east, and spread on south and south-west to Yunnan.

A peasant from the countryside around Guilin returns home from market carrying a pig on a shoulder pole. Pigs are kept by almost every peasant household in China.

(Right)
Fish was an important part of the Chinese diet in neolithic times; now it is still significant, but far less important than grain. The terracotta figure opposite dates from the Han Dynasty (206 BC-AD220).

To make up five regions the Chinese usually divide the north into 'old north' and 'far north'. They consider both of them dull compared to the far south, the south-east and the west. Henan in the Yellow River basin, the ancient heart of Chinese civilization, is thought the best area of either region, drawing on the eastern imperial traditions of Luoyang and Kaifeng. Here the staple grains are millet and wheat. This is also the home of sweet and sour dishes such as the Henan yellow fish, which is served on a bed of handmade noodles, thin as hair and quickly fried. Everyday food is mainly pancakes, steam-bread, dumplings and millet congee, a form of thin gruel.

In Beijing and throughout the far north Mongolian influence shows in the predominance of fire-pots and of barbecued meats. The north in general, and the 'far north' in particular, use a great deal of mutton as well as garlic, onions, chives, ginger and other sharp, strong flavours.

Because the Chinese of the north cut down their forests so early they have long had to rely for fuel on thin branches of shrubs which flare and burn out rapidly. Since the New Stone Age Chinese cooking vessels have had an unusually efficient system of heat-flow built into their design. By contrast with the Western saucepan with straight sides, which tends to make for a dish burned at the bottom and less than fully cooked at the top, Chinese cooking vessels have always flared at such an angle that the hot air rises evenly, neither rushing away rapidly nor burning parts of the food. The tools used in cooking are also economical and tend to be all-purpose. There are few pots and pans, and even a professional chef usually manages with a single cleaver rather than a multiplicity of knives.

Stew was once the primary dish of Chinese feasts. It was cooked in a tripod cauldron (*ding*). Among those recorded on the bamboo menus found at the Mawangdui burial site, which dates from 168 BC, are 'ox, mutton, venison, pork, suckling pig, dog, chicken, pheasant and wild duck.' When food was stewed, it was cooked for so long that it could be pulled apart without a knife. Perhaps partly to save fuel most food was cut up before it was cooked: the practice is of such ancient origin that in Zhou times the phrase used for the art of cookery itself was 'cutting and cooking'(*gepeng*). This, together with the practice of long stewing and the predominance of grain, has enabled Chinese food to be eaten from the earliest known times with a spoon and a pair of chopsticks.

Boiling and steaming are the usual methods of cooking grain and grain products. Wheat buns and loaves are steamed. Rice, soup noodles and soup dumplings are boiled. Steaming probably started with a colander-like dish filled with millet and fitted above a pot of stew. Both were covered, and the stew vapours went up through the holes in the colander to steam and flavour the grains. The practice of steaming grains over meat seems to have disappeared about the end of the Stone Age, but the method was not abandoned, merely reversed. Today people cook grains in a 'kettle', put small dishes of fish and vegetables on top, cover the kettle, and let the steam cook the dishes. They also use bamboo steamers which can be stacked up six at a time over boiling water, to cook the many varieties of dumplings known

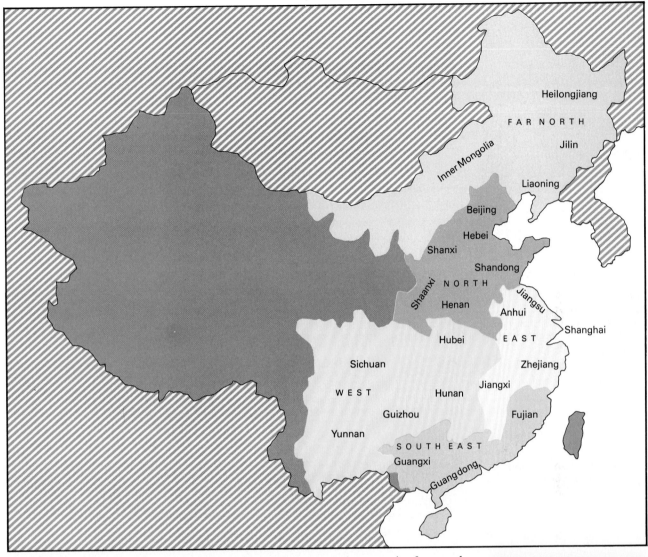

as *dimsum*. These devices all enable the Chinese to cook a meal of several dishes and yet use the fuel, time and effort for one.

In many cases, to preserve the fresh flavour of the separate ingredients as well as to save fuel, small pieces of separately sliced, cubed or shredded food are very quickly cooked and only afterwards blended together with the flavouring ingredients and sauces. This method is called 'stir frying'. It is a comparatively recent method in Chinese terms, coming in about the time China was unified. The invention of cast iron enabled the armies of Qin Shihuangdi to use iron-tipped lances, arrows and crossbow bolts: the wok, the shallow conical frying pan in which stir-frying is done, made of thin-beaten iron, was a peaceful product of the same age.

Particularly in stir-fry cooking there is a long tradition of using 'flavoured fat', created by frying fats or oils with what is called the 'trinity of Chinese cooking' – scallion, ginger and garlic. It probably dates as far back as the

An iron wok, with its distinctive flared shape, is a mainstay of the Chinese kitchen. Set on a small brazier or stove fuelled by straw and wood chips, the wok distributes heat evenly up its sides, enabling the finely chopped ingredients to be stir-fried quickly in a small amount of seasoned oil. The benefits are twofold. Scarce fuel is saved and the food retains its taste and nutritional value.

times when cooking was mainly done in cauldrons. When animal flesh was stewed, thick layers of chicken fat, dog fat or beef fat accumulated on the surface, and they were early on distinguished carefully by the Chinese. This is 'the first layer' in the preparation of a Chinese dish. Into it the second layer of flavouring ingredients is stirred: salted soya beans and soya sauces or soya pastes, with sugar, wine or stock. The 'third layer' of cooking consists of the main ingredients, which are chosen above all for their freshness.

Chinese cooking can involve skills more usually found on the sportsfield or indeed the battlefield than in the kitchen. The cook may have to be highly mobile, to be able to toss and catch food in a wok with a flick of the wrist, and to manage sudden fireballs of flavoured fat as they explode from stir-fry cooking. Professional cooks were until recently nearly all men, especially in the north. Cooking in the home was done by women, who were expected to be frugal; they were not thought likely to be capable of adapting to the more lavish approach required of a good restaurant cook. Although most women work full-time today, and some are restaurant cooks, they still do most of the cooking at home.

Many recipes for Chinese dishes are the same today as they have been for many centuries. Yuan Mei (1716-98), who with Li Yu is among the best-known gourmets in Chinese literature, has left behind a wide variety of recipes, including these:

Sea-slug (Bêche-de-mer)
It has a neutral taste with a slightly fishy smell. It should first be thoroughly cleaned and then boiled in thick chicken broth. It may be mixed with fungus and mushroom. In summer, it may be consumed cold, shredded and taken with chicken stock and mustard. It also goes well with bean curd and mushroom.
Shark's Fin
Shark's fin must be boiled for two days before it is tender. One way is to cook it with a good ham and chicken stock, with a small quantity of bamboo shoots and rock-sugar. Another way of preparing it is to boil it in chicken soup until the 'needles' are separated, and add [celery] in long, slender slices so that they become indistinguishable from the shark's fin.
Stir-fry Sliced Chicken
Mix sliced chicken with soya sauce and sesame-seed oil. Add oil and pour meat in. Stir, add ginger slices and spring onion. For best result, use only about six ounces of meat for an ordinary-sized wok.
Steamed Duck
Take away bones from duck; stuff it with a mixture as follows: one cup rice wine, some ham, cloves, mushroom, bamboo shoots, soya beans, spring onion. Add chicken broth and steam till tender.*

Yuan Mei was a severe critic of misplaced gourmet enthusiasms: 'There is a common saying, "The right girl for the right husband." The art of cooking follows the same principles. No single ingredient is self-sufficient . . . I have often seen people mix crab-meat with swallow's nest, and lily-flower with chicken and pork. It is . . . quite unnatural.' He also frowned on sloppy habits in the kitchen: 'The knife that has been used on onion should not be used to cut bamboo-shoot. Vegetables take on an unpleasant smell if wiped by a piece of unclean cloth or cut on an unclean board. Similarly affecting the goodness of vegetables are tobacco ashes, sweat on your forehead, ants and flies, and chips of charred leftovers in the wok.'*

He was attentive not only to the cleanliness and the flavour of food, but also to its appearance. 'The eyes and the nose are neighbours to the mouth and act as middlemen,' he wrote. 'A good dish strikes the nose and eyes first. Sometimes it is clear like autumn clouds and beautiful like amber. Its flowery flavour tells the secret before being tested by the mouth and tongue.' The Chinese still speak of 'the three appeals' of food – to sight, to smell and to taste – in that order. There is a beautiful art of flower-shaped, bud-shaped and butterfly-shaped arrangements of food, achieved either by carving vegetables for decoration or by layout. This is normally done only for feasts and banquets.

For ordinary people throughout China today a good meal involves a grain, soup, a steamed dish and a stir-fried dish. If one dish is left out for economy – and one of these usually is – it is likely to be the stir-fry. Meat and fish are more likely to be dispensed with than vegetables.

In the early part of the twentieth century nine-tenths of the population ate virtually nothing for most of the year but grain and coarse vegetables, 'yard-long bean' and soya bean, the last a vital source of protein, since they hardly ever had meat. Poor people today may live on sweet potatoes or other vegetables, going without grain for months at a time. One reason, no doubt unconscious, behind the Chinese devotion to periodic feasts such as Chinese New Year is that they give many people their only chance to eat certain essential minerals and vitamins.

Soup has never been regarded as dispensable. As Li Yu put it: 'As long as there is rice there should be soup. The relationship between soup and rice is like that between water and a boat. When a boat is stranded on a sand bank, only water can wash it back to the river; rice goes down much better with soup. I would go as far as to say that it would be better to go without all main dishes than to have no soup.'*

One reason why a traditional meal without soup is almost impossible to imagine is that Chinese water is generally undrinkable without boiling, a fact not unconnected with the widespread use of night-soil as a fertilizer in the fields. Drinking soup is the usual way people quench their thirst. In summer, the Chinese drink several bowls of it at meals and seldom drink anything else, though they eat fruit, especially watermelon. Summer soups are thin and watery. In winter people like thick soup.

Tea came into China in the Han Dynasty (206 BC–AD 220), and became widespread among the rich in the Tang (618-906). It was treated with ceremonial reverence, and there were cults of tea-drinking,* of which the best-known record is a book, again by Li Yu, entitled the *Tea Classic* (*Cha Jing*). In the Song Dynasty (960-1279), tea remained an object of connoisseurship and cult, even though it was drunk as widely as it is in England today. Since then, despite the Western phrase about 'all the tea in China', it has become something of a luxury again.

The standard Chinese invitation to tea is an invitation to drink hot water; and some poor people actually do drink only plain boiled water. When the

Two ritual bronze vessels, one a cauldron for cooking and the other (below) a fanciful wine pourer, testify to the importance of food and feasting to the Chinese from the earliest times. In the shang period (c. 16th century–c. 11th century BC) such vessels were among the grave goods buried with members of the royal family and nobility to ensure that all their needs were taken care of in the afterlife.

Tea-houses in China are traditional refuges for men. Customers in this tea-house in Shanghai pay a small amount for a place to sit, a cup of tea and as many refills as they like. Many tea-houses provide entertainment as well, from musicians, singers and storytellers.

(Right)
The 8th-century poet Li Bai (Li Po), celebrated for his love of wine as well as for his verse, is escorted by two attendants after a drinking bout. The wine he drank would have been rice wine, still common in China today.

Chinese make tea, they pour in water that is not at boiling point, so the leaves tend to float in the tea. Usually tea is pot-brewed and the first pot is thrown away; then infusion after infusion is made and connoisseurs observe how the taste and fragrance change until it is very weak.

Each province tends to have its favourite tea, sometimes from another region. Special waters are required for the brewing of the ideal teas. For example the Nine Dragon Spring Teahouse in Guangzhou, which has long been a favourite meeting place for artists and writers, is famous for the water from its eighteen-hundred-year-old well which, in the opinion of connoisseurs, suits one of the local teas particularly well.

The Chinese have one word, *jiu*, for most alcoholic drinks. It is usually translated 'wine' but this does not mean that it is necessarily connected with grapes. These came late to China, in the Tang Dynasty, from the north-west frontier region of Xinjiang. Most Chinese wine has been brewed from grain, either millet or rice. Rice-wine was drunk in quantity by the great Tang Dynasty poet Li Bai (Li Po), and it is still common today. The Chinese also use the word *jiu* for hard, highly alcoholic spirits such as *mao tai*, the hazard of Chinese banquets, object of countless cries of *gan bei* from hosts and guests in turn. Beer is brewed mainly in the east and owes its origin and flavour to the German presence in parts of Shandong Province before the First World War.

The Chinese appear to have been heavy drinkers through much of their early history. In the Southern Song capital of Hangzhou people were drunk frequently.* Since those times, neo-Confucian moralists have waged and won a battle against alcohol, and today the Chinese seldom drink without

food, while it is very rare to see anyone drunk in the streets. It would not be easy for the poor to drink a great deal even if they wanted to, since alcohol is expensive. What heavy drinking does occur is mainly done at banquets, where officials unwind at restaurants and toast each other in *mao tai*, or at family feasts.

Much of the excellence of food in China may well be due to the role it has played in celebration and ritual. No people know more about feasting or about the social side of eating than the Chinese: indeed there is probably no civilization where eating plays so central a part in festive life. Whether the occasion is a business deal or a family gathering, a birthday or a New Year festival, the Chinese love to celebrate it at the table.

The capital of the Northern Song Dynasty (960-1126), Kaifeng, was famous in its heyday for its bustling market places and as a centre for good living. According to a contemporary account the city had 72 restaurants which served food day and night. In a scene from the 12th-century painting, 'Life Along

122

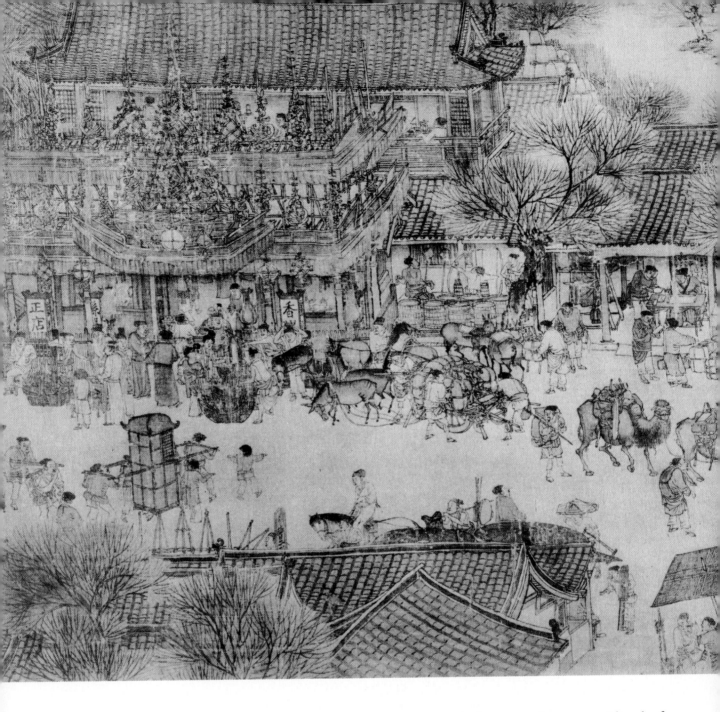

the River on the Eve of the Qing Ming Festival', citizens throng a street lined with restaurants and shops selling wine, food, herbs and many other goods. Well-to-do customers sit in the large two-storey restaurant decorated with banners, while on the street a small crowd has gathered to listen to a storyteller.

The emperor's food and drink in particular were always considered of great importance. In ancient Chinese tradition only he could make sacrifices to Heaven; he was its Son. Much of his time was spent moving around in ceremonies in measured steps from dawn to dusk; and many of the rites with which he was associated involved food. In the Han Dynasty the kitchen staff of the palace included some thirty ice-men, a hundred men to deal with vegetables and about three hundred to handle wine; the division of labour and the number of attendants have been compared to those at Versailles. Imperial Chinese law contained numerous provisions for the preparation of the emperor's meals. The sixth article of the Tang Code, recalling an earlier passage in the *Rites of Zhou*, stated that if the food-doctors in charge of the eight flavours of the ruler's food left any dirt in it, they were to be punished by two years' penal servitude; if the flavours were wrong or the food had not been tasted the penalty was 'one hundred blows with the heavy stick'; while if they did not follow the standard cookery book, they were guilty of 'capital irreverence' for 'violating the dietary proscriptions'. Examples cited included mixing dried meat with millet or rice and, worse, serving green vegetables with tortoise. Not only were green vegetables and tortoise thought poisonous if eaten together but, according to the Song Dynasty *Instructions to Coroners*, 'this combination produces tortoises in the stomach of the person who eats them together'. All such crimes were punishable by strangulation.*

The Manchu emperors added a personal preference for frugality to the other imperial tradition of lavishness. The Qianlong emperor, for example, ate only two meals a day, each lasting fifteen minutes. The dual tradition persisted into the twentieth century: according to the autobiography of the last emperor of China, Puyi, the eunuchs of his retinue would always formally announce what he had eaten in the same way: 'The Lord of Ten Thousand Years consumed one bowl of old rice viands, one steamed bread roll and a bowl of congee.' Meanwhile the Emperor was sending back untouched vast banquets daily, so that his official menu included each month more than 1000 pounds of meat and 240 chickens and ducks. Privately, in the practical Chinese spirit, he was all the time eating something different again: delicious, small meals, cooked specially for him and exactly to his taste, by the chefs of his favourite concubines.*

Food for the imperial palace was transported from other parts of China packed in ice, and had been since the Han Dynasty. Besides unrefrigerated cargoes of swans, pickled vegetables, cherries preserved in honey and cormorants, the Directorate of Foodstuffs in the Ming Dynasty (1368-1644) shipped iced plums, loquats, bamboo shoots and shad more than a thousand miles along the Grand Canal to the kitchens of the Forbidden City. Today refrigeration is rare in China; electricity is in short supply.* The traditions of salting and pickling food and of drying meat for winter continue; and, as in the past, most people rely on their own local diet for staples. Together with the Chinese preference for very fresh food, just dug up from the garden or just caught in the river, this helps to maintain regional identities.

There have always been street hawkers, however, who have made a living by presenting in one part of China the local specialities of another. The Yuan drama *Baihua Ting* (about 1250) has a character in it, a fruit vendor, who offers delicacies from five separate provinces, including 'juicy-juicy sweet, full-full fragrant, sweet-smelling, red and watery fresh-peeled round-eye lychees from Fuzhou; from Pingjiang some sour-sour-tart, shady-cool, sweet-sweet luscious yellow oranges and green tangerines with the leaves still on; [and] some supple-supple-soft, quite-quite white, crystal-sweet, crushed-flat candied persimmons from Songyang.'*

Restaurants were an early feature of Chinese society. The poet and statesman Jia Yi in the second century BC argued that, 'when the Xiongnu have developed a craving for our cooked rice, *geng* stew, roasted meats, and wine, this will have become their fated weakness.' He proposed a chain of restaurants on the northern border, each with a first-rate menu, in order to attract China's chief barbarian scourge to the side of civilization. Had his idea been put into practice it might have provided the first instance of Chinese take-away; though the nomad horsemen would more likely have left with the cooks than the cooking.

In the Song Dynasty capitals of Kaifeng and Hangzhou it was possible to get food, tea or wine at almost any hour of the day or night. Restaurants, tea-houses and wine-shops can be seen in profusion in the great scroll showing the Spring Festival on the River Huai at Kaifeng, the *Qing Ming Shang He Tu*. From a little later a description survives of a room full of diners in the Southern Song capital:

The people of Hangzhou are very difficult to please. Hundreds of orders are given on all sides: this person wants something hot, another something cold, a third something tepid, a fourth something chilled; one wants cooked food, another raw, another chooses roast, another grill. The orders are given in a loud voice, all are different, sometimes three different ones at the same table. Having received the orders, the waiter goes to the kitchen and sings out the whole list of orders, starting with the first one. He never mixes them up, and if by any unlikely chance he should make a mistake, the proprietor will launch into a volley of oaths addressed to the offending waiter, will straightaway stop him serving, and may even dismiss him altogether.*

One unusual feature of Hangzhou in that period is that there were establishments that served human flesh. That of women, old men, young girls and children was served in separate dishes, since each had its distinctive taste. The food in general was referred to as 'two-legged mutton'.* A contemporary author says the habit came in when people from north China, accustomed to cannibalism after the wars and the distress of the early twelfth century (when the Tartars and Mongols were ravaging the north), had opened restaurants in the southern capital. The great romance *The Water Margin*, which is set in the late years of the Northern Song Dynasty, refers in several places to steamed dumplings 'filled with human flesh, sold only at the so-called "black deeds inns" where evil and violent persons gathered to plot crimes'. At one point the hero Lin Chong comes to an inn and is confronted by a big man, who explains:

Humble one has been ears and eyes for Wang, the leader of the robbers. My surname is Zhu, my name is Gui, and I am originally of Yizhou in Yishui County. The ones in the lair have commanded this humble one to keep the wine shop here as a pretence, in reality to discover what merchants pass through these parts. It is only if they have money that I go and make it known in the lair. . . . If one guest comes along here and he has no money I let him pass on. If he has money and if he is to be treated lightly I only give him a sleeping draught, but if I am to deal with him more severely then I really kill him. His lean meat I cut into strips to make dried meat to eat and his fat I render and we burn it in lamps.*

There are instances in historical times in China of people eating their enemies in anger.* Human flesh and blood have also been thought of as potent remedies for disease and debility. In a story called 'Medicine', Lu Xun,

An illustration to a 17th-century edition of The Water Margin *shows the hero Wu Song and an escort of two soldiers at an inn where the innkeeper's wife is in the habit of serving the guests drugged wine, killing them and selling their bodies for meat. The two soldiers die. Wu Song discovers human hair in his dumpling and escapes.*

125

Famine has been a constant feature of Chinese life throughout history in a country where the pressure of population on the available agricultural land has always been intense, and drought and flood have been constant threats.

China's greatest twentieth-century writer, tells how Old Xuan, a tea-shop owner, tries to save the life of his consumptive son by procuring some *mantou* (steamed bun) dipped in the blood of an executed revolutionary. One of his customers assures him: 'This is a guaranteed cure! . . . Just think, brought back warm and eaten warm! . . . A roll dipped in human blood like this can cure any consumption.' The idea of cannibalism as a last resort in hunger may not have disappeared in contemporary China, when so many people have sometimes been close to starvation.*

Threat of starvation has also been the reason why the Chinese know so much about the leaves, herbs and even insects that can provide nourishment in times of emergency. The exceptional number of dishes in Chinese cooking is the result of a curiosity that has never been wholly a matter of connoisseurship, but which has had the dry wind of famine behind it also. In the early twentieth century famine foods included 'flour of ground leaves, sawdust, thistles, cotton seeds, peanut hulls and ground pumice'.* More recently they have been cassava (although it is potentially poisonous), grass roots, locusts, weeds, stalks, husks, sugar cane waste, sweet potato and in the south the oil squeezed from rice husks. In the hungry years that followed the Great Leap Forward of 1958 peasants were exhorted to eat 'Leap Forward Flour', which consisted of corncobs, corn silk, rice husks and wheat husks ground together.* Some of these foods have no nutritional value but merely still the pains of hunger.

A woodcut by the artist Zheng Yefu illustrates a heavy flood in 1947.

In a room decorated with pin-ups of Shanghai film stars, a family in a southern village today enjoys a midday meal.

In general, however, the diets that the Chinese have evolved when they have had enough to eat have been nourishing and balanced. There are good reasons for the rest of the world to look closely at the story of Chinese eating, besides the pleasures in store for those who learn new recipes from Guangdong, Sichuan, Shandong, Beijing or Henan. The largely vegetable diet on which the Chinese live is one that the rest of the world may soon be forced to adapt to, as other countries go through the now ancient Chinese experience of increasing densities of population and decreasing natural resources. Some of the ways the Chinese have evolved of making every inch of ground and every fragment of food nourish human life are 'classical' in the sense that needy people have voluntarily preserved them for centuries because they worked well.

LIVING

LABOUR AND HARVEST

In China, agricultural work has always occupied the vast majority of the population. But in a country of such continental scale agriculture has meant rather differing activities in the north and the south. North China has a severe winter climate during which for nearly three months the ground is frozen to a depth of more than a foot, and all agricultural work outside is impossible. It is also a very dry climate in which the rainfall is concentrated into less than three months of summer, apart from light, variable and sometimes scant rain in April, vital for the seedling crops which have lain dormant through the dry, cold winter. Work is therefore intense and strenuous at certain seasons, but at other times impossible. In high summer it may rain, violently, for a week or more at a time, producing floods which may sweep away the crops. Alternatively, the summer rain may be erratic or may hardly fall, so that the crops fail through drought. It has been said that one or other of these calamities strikes the northern provinces every three years. Sometimes the disaster is not general throughout the region but is intense in one province. Thus the northern farmer works under the constant menace of a capricious climate: although the onset of seasonal changes has an almost clock-like precision, this does not guarantee that any season will be normal.

The prevailing crops of north China – millet, sorghum, wheat and maize – do not depend on irrigation, though they can benefit from it; in north China hydrology is mainly concerned with keeping the raging summer floods within the high dykes which line the rivers, rather than irrigating fields which are in danger of being flooded in any case. Work for the northern farmer means not only ploughing, sowing and reaping, but constant care and attention to river banks and dykes.

Today 'the south' is often used to mean Guangdong and its neighbouring provinces, Guangxi and Fujian, but historically the real divide was between the land of millet and wheat to the north and the land of rice to the south of the northern watershed of the Yangtze, which is significantly named *Dabieshan* (The Great Dividing Mountains).

Where the land is flat in the south it is an unbroken rice field, divided by narrow dykes which also serve as footpaths and wheelbarrow ways. Streams are linked with small canals, navigable by boats. Villages are often strung out along a dyke, in order to save the precious land for rice. In the north they are

Much of north-west China is rugged upland covered with a thick layer of loess, a fine yellow soil which is easily eroded. Terracing has allowed cultivation to spread up the hillsides where millet and winter wheat are grown. With limited rainfall, the area has long been one of the poorest in China.

山邨水郭聽吳歌家
是江南佳勝多必不
榜秀土埃而裏与有菜
柘晚秦逸秧針挿遍
青千頃蘭簇堆來白
氎寬冷梁七云悰樂盈
田平樂畜在人和
乾隆御題

四月江南農事興
泡麻漫榖有常
程菜言婚細全
無事一夜繰車
響到明唐寅畫

子畏畫品在文沈間卓踔自成一家非一時流輩所
能全及此幀神韻溢出尤其入意者不可多得矣
識者寶之
醉鴎題

130

compact, fortified and built of mud brick; in the south of bamboo. In the south, even in its northern confines – the Yangtze valley – winter, though chilly with some light falls of snow, is short: December and January. November is still autumn, March already spring. Frost is only occasional, and at night. There is a fairly constant light rain in the winter and spring months. Agricultural work is therefore continuous.

When the winter crop has been harvested in April the fields must be prepared for the sowing of rice, or rather transplanting the seedlings, which are grown in separate beds. This means that all bordering small dykes and banks must be repaired to hold water. Then the fields are flooded to soften the ground, and ploughed. Water buffalo, powerful animals, are well adapted to this work, which is still laborious for the man guiding the plough in the soft mud.

By May the weather is getting hot, and continues to be often rainy. The seedlings must now be transplanted. This requires a large number of workers, as the little plants must be placed by hand in the soft mud beneath the water, and in orderly line. Men, women and children are all impressed for this long and hard work, lasting with brief intervals from dawn to dark, and continuing for several days. It is of great importance to complete it before the sun grows so hot that it would shrivel the seedlings. Once these are planted, however, the southern farmer, in contrast to the northerner, can take life more easily in the hottest season. The main work is to care for the dykes and irrigation, weed the rice fields a little by hand or by foot, and watch the rice grow. This is just as well, for the day temperature is sometimes over 100°F (39°C) in the shade and the humidity ninety per cent. There is rarely any wind or even breeze. When the rice is ripe the fields are drained, and the work force assembles to reap the harvest; and as soon as this task is completed the fields must be cleaned and ploughed again, this time dry, for the planting of the winter crops. Though these are usually beans, in the extreme south, wherever the warm winter permits, there is a double and in the far south often a triple rice crop.

In addition to rice, which is by far the main crop, maize is grown on hillsides where irrigation is difficult or the available ground too restricted to make terracing and irrigation worthwhile. A striking feature of the landscape in many parts of China is the ladder of terraces, diminishing in size, that climbs up the valleys almost to the summit of each ridge. In the south that summit is left forested to gather the rainfall which, as it flows down in streams, is diverted from terrace to terrace to irrigate the ground. Often this reworking of the topography of the valleys has taken centuries of steady development.

The south-east provinces – Jiangsu, Zhejiang and Fujian – are also the main producers of tea and silk, with bamboo an important crop as well. The people of a southern farming village may therefore be at once rice-growers, tea-growers, silk-spinners and foresters. Tea gardens can be planted on hill slopes, which are the natural habitat of the camelia bush, a plant that grows wild in the south-eastern mountains. Those camelias grown as ornamental

A spring scene in the rice-growing lands south of the Yangtze River.

shrubs for their flowers, in China as in the West, are the same plant as the tea bush, which has simple white flowers. Tea, like wine, depends for its quality on the particular aspect of quite small areas of land. Certain gardens were, and still are, famous throughout China for their tea. Apart from keeping the gardens free from weeds and caring for the plants, tea-growing is not labour-intensive until the season for picking the leaves arrives. This is skilled work, and requires the work of many people, usually women.

The mulberry trees on which silkworms feed are grown in the same areas as tea, and usually also on hillsides, since all the land that can be irrigated is reserved for rice. In some areas silk cultivation has been combined for many centuries with fish-farming: mulberry trees are planted round the edges of carp-ponds and the fish fed on the silkworms' droppings. The skilled work of rearing silkworms so that their cocoons can be gathered for spinning silk is traditionally also entrusted to women. Though the spinning of the silk is sedentary, the work in the fields requires the active participation of women without the artificial impediment of footbinding; hence broadly speaking the peasant women of the south escaped this mutilation, which most other Chinese women suffered for a thousand years.

The fertile, warm southern provinces also produce a great variety of fruits, some of them peculiar to China. It seems probable that China was the original home of the citrus fruits, of which there are many domestic varieties, large and small, edible and ornamental, particularly in the south-west provinces, with their mountain country – Sichuan, Guizhou and Yunnan. The lychees of the far south, Guangdong Province, are grown in large orchards which are prominent near the border with Hong Kong. Formerly fresh lychees could be found only here or in the nearby regions, for the fruit did not easily stand long journeys, though the most famous beauty of the Tang Dynasty, the emperor's favourite Yang Guifei, insisted on having them brought to the capital at Chang'an (Xi'an) in the north-west. Now this delicious fruit is sold far more widely and is available, in season, even as far as Urumqi near the dry borders of central Asia.

The major transport networks of China were organized by the state

Silk-making has traditionally been one of the activities basic to the livelihood of people in the countryside of the eastern provinces. A scene from a 13th-century scroll shows workers pruning mulberry trees, the leaves of which are fed to the silkworms. Making the silk from their cocoons is delicate work and has usually been done by women.

mainly to carry rice and other supplies to the court and to the officials in the capital, and also to the armies, which usually had to be concentrated in the north to face the threat from barbarian invaders. The Grand Canal, constructed in the Sui Dynasty (590–618), connected the Yangtze to the Yellow River, thus linking the grain-producing regions in the south-east with the capital in the north. Even when the capital moved to the north-east, to Peking, the canal was safer than the sea route, which was exposed to the activities of pirates along the Shandong coast, and to the typhoons of summer and the freezing storms of winter, which can close the gulf of Bohai to shipping.

The Grand Canal was an extension of the southern system of transport, which was mainly by boats and barges. The Yangtze, navigable for more than sixteen hundred miles for small craft and for two to three hundred miles for seagoing vessels, provided the central line of communications for the six provinces through which it flows. In addition, its great tributaries – the Han from the north, the Xiang and the Gan from the south – linked it with further provinces. Local transport in the near vicinity of a large river was also largely by boats on the tributary streams and small canals.

In the rice country the only other means of carrying goods was either by porter or by wheelbarrow. The Chinese wheelbarrow, which distributes the load in two halves, one on each side of the central wheel, is able to carry

A painting of the Yuan Dynasty (1279–1368) illustrates the frenzied activity of the rice harvest, when all but the old, lame and blind work from dawn till dusk to cut, thresh, dry and store the grain. In areas where two crops of rice are grown each year the fields must then be ploughed and flooded before the new rice seedlings are planted out.

133

much larger and heavier loads than the European type, where the weight is so largely borne by the arms of the pusher. From the earliest times the understanding of balance has been characteristic of the Chinese: an aspect of the broader principle of *wu wei*, letting nature do the work, guiding it or being guided by it with the minimum of effort. In the Hankou region wheelbarrows were often used to carry people, especially girls and women, many of whom still had bound feet in the years after the First World War and could not walk any distance. In the 1920s, when the workforce for the textile mills at Hankou was mainly women, the approach to the mills would be thronged in the early morning with wheelbarrows bringing in the girls to work. They sat, two on each side, and the pusher seemed to suffer no severe strain from a load of four girls.

In the mountainous provinces of south-west China goods were shifted by mule, packhorse or porter. Caravans of more than a hundred mules would be used, with loads on each side attached to a wooden saddle. The loads on their frames could be detached without being unbound, as they slipped into wooden slots on the saddle. Thus a load could be made up at Bhamo in Burma, or Suifu in Sichuan, and transhipped at Bhamo for Rangoon and thence Calcutta, its final destination. Four or five men would control a caravan of more than a hundred mules. The muleteers were all Moslems, a long settled community in Yunnan, dating back to the thirteenth century.

The movement of salt was a significant occupation in these regions, since salt was lacking in the far south-west itself and almost all the salt consumed in the south-western provinces of Yunnan and Guizhou was imported from Sichuan Province. In the interior of China a great part of the salt was recovered from salt wells, the most famous being Ziliujing ('The Self-Flowing Well') in Sichuan, where an elaborate system of bamboo pipes and water-power brought up brine from a great depth. It was evaporated in large iron pots, frequently replenished, and the process was continued until the pot was filled with pure salt. The contents were then removed and divided by saw into two pieces, one of which formed the load for a porter. The salt lump was tied onto a wooden frame which fitted into the pack frame on the porter's back. Such loads were heavy, and the men who carried them the poorest of the poor. Their lives were short: they could not sit down to rest, but propped up the load on their backs with T-shaped wooden sticks. If they fell they could not rise again, and their fellows could not help them to do so. In frosty or snowy weather in the mountains of Guizhou and southern Sichuan it was commonplace in the years before the Second World War to find four or five of them frozen to death where they had fallen over.

Transport provided employment for large numbers of workers in other parts of China also. In the north, where the rivers are not for the most part navigable, carts were the main means of transport, both for goods and men. The Chinese cart has generally been two-wheeled and drawn by horses or mules, in tandem, or in threes or fours in triangular or diamond formation, if the load is heavy. Their iron-rimmed, many-spoked wheels have cut deeply into the yellow crystalline soil of the northern plain, and in the course of the

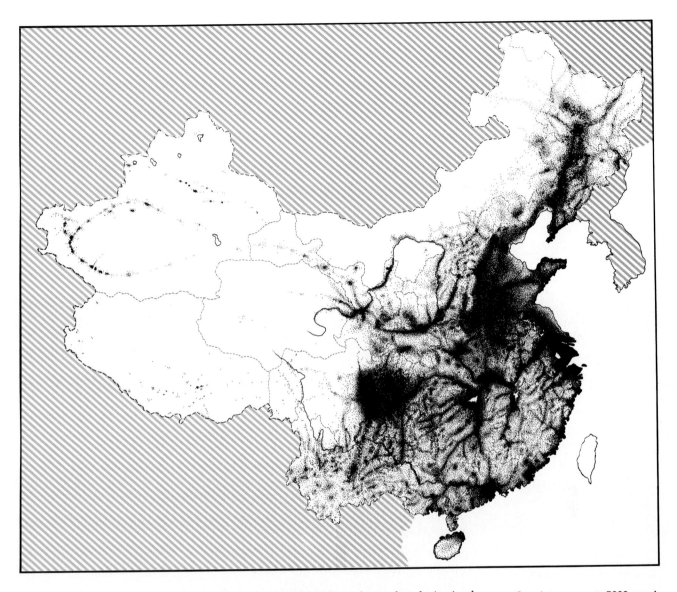

One dot represents 5000 people

centuries many roads in Shaanxi, Henan and Hebei have been deeply incised into the ground, to a depth of ten or twelve feet. Carts are slow; fifteen miles has long been the limit of a day's stage. Consequently the movement of large quantities of goods required the work of many men. The ancillary services – large inns with fodder for the animals and lodging for the men – provided a good part of the employment in the small cities and large villages which were regular staging points in pre-revolutionary China.

The impression of timelessness that Chinese rural life may at first convey is deceptive. In reality, both agriculture and the landscape underwent significant changes, and these in turn led to sometimes dramatic changes in population and to gradual alterations in the balance between north and south. Until well into the first millennium AD, the southern provinces were largely undeveloped wild forest with very light inhabitation, whereas the

Yellow River basin had then been cultivated, and its forests denuded, for more than two thousand years. During this time the north, with its superior civilization, was able to dominate the south; in doing so it introduced or stimulated new methods of irrigation or of agriculture in the south, and these led to massive increases in the productivity of the south, and in its population.

One striking example of this process is the taming of the Min River at Dujiangyan, close to Chengdu in central Sichuan. The province of Sichuan forms a fertile plateau in the central south-west, near the early big confluences of the Yangtze. It has a population of a hundred million people, more than Japan. With its sheltering ring of outer mountains and its variety of heights and terrains, it can today support almost all the crops grown in China, and for more than two thousand years it has been a massive grain-bowl for the rest of China, largely because of the policies of the state of Qin in the early third century BC.

The Dujiangyan irrigation scheme is one of the greatest feats of early engineering in the world. In 316 BC the Qin generals Zhang Yi and Zhang Ruo conquered the state of Shu, now Sichuan, as part of the Qin expansion that led in the next century to the unification of China. According to the historian Sima Qian, 'Li Bing, the governor, cut through . . . the "Separated Hill" and abolished the ravages of the [Min] river, excavating the two great canals in [the plain of] Chengdu.'* The plain had previously been of little use for agriculture: either flooded or too dry, and neither predictably. A text that Li Bing left carved at the site in 294 BC is still there: 'Dig the sand-beach deep, so that there will be enough water for agriculture. Make the overfill spillway low, so that surplus water can run off and not cause floods.' The works were completed by his son, Li Erlang, and there is a temple to them beside the river. A watermark, a piece of sculpture in the form of a heroic figure carrying a spade, was used to tell the engineers when the flood waters were about to spill into the relief channel, once the original course of the river. The main channel would thus be kept at the same maximum height throughout the year, and the stabilized flows of water made to irrigate the plain of Chengdu. The system is used today much as it was designed.

The Qin state peopled such reclaimed land with peasants, and taxed them directly, eliminating the feudal lords who were rivals to its central power. Its Legalist philosophers prepared agricultural handbooks to distribute to peasants and argued for low farm taxes and high grain prices, with government grain stocks to minimize price fluctuation. Later Chinese emperors continued the policies of settling peasants on conquered or reclaimed land when they could, and of promoting agriculture, which long provided them with their main revenue in taxes. In the Song Dynasty the court constantly exhorted the people to improve food crops and to try out new methods of cultivation, and it took a lead in experimenting with early-ripening rice, in particular champa rice, a relatively drought-resistant variety which had been recently imported to Fujian from central Vietnam. When the rice crop failed in the lower Yangtze and Huai regions in 1011-12,

The Leshan Buddha, a colossal statue carved out of a cliff, overlooks the confluence of three rivers near Chongqing. It was built in the hope that its watchful eye would protect river boatmen and prevent the turbulent waters from flooding. A zig-zag path leads down from the crest of the hill to the Buddha's foot (right).

Emperor Zhenzong gave orders to have champa rice distributed to the peasants of the drought-stricken areas. Hillsides which had been barren were turned into terraced fields and vast areas of land outside the river valleys were gradually brought under cultivation. In the course of the eleventh and twelfth centuries farmers succeeded in isolating varieties which matured in sixty days, ensuring a double, sometimes even triple rice harvest, and in one place, the marshlands of Jiangsu, a particularly flood-prone area north of the Yangtze, thirty-day varieties were eventually discovered. These and similar strains of rice did much to mitigate the effects of the greatest of all recent Chinese floods, those of 1720-1 and 1834-5.

The discovery of early-ripening rice was the first of two great revolutions in Chinese agriculture, and it led to East Asia's first population explosion in the tenth to twelfth centuries. In the Yangtze valley numbers increased at a much faster rate than in north China, and the southern provinces, with their milder climate, long growing seasons and abundant water gradually became the richest parts of China, while the older-settled northern provinces, dependent on one main crop a year – millet or wheat – and more at the mercy of the climate and limited by the shorter growing season, declined.

The second revolutionary change in agriculture was the introduction to China of American crops. Maize and the sweet potato were brought from the Philippines by the Spaniards and thence to China in the seventeenth century; the potato arrived at the same time through the Dutch in what is now Indonesia, together with snowpeas or *mange tout,* which are still called Dutch beans by the Chinese. Cotton was introduced earlier, about the thirteenth century, and was widely grown in the southern parts of the Yellow River basin.

The main object of imperial agricultural policy was to create a rich peasantry, who would in turn provide plentiful taxes. However, the results of the development of early-ripening rice were not all beneficial for the poor. Early-ripening strains of rice were used mainly to deal with exceptionally unfavourable natural conditions, and in the rich lower Yangtze area, where a network of streams and canals allowed an elaborate system of irrigation, and where only the ancient form of rice (*geng*) was cultivated, land was still severely limited. Apart from its heavier yield per acre such rice was also considered superior in quality, because of its high gluten content; it was called 'aromatic rice' and was eaten by the imperial family, the bureaucrats and the army. Consequently it was in this kind of rice that taxes in kind had to be delivered by the peasants. But because it grew only on rich soil, made still scarcer by the explosion of population and the pressure on good-quality land from the newly enriched landlords of the Song Dynasty, the peasants who had poor soil often had to pay in cash for their tax rice and thus had to borrow money. Increasingly they were drawn into a monetary economy in which they could easily find themselves victims of fluctuations in prices; their land could then be taken by moneylenders. The Southern Song poet Fan Chengda, in his poem 'The Toil of Farming', wrote of the peasants of his time:

(Previous page)
A 17th-century scroll records a tour of inspection by the Kangxi emperor (1662-1722) during which he witnessed the building of a dyke to contain the waters of a rising river. Labour such as this has been the responsibility of every household in times of emergency.

[They] do not grudge tending the rice in spring
But fear the payment of taxes in the autumn;
The evil officials act like sparrows or rats
And the thieving clerks like locusts or caterpillars;
They take extra with their enlarged measures . . .
People cannot avoid being flogged to make them pay up
And are further oppressed with private debt;
No smoke rises from the abandoned homesteads,
Never once in their lives have they tasted
Rice clean and bright as the cloudstone;
Those who eat it are always the idle . . .
The mouths of those who grow it are forever watering.*

For those who were not beneficiaries of the state transport system, primarily designed for officials and soldiers, food supply in China has always been extremely precarious. The worst areas of China for famine, though it may strike anywhere, are probably the lower basin of the Yellow River (Huang He) – especially Henan – and Anhui, where floods are a constant danger; and the *huang tu* or 'yellow soil plateau' of the north and west,* formed over the millennia out of pulverized rock carried by the wind from the Gobi and the mountains of the far west, which in the violent alternations of temperature characteristic of northern China crack and give off a hard, crystalline yellow dust, called by geologists 'loess'. Floods and drought may strike other areas also, including Yunnan in the far south-west, and even the Yangtze river valley. The great drought-famine of 1877-9 covered virtually the whole of north China. It is thought to have killed between nine and thirteen million people. In 1888 nearly the whole of Henan was flooded and between one and two million people died. As recently as 1928 five million people died in north China – Shaanxi, Gansu, and Henan – from drought.

When the Communist Party came to power in 1949 its declared aim, in the ancient tradition of government but with new methods, was to improve the lot of the peasants and to solve the problems of famine, undernourishment and poverty. It set out to transform the Chinese countryside; but it transformed it not once but four times in its first thirty years of power, each time in a radically different way. First the Chinese farmers were banded into co-operatives; then in 1958 into communes of tens of thousands of people, with all income shared and with work, eating and some housing collectivized; then in the early 1960s they found their lives organized by brigades and teams, subdivisions of the communes; and about the end of the 1970s they were told to till their family fields again under the so-called Responsibility System. Meanwhile they sustained the impact of the Cultural Revolution of 1966-76, with its power-struggles in the Party and in government at all levels, and often with a breakdown of law and order in the countryside. In between all these changes, they were also expected to produce food.

Up to the end of 1957 the Agricultural Producers' Co-operatives, in which almost the entire rural population had been organized, were regarded as the most important institutions of the new social order. They were usually about the size of natural villages and were often identified with them, incorporating some three hundred households. Members and their families lived in their own houses. Household tools, small animals and vegetable gardens were also privately owned. Machines, larger tools, draught animals and cultivated land were collectively administered. Peasants were paid according to their work. In September 1957 the government told the Agricultural Producers' Co-operatives that there would be no more change for the next ten years.

But Mao was drawing away from Russia and from the Soviet model of economic development. He wanted China to follow her own path, and in view of the diminution in Soviet economic aid since 1956 he decided that China must be self-reliant. The country might be short of capital, but it was rich in human labour. Now, in the 'war against nature', he believed he needed only to mobilize the peasants and China's millions would overcome all obstacles.

Many people were set to work without pay to complete the large Ming Tombs reservoir, near Beijing, in six months. Such periodic campaigns for large-scale works, familiar from imperial times, have usually been dreaded by peasants because they did not bring them immediate income: they have been popularly called *mangmu gan, bailiu han,* 'blind work and useless sweat'. Then in March and April 1958 some regions of Sichuan and Hunan were required to merge their co-operatives into units on average thirty times as large, 'communes'. During the summer Mao toured China promoting the new movement, the 'Great Leap Forward' and by the early autumn all China's three-quarters of a million co-operatives had been amalgamated into about twenty-six thousand rural communes, and their land nationalized. Each commune contained a number of brigades, further subdivided into production teams, but the main power was at commune level.

Under the commune system, agricultural tasks were done by large groups of people, so that individual fields were no longer tended by the peasants who knew them. Working hours in most communes were twelve hours a day except at harvest time, and then sixteen or eighteen hours a day. Meals were taken in mess halls; children and babies were supposed to be cared for in crèches and nurseries; and the old were put to light work in old people's homes. In some communes the family houses were demolished and people had to live in barracks, the sexes separated.

The country people were also expected to build thousands of small-scale factories and primitive clay steel-furnaces in the villages. But so much labour was being mobilized for the construction of these rural steel-furnaces, and so many meetings were being called to work up popular enthusiasm for the Great Leap, that there was little time left for farm work. During the autumn harvest of 1958 in many regions only two-fifths of the peasants worked in the fields. At the same time the statisticians were ordered to produce evidence that would spur people to even greater efforts. By the summer of 1958 reports had begun to appear of ten- and twenty-fold increases in grain production in certain areas, and in September Mao declared that the national grain output had more or less doubled; the following year it might be

The use of massed labour for public works, characteristic of imperial China, continued under the People's Republic, notably in the Great Leap Forward and the Cultural Revolution. Here young townspeople 'sent down to the countryside' hump loads previously familiar only to the peasants.

'Digging a Well', a painting in the naïve style much promoted in the communes during the Cultural Revolution. The slogan on the rig, 'In agriculture, learn from Dazhai', encourages peasants to emulate the achievements of a supposedly model commune, since discredited as a figment of statistical exaggeration.

expected to double again, so that soon there would be too much even to feed to the animals. Mao's figures were believed at the time by many Western analysts. But as 1958 ended the Chinese peasants realized they had been led into disaster.

It appears that the water table in the North China Plain was raised, and that this was done accidentally in an attempt to extend the northern limits of rice cultivation to what they had been in Neolithic days, when the climate was wetter. This resulted in the destruction of much valuable pasture land and the 'alkalinization' and ruining of arable land previously useful for wheat. Meanwhile policies of intensive rice cultivation in the south of China also changed water levels. As one peasant put it when ordered to take part in the then fashionable practice of deep-ploughing, 'Before, the water in the paddy used to be above the ankle; now it went above the knee. But deep down the soil is no good, too compact. Only four to five inches on the surface are good. It wasn't correct but we couldn't help it. We got orders.'* By November 1958 many peasants were secretly cooking meals at home and taking their children out of the nurseries and crèches. In December 1958 there were insurrections in the provinces of Guangdong, Hubei, Hunan, Jiangxi, Gansu, Sichuan and Qinghai.

Mao was now held responsible for the economic and social chaos that succeeded the Great Leap. In late 1958, as already arranged, he stepped down from his position as head of state in favour of the more pragmatic Liu Shaoqi, though he remained as chairman of the Party, and it was publicly stressed that the change was intended to give him more time for theoretical work. It was too late to save many millions of Chinese peasants. The campaigns of 1958 were followed by the so-called 'Three Years of Natural Disasters' of 1960-2.

The Party now reversed the policies of the Great Leap. The role of the commune was reduced in favour of the lower levels of organization within it: brigades and teams. Peasants received a portion of crops and cash income according to the number of 'work-points' gained, mainly from time spent on the collective land. Some 'sideline occupations' were permitted again, free markets were expanded a little, and peasants were given back the small 'private plots' that they had had before the Great Leap.

Initially, after the failure of his Great Leap, Mao seems to have envisaged a new bid to reassert his authority by rallying the peasants, with whom he felt deep affinities, and the army, which he had formed. In 1959 he threatened to raise another army in the countryside if his colleagues in the Party did not follow him.* But he was disheartened by the peasants' dislike of ideology. 'In the end,' he remarked, 'peasants are only peasants.'* Faced with hostility from his colleagues, and without clear control of the Party, he seems gradually to have thought of mobilizing the older children and adolescents: and he began to do so in late 1965 and early 1966, calling them Red Guards. When they went further than he had planned and began to call the system itself into question he tried to contain them. His solution was the 'Downward Dispersal Movement' (*xia fang*). The army, his best ally, dispatched Red Guards to remote, underpopulated areas of the countryside where hard labour was expected to cool their heads. Officials who had allegedly committed excesses were sent to 'rural cadre schools' in the countryside, and other town dwellers were also sent to the countryside to learn from the peasants. Few peasants welcomed these reluctant apprentices of the hoe.

After the turmoil of 1966-76 the new leaders of China under Deng Xiaoping held a sober review of the events not only of the previous ten years, but also of the previous thirty years. In the first place, they considered the problem of undernourishment in the countryside. Since 1949, population had kept pace with increases in agricultural productivity, and, while 450 million new mouths had been added, land under plough had actually diminished through a combination of urban expansion and the consequences of state planning. For each member of this much larger population, even though life expectancy had increased substantially over recent years, there was no more food than there had been a quarter of a century earlier.

In 1982 the area of farmland available per head was little more than half what it had been in 1957, despite much land reclamation. Population had increased by about a half, and industrialization, urban spread and soil erosion had taken away a tenth of the farmland in that time.*

Because of the heavy work that Chinese peasants are required to do, the authorities reckon that they need a minimum diet of 2600 calories a day. Most of their food comes from grain, and the government says that a peasant needs a minimum of about half a kilogram of grain a day, which is half to a quarter of what peasants seem to like to eat if given the chance. Because grain is low in protein, and peasants get little meat or fish, it is vital for them to have protein from some other sources, mainly bean-curd and other soya products: the authorities reckon that they need 75 grams a day. Even by the official minimum standards they were not adequately fed in the late 1970s, and they had not been getting better off over the previous twenty years. Deng Xiaoping's leading spokesman, Hu Qiaomu, said of grain production per head that, 'in 1977 it was the same as in 1955 – that is, the growth in grain production was only about equal to the growth in population together with the growth in the grain requirements for industry'.

The most important element of real income in Chinese villages for three decades after 1949 had been the grain ration. According to the New China News Agency, in some areas of China in the late 1970s it was less than 16.7 *jin* (about 9 kilograms) a month. The inequalities covered by this broad average concealed greater dangers than the low average itself. The Central Committee of the Communist Party reported in 1979 that more than a hundred million people in rural areas suffered from lack of grain. And even where the figures looked less bad, the practice of mixing less nourishing and less popular foods like maize and sweet potatoes into the rice or flour had eroded the quality of the grain ration over these decades. There was also evidence of a decline in the proportion of vegetables and fresh fish and meat in the diet of the Chinese over the twenty years to the late 1970s.

In 1978 the State Statistical Bureau estimated that average food consumption for China had been rising and had reached 2311 calories and 70.8 grams of protein a day. As early as the 1920s a widely-respected study by John L. Buck (then husband of the writer Pearl Buck) had recorded daily average food availability at 2280 calories a day. Thus, in the supposedly evil days of 'warlord rule', there had been a level of food consumption possibly not attained until the very end of the half century of war, civil war and central planning that followed.

What was true of inadequacies in grain production and food supply was also true of income in general. Peasant income is hard to measure accurately, since much of what country people eat does not go through the market but comes from their private plots; but the authorities stated in the late 1970s that the minimum comfortable income for peasants was Y100 a year per head,* and again there were many millions of peasants who were not earning as much as this. The *People's Daily* of 26 November 1978 reported that in more than half the counties of the north-western provinces, the *huang tu* or 'yellow soil' area, average earnings were less than Y48 a year.

These were matters of serious concern to the Chinese leadership. As Song Zenting, dean of studies of the Party School of the Central Committee put it, 'If the Party is not concerned about the people in whatever it does, and does not bring the masses material improvement which they can see with their own eyes, the people after a period of time will become disappointed and feel there is no point in following the Communist Party.' If the peasants were not adequately fed, there was good reason to fear worse disasters: peasant rebellions, the splitting-off of provinces from the central authority of Beijing and even the fall of the regime could be the consequences of mass starvation.

The reserves against famine have been so slender in China that when famine has struck, with little transport and many calls on it, widespread relief has been exceptionally difficult, and local 'self-relief' has been the main recourse. This has included the traditional remedies of *kai huang* ('opening up the wilderness') and *tao huang* ('flight from famine'). The former can be counterproductive. In northern China the destruction of surviving forest and pasture land in attempts to improve grain production appears to have helped to cause something like a change of climate. The *People's Daily,* speaking of much of the *huang tu* over recent years, said, 'Desert encroached southwards, rainfall decreased, weather became unpredictable . . . Since the massive losses of water and land . . . whenever there is a rainstorm, land and dykes are washed away and irreparably lost. Basic construction on the farm has to be undertaken every year, so that reconstruction is perennial, requiring enormous investments of labour and capital with little result.'* And the New China News Agency has said that reclamation of land in the *huang tu* can be fruitless: 'The poorer one becomes, the more land one reclaims; and the more land one reclaims, the poorer one becomes.'* Despite much planting of poplars, making areas of north China look like southern France from the roads, the still largely deforested state of the countryside has meant that soil erosion has continued.

Tao huang, the practice of deserting the land, leaving women and children for half the year after the harvest and seeking food by begging in richer provinces, is contrary to the policy of the Party, which has imposed restrictions on any movement without a pass. In the 1950s 'Exhorting and Impeding Stations' were reported to have been set up along railway lines, highways, at river ports and at points of communication between provinces, to stop peasants deserting their fields.* Nevertheless many peasants resorted to this traditional practice rather than starve in the 1950s. Beggars from Anhui, silently standing in restaurants and licking the plates after the meals taken by 'cadres', or more brazenly coming up to diners in the south and touching their food, after which the cleanly Cantonese were unable to face finishing the meal, were sights that foreigners were not generally encouraged to witness. During the Cultural Revolution beggars, who were seen by Red Guards as losing face for the Chinese people in front of foreigners, could be punished for their misdoings. The red and white poles with which they were beaten were called by the beggars 'big chopsticks'.*

The persistence of undernourishment, of rural poverty and of beggars, is not only widely felt to be some sort of disgrace to China, but more practically poses a threat to the prestige and ultimately the authority of the government in the eyes of its own people. Restrictions on travel make it hard for the facts of rural poverty in one area to be known to the inhabitants of others. But the liberty that Red Guards enjoyed in the Cultural Revolution, to board trains and wander all over China, and the liberality with which sentences of exile to poor rural areas were meted out to bureaucrats and intellectuals, did much to open the eyes of members of both the younger and an older generation at that time.

When Sichuan was shaken by drought and hunger from 1976 to 1979, and by floods in 1981, young Sichuan girls were sent by their families in marriage to new communities as far afield as the distant north-east. These were predominantly male, since many of the inhabitants were ex-convicts, and until very recently almost all convicts in China have been men. The families reportedly received ration cards in return.

Since the 1950s there have been intermittent references in the Chinese press and in broadcasts to peasants leaving their fields in times of famine and drought, particularly in Shandong, Henan, Anhui and Jiangsu.* More guarded references to inadequate supplies and to the need for help for the worst-hit areas or for 'self-relief' have made clear the existence of serious hunger, for example in Anhui for nine of the eleven years from 1968–79; and in Henan for eight. The most recent of these, like the disasters in Sichuan, the far north-east, Yunnan, Inner Mongolia, Hubei, Jiangsu and Zhejiang in the late 1970s, were revealed by the authorities openly, with broadcasts and articles referring to disaster, calamity and, on at least one occasion, the word 'famine' itself.* Since then there has been some pulling back from the extremes of frankness that marked the years 1977–9.

These discouragements and disasters have prompted a major redirection of the country's economy. Since 1978 the new leaders of China have again reversed the collectivist policies of the previous period, as they did in the early 1960s, but this time on a greater scale, with the introduction of the Responsibility System. It is now followed by the overwhelming majority of peasant households in China. It varies slightly in different parts of the country, but in the broadest sense it means that each production team and in turn each household is allotted a certain amount of land to farm, or certain other production responsibilities to fulfil. The families agree to produce so much rice, wheat, cotton, tea, bamboo, wood or a similar crop, depending on the main products of the area. Whatever they produce over and above the agreed amount they may either keep for themselves or sell to the state or in the rural markets. If they fail to fulfil their agreed quota then they have to pay compensation out of their own pockets.

The peasants used to say, 'The collective earth is an orphan, the private plot is a child.' Food production and calories are believed to have gone up dramatically in the period immediately after the Responsibility System was introduced. Certainly the statistics went up, and they are plausible: the government announced that between 1978 and 1982 the calories consumed by the Chinese had increased by more than fifteen per cent, to an average of 2666 with 78.8 grams of protein, per day.

If all the food in China were distributed evenly, the margins for error would still be uncomfortably small. The situation becomes alarming when it is realized how very unevenly income and food are in fact distributed, and with what inherited problems and what slender reserves the Chinese must manage. How will the poorest fare if the means of raising the average levels is to stimulate incentives through permitting inequality? How will they fare if transport is not radically improved to allow rapid relief in case of famine, and unless a fairly uniform system of taxation at quite low income levels is introduced to permit greater equalization? How will the infrastructure for future growth in productivity be provided if the new Responsibility System returns power to people at the level of the family, where they may have little interest in financing large-scale public works, regarding them – sometimes rightly but sometimes wrongly – as 'blind work and useless sweat'? And finally, how is the rate of population increase to be kept even remotely in line with agricultural production, let alone far enough below it to allow more food for everyone, when many families are still likely to want at least one male child, which in practice must mean trying to have on average at least two if they can get away with it? The greater liberalization that is likely to accompany the Responsibility System and free markets is likely to collide with the greater repression and control needed to enforce large scale works and the one-child family. This is perhaps the central paradox of contemporary rural China.

Some of the results of change can be seen in a village such as Maoping in Zhejiang Province. Maoping is reached by an unpaved road that winds along the Fuchun River, through mountain country, from a small town called Qililong – Seven Mile Dragon – which lies about sixty kilometres from the provincial capital, Hangzhou. Zhejiang, on the east coast south of the

The village of Maoping lies in a picturesque valley in Zhejiang Province, surrounded by forested slopes which provide the villagers' main source of income. Timber, firewood, charcoal and bamboo are sold to the state, while rice and other crops are grown on fields farmed under the Responsibility System and on family private plots.

Wheat noodles hang to dry at the grain processing station in Maoping. Here, for a small charge, families can exchange the wheat grown on their 'Responsibility' fields or private plots for the same weight of noodles. The station also processes maize, rice and barley.

(Right)
Using forked branches to balance their load, young men from Maoping carry trunks of bamboo down the hillside to the receiving station in the village. They receive half the value of the bamboo they cut, the other half going to their production team's welfare fund.

Yangtze River, is one of the most favoured provinces of China, with plenty of rain and rich harvests of rice, tea, vegetables and bamboo. It has a population of just under forty million.

In a country of China's diversity it makes little sense to speak of a 'typical' village. Maoping is more beautiful than most villages, and can rely on a more predictable climate than many. But its income is close to the average country income for China, which in 1981 was Y223 per head: in that year, average income in Maoping was Y193. Rural income statistics are not on the whole consistent across China and can be taken only as a broad indication of relative standards of living. They include a value imputed to the grain and fuel issued by the collective, usually from Y60 to Y90 per year, and they record an average Y100 a year in cash spent on food, but they do not include the produce of private plots, an important source of food for most families. Yearly incomes vary from Y50 to Y1000 in different parts of China. Even within a single brigade, differentials between one team and another can be 3:1. Within a commune, one brigade may be five times as rich as another. The majority of brigades have average income levels between Y150 and Y250.

The village of Maoping is one of four which make up Maoping brigade, which in turn forms part of Luci, a small commune with twenty-four villages and a population of just over 3600. Maoping's staple crop is rice, but the main cash income derives from forestry and its by-products, charcoal and firewood. There are only 800 *mu* of arable land as against 63,000 of forestry land. (A *mu* is a sixth of an acre.) Until 1970 the brigade did not have enough grain to feed itself, and had to rely on 10,000 kilograms bought from the state each year. But for the past dozen years there has been more than enough. Besides two rice crops a year, the brigade members also grow wheat, barley, maize, sweet potatoes, soya, sesame and tea.

In Maoping the people tell visitors that after the fall of the 'Gang of Four' at the end of 1976, when policies became more relaxed, agricultural production increased, and people became gradually better off, in spite of a flood in 1977. The greatest change came in 1981 when everyone in the village changed over to the Responsibility System.

Maoping is primarily a forestry area, and thus different from many parts of China. Out of the average income per head of Y193 in 1981, Y123 had come from forestry and connected enterprises, and only Y70 from agriculture. The state did not expect the brigade to provide it with any grain at all, but it had to supply a certain amount of tea and wood, including some bamboo.

Under the Responsibility System the arable land was allocated to each man, woman and child in the brigade, with each person irrespective of age receiving 0.6 *mu*. This included good, medium and bad land, which was to be rotated every three years. In Maoping, a small cash sum of Y4.5 per *mu* per year had to be paid as a tax. Whatever the family produced on the land then belonged to it. Although many peasants in China sell their surplus grain, this was not the case in Maoping: because they were too far from any rural market what they did not eat themselves they gave to their pigs.

In addition to Responsibility Land each household had its own private plot on which to grow vegetables and extra grain for the family to eat. In communes round the big cities of China private plots are often as small as 0.1 *mu*. In Maoping people could have as much land as they wanted, provided that they did not usurp brigade arable or forestry land, though most people did not want land that was far from their home or from a water supply. On these plots people grew cabbages, onions, beans, chillis, sesame, soya, maize and sweet potatoes. The maize, together with the wheat, rice and barley produced in the main fields, could be taken to be ground at the grain-processing station for a small charge, or exchanged for the same weight in wheat noodles. Grain husks were taken home to feed to the pigs, which were given three meals a day.

Before the advent of the Responsibility System women as well as men had to work in the fields for eight hours a day, and in addition to this the women had taken care of the household chores. Under the new system they generally seemed to work either in the fields or in one of the brigade-run enterprises until after the birth of their first child, and then, except during the busy season, they became full-time housewives, looking after the family's private plot and tending the pigs. There are few domestic appliances in China, and housework took up much of their day. The clothes had to be taken to the river or to the standpipe to be washed. Vegetables had to be fetched from the private plot, washed and prepared. Most women cooked three hot meals a day, and four in the busy farming season. This took about an hour for each meal for some women; for others it took most of the working day. The main method of cooking was to stir-fry the various dishes in one of the built-in iron woks, heated from underneath by firewood, while the rice was first boiled and then resteamed in the other wok. Some of the new houses had stoves with white tiles which were easy to clean, but in general the stoves were heavy stone objects built into the kitchens, which were blackened by years of smoke and frying.

The family's clothes had to be sewn or knitted, soles for the traditional shoes sewn, and food prepared for the pigs. If the weather had been dry the vegetables in the private plot would need water. Although, unlike many areas of China, Maoping has abundant water, in most of the households all water for domestic use had to be carried from standpipes, using heavy buckets suspended from shoulder poles. Most of this work, in 1982, was done by the women.

The head of women's affairs in the brigade, who had to see to the health and welfare of the women and encourage them to play their part in village life, spent much of her time in propaganda for the one-child family policy. In Maoping there had initially been much opposition to it. The young women were now, for the most part, content to settle for one child, but their parents were less happy, particularly if the child was a girl. Few rural work-units are yet rich enough for peasants to have pensions; they must rely on their children and in time their grandchildren to support them.

In Maoping the brigade had an allocation of fifteen babies a year. When a couple decided to have only one child they signed an agreement to say so and they then received a certificate and a reward of Y30 from the county and Y30 from the brigade. Families who had only one child were supposed to receive more housing space, and their child was supposed to have better education and better job opportunities. These would have been strong inducements, perhaps, in the crowded and competitive towns, but hardly in Maoping. If a couple broke their agreement and the woman conceived again, they were subjected to criticism, and the woman would be persuaded to have an abortion. In Maoping the system was slightly more flexible than in some parts of China. If a couple had produced a girl and the brigade's annual baby-quota had not been filled, then the couple could apply to the commune authorities to try for another child, and permission might be granted. In 1981, for example, there were eleven first-born children, and two second-born. Even if the second child was also a girl, officially they had no further chances.

According to the head of women's affairs, out of some 200 couples of child-producing age in the brigade, 118 of the women and 18 of the men had been sterilized. Twenty-one women had coils, four used the pill and the remainder used other methods of birthcontrol including a monthly injection. Sterilizations were performed by a mobile medical team. The midwife delivered the babies in the mother's own home, unless there were known to be complications or the woman was over thirty, in which case she went to the hospital at Seven Mile Dragon.

Families with several working adults are always the richest; those with small children are the poorest. The wealth of the richest families in Maoping was reflected in the handsome new houses which they built. Chinese village families usually own their own houses. Building even a large house in Maoping did not cost more than Y1000, less than a year's income for a prosperous family with three or four people earning wages. Even in other parts of China, where wood is not plentiful, houses are still relatively cheap: in the early 1980s a new house in a village cost, on average, about Y2000.

The outer walls of the houses in Maoping were a mixture of earth and sand, tamped down hard between two planks of wood. Most of the labour of building a new house was done by the family, with help from friends and neighbours, who received no payment but were fed and given alcohol and cigarettes on the understanding that the favour would be returned when they needed to build a house themselves. Often a new room would be built as it was required, butted onto an existing house, and in some cases a whole new house for married sons would be put up next to the main family dwelling. This is the ancient pattern of house-building in Chinese extended families, and it has given rise to the courtyard, the main form in which houses have long been grouped in China. The village courtyard house has set the model for dwellings in cities, including the capital, where the Forbidden City, a great complex of palaces, is itself built up from the simple elements of the courtyard house, facing towards the south, and with lesser courtyards for peripheral members of the family and household grouped around the main imperial buildings.

The headquarters of the brigade's management body in Maoping village was a beautiful old house which had formerly belonged to the local landlord. There were some 1300 people altogether in the brigade, in 332 families, living in 4 villages and divided into 10 production teams. Six of the teams were situated within Maoping village itself, together with the main centres of brigade activity: the hydroelectric power station, the small factories for bakelite and roof-tiles, the two shops, the primary school, the grain-processing station and the receiving station where the bamboo was brought to be assessed, paid for according to the Responsibility System, and sold.

With the exception of bamboo, a team-run enterprise, all the forestry products were managed by the brigade as a whole. When a person carried down 50 kilograms of charcoal from the mountain it was duly weighed and recorded in the books, and he was subsequently given four-fifths of its value. The brigade and team took 10% each. A person who had cut and carried 50 kilograms of bamboo got only half its value; the team got the other half. The percentage taken by the team and the brigade went into their respective welfare and accumulation funds to cover education, health care, caring for the poor and elderly dependants, cultural and recreational activities and agricultural improvements.

In 1981, of the total brigade income of Y267,514, some Y18,000 came from the power station and Y17,000 from the bakelite factory. The employees of the bakelite factory were paid a monthly wage of about Y30, with small additional sums for working the night shift. They were chosen to work there partly according to the wealth of their families – with the children of poor families favoured – and partly for their ability to learn a technical skill and to abide by strict timekeeping, a concept alien to many peasants, in China as elsewhere.

The brigade leaders were responsible for making sure that the teams and the households carried out instructions and fulfilled the production norms issued by the commune leadership. Every year a state plan was drawn up according to the country's estimated needs for grain, cotton and other crops. Each province was given a quota to produce, and quotas were gradually filtered down to the lowest levels. Meetings took place between the leaders of the commune, the brigades and the teams to discuss how to implement the plan. Commune leaders had lost much of their power in the early 1980s with the coming of the Responsibility System, when the administrative power was given back to the townships from which it had been taken, but they still retained considerable authority in the implementation of economic plans.

Luci Commune had the three levels of militia common all over China: ordinary, 'backbone' and armed. People over forty formed the ordinary, those aged thirty-five to forty the 'backbone', and the young and strong the armed. The local units of the People's Liberation Army were responsible for training the militia. Mediation committees sorted out small disputes, while serious cases had to be tried by the county courts. In general there are no policemen, in the sense of members of the Public Security Bureau, in the Chinese countryside.

On the morning of a traditional wedding ceremony in Maoping friends of the groom carry the bride's belongings through the village to the young couple's new home. Among the furniture and gaily coloured quilts which are the bride's contribution to the household is a sewing machine, a present from the groom to his young bride.

Members of the all-female local opera company give a performance in the old village temple in Maoping. The troupe visits the village once or twice a year and is immensely popular, especially with women. The operas are based on traditional stories which are well known to the audience.

In Maoping there was a seven-person Party Branch Committee, drawn from the thirty-nine Party members in the village. Each of the seven was paid Y40 per month from brigade funds. Each had a separate area of jurisdiction: agricultural production and planning, health and welfare, brigade-run industries, law and order, the young, culture and recreation, and education and the training of the members of the brigade in socialist virtues.

Those high up in the brigade administration were generally Party members. The Party secretary, Fang Benren, spent much of his day attending to the practical details of agricultural production, but also saw it as his duty to do propaganda work among the people. He admitted that many of them were 'politically backward', and were interested only in getting rich. However this did not cause excessive concern as the Party and government were also encouraging the peasants to get rich, within the bounds of legality.

The deputy-secretary in Maoping, a woman called Wang Dongmei, was responsible for brigade enterprises. She had started the bakelite factory herself. Having married into the village from a neighbouring county, she had gone back to her home area's bakelite factory to learn the techniques, returned with blueprints and trained the workers.

The primary school was run by Maoping brigade, but children from other brigades could also attend. Maoping brigade had no say in the curriculum, which was decided by the state, but it was responsible for the upkeep of the buildings and the equipment, the purchase of books and other necessities, and for paying half the salaries of two of the six teachers. The other four teachers were paid for wholly by the Education Bureau of the county, Tonglu, which also paid the other half of the salaries of the remaining two teachers.

Children started in primary school at the age of seven and in theory stayed until twelve. The tuition fee was Y2 per term, but some thirty per cent of the children were exempt from paying this because of family circumstances. The fees were ploughed back to buy equipment for the school. The school also had an area planted with tea bushes, and the income engendered by the sale of the tea was used to help with the upkeep of the school.

There was no junior-middle school in the brigade, and the children had to go to the commune's headquarters in Luci to attend. More than ninety percent of the children in Maoping went there for three years, a high percentage for the rural areas of China. However, with the new Responsibility System in operation, fewer children were going on to junior-middle school, as their parents wanted them to help in the fields. It appeared that the number of places available in junior-middle school was being deliberately curtailed. Very few children went on to senior-middle school, located in Tonglu, many kilometres away.

The brigade clinic was run by 'barefoot doctors', as they used to be called, now called 'paramedical workers'. They had had about two years' training in public health medicine in Tonglu, and practised a mixture of Chinese and Western medicine. While working in Maoping they were paid Y36 per month by the brigade. There was a co-operative medical scheme in operation. Everyone contributed Y1 a year towards medicines, and the brigade and team each contributed another Y1 per person. In addition there was a fee of 5 *fen* (.05 of a yuan) for every consultation. If someone needed medicines or an operation he paid for half himself and the brigade paid the other half, no matter how expensive the treatment might be.

Television was the most popular entertainment in the evenings at Maoping. There were six colour sets dotted around the brigade, some in the larger houses, some in public places where there was room for many people to watch. About four films were shown in the brigade each month, sent from the commune on distribution from the county. Many of the young people liked to go by bus or bicycle to the small town of Seven Mile Dragon to see the films regularly shown there. Adventure films and love stories were the favourites. Besides these forms of entertainment, people did a lot of chatting and card-playing, and the men in particular drank a certain amount in the evening, either at home or in the small brigade bar.

The county opera troupe visited the village once or twice each year. The type of opera which they performed, in which all the roles are played by women, is peculiar to the region and is called *Yueju*. The local troupe was partly subsidized by the county government and partly paid by the villages it visited. The members of the junior troupe trained from the age of eleven to seventeen, when they entered the senior county troupe. The stories enacted were traditional and familiar to everyone. The opera was extremely popular, especially with the women, and people came from miles around to see it. Over two thousand people would pack into the old village temple for a performance, where the colourful costumes, the bright lights and the dissonant music provided a dazzling contrast to the somewhat monotonous grind of the peasants' daily life. After the performance the floor would be ankle deep in melon seed husks, corncobs, orange peel and cigarette ends, a testament to the irreverent gusto with which the Chinese enjoy opera. It is something of the people and for the people, and they can identify with the joys and sorrows of the characters, with whose names they have been familiar since childhood.

WORKING

工
作

COAL STEAM AND STEEL

Datong, on the Mongolian border, makes steam engines and it also mines coal. In China both industries – railways and mining – are run by the state.

The name 'Datong' – literally 'Great Harmony' – evokes Utopia; it was the name of the ideal stage of society imagined by the Confucian philosophers. But Datong has never in fact been noted for its harmony. In imperial times it was a frontier town between two cultures, Chinese and Mongolian. It lies just inside the 'Great Wall', and beyond was the domain of the horsemen who under Genghis Khan invaded the north and under Kublai Khan conquered the whole of China. Even today the closeness of central Asia is evident in the biting wind from the Russian steppes that blows for much of the winter, and in the city's one exotic sight, Bactrian camels slow-marching through the streets with panniers of coal on either side of their humps.

The Japanese lack coal. They conquered north China in the late 1930s, and opened up the mines on a great scale. Today memories of the Japanese occupation are kept alive by the authorities: they help to make people appreciate the present. Thus at the edge of a grim hole in the hills outside Datong, on a sunny day in May 1982, a rest day for the miners, a group of them had been gathered round an older colleague to engage in what is called a 'speak bitterness' session. The old miner said:

I am Wang Futian and I came from Yidu County, Shandong Province. Our whole family fled from famine in 1939. We came here begging for food. Collaborators with sweet words captured us and forced us down the mines. We worked thirteen to sixteen hours a day. They whipped us every day. The Japanese imperialists did not treat the workers like human beings, but like animals. 'Exchange coal with Chinese people's lives,' was their slogan. They used to say, 'There are so many Chinese. Killing them is like killing chickens. When you kill one there are always more.'

The workers had to drink the stinking water at the bottom of the pit. When people became seriously ill they tied their legs and arms, carried them away on a thick carrying pole and kicked them into this hole. No space was wasted in the hole; it was completely filled with bodies. Numerous dogs were waiting down there, biting and tearing the bodies to pieces. It was not long before the collaborators broke my father's leg and threw him into the 'Ten Thousand Men's Hole'. My father was only thirty-six years old, but he died only a few days after he arrived here. When he died I was nine years old, and I was sent to work in the coalpit. I was always beaten by the Japanese, because I was a child and I couldn't do hard manual work.

Once I was ill and became unconscious. They carried me to the hole and threw me in. Down there the dogs barked and howled and there were litters and litters of small dogs. I cried very loudly. There were so many people in there, crawling and grasping one another. I was so

A new steam locomotive is produced each day in the northern industrial town of Datong. Railways are the main form of modern transport. Seven trains out of eight in China are hauled by steam locomotives.

frightened that I cried madly, shouting 'Mother! Mother!' It happened that a poor man was nearby. Hearing a child crying in the pit, he took me out. He asked me if I had any relations. I told him my mother was begging for food not far away. He took me to my mother in a desolate place. Both my mother and I held each other, crying. That is how I was brought back to life.

There is no knowing how typical such experiences were. In the increasing chaos of war, production virtually dried up by the time the Japanese left in 1945. Then there was civil war. In 1949, with the communist victory, came a system of centrally planned industry modelled on that of the Soviet Union. In 1960 China broke off her friendly relations with Russia, and since then has been trying out alternative ways of organizing work at factory level, but until the end of the 1970s she had left the Stalinist system of centrally planned heavy industry untouched. Since then this too has come into question. No one can tell what the outcome will be of the conflict between the innovative ideas of Deng Xiaoping's government and the bureaucracy entrenched in the heavy industrial system.

Since variations in wealth, climate and environment are so great in China, a person's place of birth and 'work system' (*xitong*) do much to determine his or her material life. In China the most privileged place to be born, outside the capital, is an industrial town, and one of the most privileged work-systems to become attached to since 1949 has been that of the heavy industries run directly by the state. Employment in a powerful and flourishing unit (*danwei*) within that system has been the next most important step in determining a prosperous life. The most revealing first question when two people meet in China is, '*Ni shi nage danweide?*' ('Which unit are you from?').

Whatever their unit, those who work in heavy industry in China belong to an elite. There are thirty million of them, no more than the membership of the Communist Party. They constitute fifteen per cent of the Communist Party itself, although they are only three per cent of the population; and they are the people most likely to be promoted through the Party bureaucracy. Both Marxist theoreticians and Chinese central planners treat them as the vanguard of the nation, the most 'advanced' and the most responsible class. Until recently they had the highest wages in China: more than Y800 a year on average in 1982 and over Y900 a year in Shanghai. They still earn a third as much again as workers in light industry. But some peasants, particularly near large cities, have begun to outdo them with their earnings under the Responsibility System. Selling surplus farm produce in free markets in the cities can be highly profitable: workers spend more than half their income on food. In the early 1980s the state was diverting between a sixth and a third of its budget revenues to the city dwellers as income supplements to help maintain the living standards of the industrial elite and avert discontent.*

State enterprises provide their workers with subsidized meals, clinics, housing and education for their children, and they run nurseries and kindergartens. They build most of the new housing, and workers in state industries therefore have the best chance of getting somewhere to live, an important privilege since there are severe housing shortages in most Chinese

(Previous page)
The end of the working day in Datong. Despite its vast size China has no time zones; everyone goes to work and returns home by Beijing time. Together with its rural suburbs Datong has a population of 872,000, of whom two thirds live in the city itself. There is a six-day working week in China, and in Datong, as in other Chinese cities, workers' rest days are staggered to relieve pressure on shops and leisure facilities.

162

cities, and even after they have had a child many people have to go on living in their parents' house or flat. Most Chinese do not get pensions of any kind: retired workers from state industries receive pensions of up to seventy-five per cent of their last working wage, depending on seniority. If a worker dies because of illness or injury, the enterprise pays his funeral expenses: and in any case it organizes his funeral, lays on speeches praising (and criticizing) the deceased, and invites the family to attend, as guests.

Most of the people with jobs in this protected system have got them in one of three ways. Until the early 1980s the units could decide how many workers they needed, subject to allocations made in the central planning department, in Beijing; planning committees at various levels communicated with schools, and assigned new workers to enterprises. After a year's probation these workers achieved what was called 'formal work' (*zhengshi gongzuo*), which, until recently, meant that they had an 'iron rice-bowl': they could not be sacked, only transferred to another job. (To have a job is to 'chew grain'; to have lost one's job is to have 'broken the rice-bowl'.) A few workers also got into the system by applying to labour exchanges and entering on a more extended probation. The other main means of entry was by *dingti* or 'replacement policy': children could inherit a secure job when either of their parents retired.

One beneficiary of the *dingti* system in the early 1980s was Gong Peihua, a young apprentice welder in the Datong locomotive manufacturing plant. She had inherited the job from her father. As with other employees on the morning shift, she often had to ride to work in the dark, pedalling along in the freezing mist with a small box for snacks under her arm or tied to the back of her bicycle. Despite China's vast size there are no time-zones; the further west people live the darker it is in the morning. When asked about her attitude to her work, Gong Peihua was self-critical:

I accepted the welding job the leader of the factory assigned to me. I didn't like it at the beginning because I had to climb up and down all the time. However, my apprentice-master was very kind to me and I thought since I was young I ought not to be afraid of hardships. Little Chen, my colleague in our section, was much more vigorous in her work than I was, and the other workers never complained. So I thought, 'Our factory is the only steam locomotive manufacturing plant in the whole country.' I told myself, 'When the locomotives leave the factory the "Datong Factory" plates have been welded by me.' When I thought this, I felt quite proud of myself.

As an apprentice Gong Peihua's prospects for promotion in the early 1980s depended to a considerable extent on the report of her 'master', but to an even greater extent on her relationship with the workshop branch of the Communist Party of China. Party members are organized into small groups on each shop floor in heavy industrial enterprises in China. In such a work-place, if there is a national 'wage readjustment', local work-groups, generally with a powerful Party voice, assess the performance of their members and send up nominations for individual increases. These depend not only on 'good work contribution and good technical skill' but also on 'good attitude'. Work-group leaders must report regularly on the behaviour

Gong Peihua, an apprentice welder at the locomotive factory in Datong, works side by side with her apprentice-master. She inherited a steady job, which in China is referred to as an 'iron rice-bowl', when he father retired through illness.

of their subordinates, and these reports – especially any political 'mistakes' such as rebellious attitudes or unorthodox opinions – become part of the worker's permanent dossier (*dangan*). This file is examined when the worker is being considered for a pay-rise or for promotion, and can influence the admission to university or the job assignment of his or her children. The files are kept by the Party staff in the personnel department of the enterprise. Workers are not entitled to see their files and never know what incidents have been noted there and how they affect decisions made on their future. But they do know that *biaoxian*, which means 'behaviour showing underlying moral and political virtue', is a vital ingredient. *Biaoxian* can mean what a person says in criticism sessions, how willingly he follows Party policy, and whether or not he volunteers to do extra work; but most workers feel that in the end it comes down mainly to their personal relationships with their assessors, the local Party and managerial cadres. Thus these relationships are carefully cultivated. The Chinese call it 'patting the horse's rump' – *pai ma pi*. Employees do favours for cadres, particularly through their connections with doctors, drivers and butchers or shop assistants, who have access to scarce goods and services: these jobs are called the 'three treasures' for that reason. People use back-door connections (*wanmen*) to get access to many kinds of consumer goods, jobs for their relations or cinema tickets, since in the cities queues for cinemas for those without friends in the right places can start at 3 a.m.

Recently the government has made serious attempts to reduce the role of the Communist Party in the running of the economy, leaving more autonomy to technicians and non-Party leaders in heavy industry and to professional planners in Beijing. Nevertheless Party control is still pervasive in large enterprises like railways, locomotive manufacturing works and coal-mines. But even if they were not under such strict Party control, state employees of heavy industry would be likely to remain loyal and devoted workers in a system out of which they do so well. A sense of pride in being a member of an elite and also a sense of the weighty responsibility this entails are both evident in the reply of Lu Zhihai, an engine driver with many years of experience behind him, when questioned about his attitude to his work:

> Railway workers like us must carry out our job according to the regulations, the plans and the procedures. According to the regulations the railway is half militarized, so the engine driver has to read out the daily orders and tell the deputy engine driver and the fireman their duties.
>
> Owing to the nature of our Party and the teaching of our apprentice-masters, after seven years and one month's training I became an engine driver. This all because the Party organization assigned me the job. It was arranged by the leadership. The individual must subordinate himself unconditionally to the job he is assigned to. Why am I saying this? Because the job of an engine driver is different from ordinary jobs. The engine driver must be highly responsible, must have a high sense of being a master of a craft and a sense of duty. What do we need to fulfill the task? A correct attitude. We must fulfill the tasks the leadership assigns to us.

Regular timekeeping and a strong sense of responsibility, such as Lu Zhihai displays, were among the prime values on which the Marxist revolutionary leadership proposed to build a new society in China, as in Russia. Marx, with his low opinion of peasants, had argued that experience of work in heavy industry was essential for forming such qualities. It has been suggested that the Russian leaders may have had beyond this a particular fondness for those forms of industry that reminded them of the atmosphere of *Das Kapital*, redolent of coal, steam and smoking chimneys. They certainly admired Henry Ford and scientific management. The early Communist Party of China inherited many of these enthusiasms, and in the 1920s it proclaimed a policy of extensive heavy industrialization in China. Although Mao Zedong always remained aware of the importance of the Chinese countryside, where he had spent most of his life, he also had a keen sense of China's strategic need for military and economic self-sufficiency, and he had something of Stalin's almost mystical reverence for steel. When he came to power in 1949 he reaffirmed the Party's commitment to heavy industrialization and launched the First Five Year Plan in the early 1950s.

At its core, the plan had 156 industrial projects, for which the machinery and skills came from the Soviet Union; and with these projects, Datong and China acquired the entire system of Stalinist industrialization. Agriculture had to be squeezed for resources for steel and machinery, though probably less than in other socialist countries. Bonus systems were introduced. The factory director and the central planner were given commanding roles. All demands for investment capital from the different industries met in Beijing, and had to be judged on supposedly rational grounds.

In later years, after the Soviet Union and China had become ideological rivals, Mao Zedong's greater stress on spreading industry into the countryside was given great prominence. It was seen as a way of avoiding the problems of urban industrialization evident in the West and the USSR, and also as a means of generating capital for agricultural investment from the countryside itself. But the core of heavy industry, essential to the economy and particularly to armaments, remained, constituting a powerful interest group within the political system of China. Apart from the difficult period after the Great Leap of 1958, it went on growing, and industrial production increased twenty-fold in the first three decades of the People's Republic.

The smoky industrial cities of the 1950s also went on growing. Datong's population, which was 110,000 in 1949 had become 872,000 by 1982. Two-thirds of its inhabitants live in the inner city, which is more than twelve miles across and contains thirty large coal-pits. Some seventeen hundred small pits are scattered around the suburbs and the neighbouring countryside, some of them little more than caves or shallow shafts dug horizontally into the hillsides. Opencast mines such as these, now being developed by the State, add to the already massive pollution of the landscape.

Coal is the foundation for all heavy industry in China. The country's reserves are among the world's largest, enough for six hundred years at the present rate of extraction. However this is too slow for current needs: power is in very short supply. For instance in Datong steel can be poured only at night, because if it were to be done during the day it would take all the power from the rest of the town.

Mining in traditional China was dirty and unsafe; digging into the earth was considered inauspicious; and it was difficult for miners to find wives. The distinctions between miner and official are explicit in this picture.

Hard and dangerous work like coal-mining cannot always attract employees easily. China's coal-miners are consistently better paid than most workers, but absenteeism and turnover are probably the highest in any industry other than construction. Many coal-miners have country cousins and disappear to help them at harvest time. Round Datong, some of the small mines are not run by the state, and workers there can earn three times as much as in the large mines. Having first acquired the skills many miners vanish in this direction, returning to see their friends with their pockets visibly bulging with People's Currency.

Like the railways, mines give their workers 'cradle to grave' care. The grave is sometimes earlier than it need be: safety in mining as in other industries in China is little regarded. As the official trade union newspaper *Gongren Ribao* complained in 1980, 'Some leading cadres say, "Production is like war . . . to be wounded or die is unavoidable."' Much machinery throughout Chinese industry is left unguarded, and even where no question of cost is involved safety standards are low: Chinese lathe-operators, for example, rarely wear safety goggles. In coal-mines fatalities are estimated to be two miners per million tons of coal, ten times the US rate. Dangers may gradually recede as mines are mechanized. Meanwhile the medical system takes the strain.

In addition to hospitals, the mines provide their workers with some social amenities, including canteens, where, unusually for China, a certain amount of drinking without eating goes on. One of the big recreation centres at Datong is deep underground. As the locals explain, looking to the north, it

Two early views of mining in China. Above: miners in Hebei Province pose for the Scottish photographer John Thomson during his travels in China in the 1860s. Left: a scene at the opencast mine at Fushun in the northern province of Liaoning early in this century.

doubles as a fall-out shelter 'in case the Polar Bear comes'. Despite this, a fondness for things Russian remains. There are occasional musical evenings where the miners entertain each other in a severely Russian style, singing songs about coal, in which sentiments that fit into an ideal picture of socialist morality are imputed to the workers:

> I am a black young coalmine worker.
> I am happy day and night.
> My face is black, my friends are many,
> And we sing the whole day through . . .
> Hai! hai! Song of coal ya!
> I look like coal and coal looks like me.
> Hai! My heart is a fire-pan.

The unit with its ideology is everywhere: it even organizes weddings. In Datong sometimes as many as sixteen couples will be married in a single ceremony, with gongs, drums and a master of ceremonies opening the proceedings by calling out, 'Hallo, Comrade Zhang Peiguo, chairman of Datong City Youth Union, Comrade Min Yilian, representative of Datong City Women's Union, and Comrade He Guiyu, leader of the Trade Union. I am going to introduce the brides and bridegrooms: Liu Zujing from the Engineering Division and his bride Liu Jinxiu; Zhu Guoyu from the Map Drawing Division and his bride Cheng Chuyu', and so on. It was traditionally thought to be hard for miners to find wives, and there is still a preponderance of men in Shanxi Province, as there is in other frontier areas of China, where in the past soldier-farmers or convicts were often sent to found womanless communities. Even today many young miners live in mass dormitories, but one of them, Guan Chongfeng, believed that prospects for marriage and for mechanization were both good: 'Electrification and modernization have been basically realized. As for social position, the working class has become the master of the state. Workers are no longer called coal-black or oil-black as they were in the old society. So now it is not so difficult for a miner to find a wife.'

In the Datong mines forty per cent of the coal is cut by machine. It is good quality bituminous coal, of the kind used in power generation. But a lot of it will still not be used, because there will be no way of moving it. Most of China's coal comes from a few fields, mainly in the north, and the key to much of China's energy problem is better transport, especially rail transport. Road transport would make sense for much of the short-range haulage that clogs up the railways, but because the state-managed road transport system sets prices up to thirteen times higher than the railway's, there is a powerful incentive to use rail. China's railways carry more goods than do India's (1066 million tons against 230 million tons), though fewer passengers (912 million against 3650 million). There is still only 1 kilometre of track per 191 square kilometres of land in China, as opposed to 1 per 53 square kilometres in India. The Great Leap Forward slowed up construction: from 1959 to 1977, new railway track laid down averaged only 200 kilometres a year, a third of

the rate achieved in the mid-1930s. Some portions of the network can meet only about half the actual need, and the main north-south line from Beijing to Guangzhou has no surplus capacity. The line from Datong to Fengtai, near Beijing, was in process of electrification in the early 1980s, but only one train in eight in China was electrified or drawn by diesel, and although railfreight had increased thirty times since 1949, the number of locomotives on the railway system had less than doubled.

Industrial trouble has been endemic on China's railways, both before and since the 1949 revolution. The railwaymen's traditional stance as the most militant employees in China dates from 1905, when those in Manchuria were involved in the first Russian revolution. It has been maintained since. Unlike other Chinese, who need permits to leave their place of residence, railwaymen travel, communicate with each other and can organize. In 1976 strikes on the railways kept coal from six important mines from being moved, and a large backlog of unused coal has remained in the north. At the end of 1981 the quantity in Shanxi Province amounted to seventeen million tons, 'some of which had started spontaneous combustion'.*

But strikes are not the only reason why coal is not moved. In the central state planning system, industry has since the 1950s been organized in 'bureaus' at regional or province level. In China every bureau has had first and foremost to survive. To survive, its enterprises have had to meet production targets set for them by the central planners in Beijing, with a given number of employees, also fixed in Beijing, and at wage levels fixed centrally also. The key to survival has thus been to get hold of investment resources. But these could not be bought. They too were allocated in Beijing, and were virtually 'free' to those with muscle enough to get them. In theory the enterprises paid a little for depreciation, but this was counted over thirty years and was in any case minimal. So in effect getting enough of the

RAILROAD CONSTRUCTION

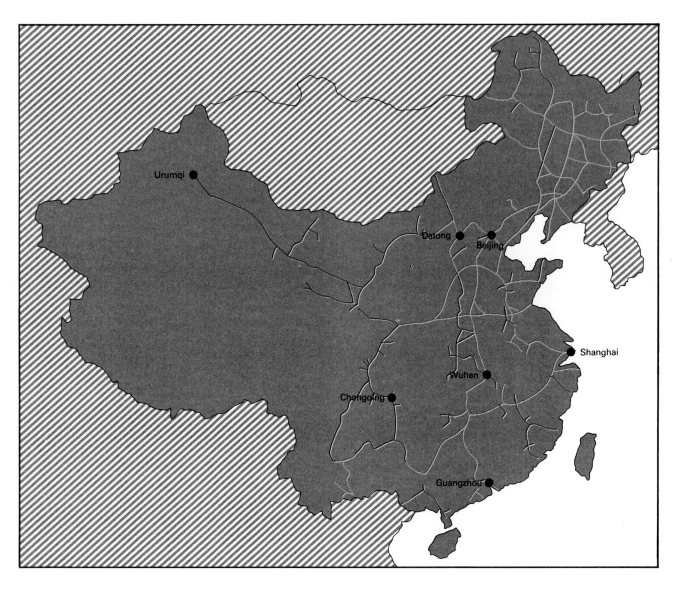

investment allocated in the National Plan was the first main need of any bureau. This need was possibly the most important determinant of the pattern of China's industry, and of the relative success of its managers. The ability to procure more or less free investment capital was the magic touch that made everything else happen cost free. There have been profit targets in Chinese industry, but profit has been calculated as a rate of return, not on the state's total capital investment, but on the year's operating costs with capital virtually excluded. Thus there have been few if any constraints on waste of capital investment. The profit targets have not in any case been taken as seriously as the physical output targets until recently. The system has been criticized by the present government, which is in the process of changing it: enterprises have been told that they will have to borrow or finance their own investment. But so far the changes have not been uniform or complete.

The railways and the mines have both been major users of China's limited resources for investment. In Datong they have competed head on: there have been frequent clashes between the Bureau of Mines and the Bureau of Railways. The railways were supposed to transport the coal. The coal was supposed to fuel the engines. It has not always happened.

After investment capital has been allocated the biggest difficulty for enterprises has been to get parts, raw materials, tools, fuel and labour during the period allowed for meeting the state's output target. Thus Chinese industries have needed to develop informal relations with suppliers and have been driven to hoard and to falsify reports in order to hide stockpiles from what is called 'the above'.

Further to avoid dependence on rival bureaus Chinese firms have produced as many of their raw materials and components as possible. Thus enterprises have tended to expand vertically and horizontally to include as many functions connected with their operations as possible. For example the railway has made its engines and also the steel needed for making them, and would like to control the supply of iron ore as well. Thus while in theory the planned economy is supposed to be a model of bureaucratically rational allocation, it appears, at least, to have obliged individual enterprises to use roundabout and even illicit methods to obtain resources.

There has been a major campaign in the early 1980s to combat 'economic crime' and to try to clean up corruption. The newspapers have been full of reports about it, though as with all such newspaper campaigns it is impossible to be sure how far they represent mainly a change in directives to editors. Radio and newspapers have constantly reported the conviction of corrupt cadres. It has been pointed out that those in high Party positions can already illegally secure advantages for their children in education and

Datong's power station uses the high quality bituminous coal produced in the local mines. Generally there is an acute shortage of power in China. Most of the coal is concentrated in a few fields in the north-east, and sometimes has to be hauled by the over-burdened railways for distances of a thousand miles.

A view of workers' housing over the rooftop of an old Buddhist temple in Datong. Most people live alongside those they work with, in housing provided by their work-units. This is one of the continuities between village life and urban life in China.

employment;* monopolize new housing built for workers;* occupy peasant land;* shield their children from punishment* take public resources for their private use; use unpaid labour to build private houses;* charge for social and public services.* They are the people who can decide which peasants are allowed the right to move to the city;* and who, through their positions in the industrial structure, can sell services, manipulate supply and marketing, and protect clients against investigation.

An immense black market has been described. For example in March 1982 the first secretary of Gansu stated that goods embezzled and stolen in his province included large machines as well as industrial raw materials, chemical fertilizers, gold and silver and medicines; and that criminals operated in gangs, often with the protection of 'cadres' of high rank.* In August 1981, a State Council work conference on smuggling in Guangdong, Fujian and Zhejiang found it 'rampant and still growing', with state enterprises, commune and brigade enterprises and government offices participating; while *Nanfang Ribao* protested that southern banks were providing smuggling funds and accepting a share of the spoils. This seemed almost a throwback to the 1820s and 1830s, when opium-smuggling in Guangdong was financed by the state's own bankers, the Shanxi banks, and when, as now, anti-smuggling patrols were involved.

Enterprise illegality and the use of the 'back door' for supplies are not the only areas where there is conflict between the central planners and the managers of units. Managers are now allowed to dismiss employees, even ones who previously had 'iron rice-bowls'. But they are also pressed to hire more people to solve unemployment. Overmanning is already widespread:

in some cases, whole factories whose output is not needed remain fully manned. Once a worker has been assigned a job anywhere in China he is considered to be employed, even if he does not go to it, and even if he remains in fact unemployed somewhere else. Most people, however, go where they are told. In the past a husband and wife, each with special skills, were often assigned to different cities, and it was left to them to arrange an exchange with others with similar skills in another city. Signs would be put up on telegraph poles in an attempt to identify such people; and though such separate postings are now less common than they were during the Cultural Revolution, the posters still appear: in most Chinese cities there is a section of wall or a set of lamp-posts where advertisements appear proposing trades in jobs or houses. Beneath the collective surface, many other such personal arrangements take place. In Beijing, for example, although most of the housing is owned by the authorities – government, municipality, ministries or factories – its actual occupation is often privately bartered.

The authorities have talked about relaxing their system of labour allocation and control, but may fear that any serious use of the market to allocate jobs would lead to a flood of peasants into already overcrowded cities. As it is, Chinese people must get the Public Security Bureau's permission even to travel to another city, and outsiders are not officially allowed to apply for jobs once they get there. Nevertheless, managers regularly hire a certain amount of unofficial labour from people without residence permits who have strayed in from the countryside, often to join relations who are workers. The existence of these extra workers is in many cases an open secret, and such labour is cheap. In 1981 about three million city dwellers were doing temporary work in state enterprises with no benefits and with lower pay than state workers; about four million country dwellers were getting temporary work in urban industrial enterprises through informal, quasi-legal means outside the state plan.

During the Cultural Revolution many unofficial workers hoped to gain equal status with the permanent employees through political activity, and they constituted a significant source of recruitment for the Red Guards. But the lower paid did not have much success in bettering their condition at that time. Although bonuses and piece rate wages were abolished, differentials were retained; senior cadres and technical personnel could still earn three or four times the average wage on the shop floor, and there were no promotions from one grade to another. According to official Chinese statistics average real wages in 1977 were the same as in 1957.

After the fall of the 'Gang of Four' promotion between grades, bonuses and piece rates were all reintroduced, though not uniformly, and there were also two general wage increases, the first since 1963. The Chinese authorities subsequently tried to shift investment away from heavy industry into light industries, hoping to mitigate the inflationary effects of the increased wages by increasing the supply of consumer goods. The most visible aspect of this change was a proliferation of television sets. Before 1977 hardly any families had their own television set, and there were not many owned by communes

A not very realistic picture of television production. The ownership of television sets, which is spreading from the cities into the countryside, and pictures like this designed to enhance their appeal, are significant aspects of the new emphasis on consumption and prosperity.

and urban units. By the early 1980s, in Chinese cities at night, except when it was too hot, most of the families were inside watching television. There were also more cameras, curly hairstyles for women and Western clothes in evidence in the city streets.

To match this shift in priorities heavy industrial factories were supposed to think up ways of converting to light industry or of producing goods needed by it. But few proved able to innovate rapidly. Some economists in China believe that, for this and other reasons, the day of the omnicompetent, all-providing vertically and horizontally integrated heavy industrial enterprise should be brought to a close. Many people in the Chinese government still defend such enterprises, pointing to the fact that they have been compatible with economic success in South Korea, Japan and Taiwan. However the current government policy is to break them down into smaller, more manageable units, and to give these units more flexibility in their handling of resources and targets. The Responsibility System, in operation almost everywhere in agriculture, is to be introduced in industry, following models from Hungarian and other East European experience.

The industrial enterprise is now partly autonomous and responsible for its own profits and losses, although it is accepted that heavy subsidies to tens of thousands of unprofitable enterprises will be needed for some time to come. The state is no longer to take virtually all the profit, nor to supply virtually all the capital free. A fixed target sum of profit is to be handed over to the state, and surplus profits are to be divided between state and the enterprise, or, in the case of smaller firms, retained wholly by the enterprise. Having fulfilled its obligations to the state, the firm is free to produce for the market, finding its own suppliers and its own customers while the state makes no further investment. Increasingly contracts between state firms within the production plan appear to be replacing ministerial allocation. But this aspect of the new policies is shrouded in ambiguous language, and the authorities may not yet have decided how far they want it to go.

As in agriculture, the small group or individual is to be given responsibility not only for a quantity of output but for quality, standards, the consumption of materials and fuel and the maintenance of machinery. Individual workers' wages have been related to their actual output. In some firms thirty per cent of managerial salaries has been made dependent on the attainment of profit targets. Managers, foremen and workers are in some cases free to form their own teams within the factory and to negotiate contracts with the firm. There is thus to be a complete 'pagoda' of contractual relationships from worker to work-group, to shop to management, and from there to the enterprise, which is to be contractually related to the bureau, the trust or the economic commission and thence to the ministry.

These changes have altered the power relationships within enterprises. Since 1949 the most influential figures in a factory in China have been the director, the chief engineer and the Party secretary. Directors were a Stalinist creation and went out of favour in 1958, but are now again the key men in operational management. Chief engineers remain at the apex of the technical hierarchy, and Party secretaries are still important, but are now told to keep out of detailed decision-making. Similar changes have been occurring lower down the industrial hierarchy. There has long been antagonism between administrative cadres, most of whom are Communist Party members with little formal education, and technical cadres such as engineers, most of whom are not Party members but who have higher educational credentials. The two groups have often clashed over production decisions. While administrative cadres are backed up by higher level bureaucrats and by the Party apparatus, the technical cadres have tended to have greater prestige in the eyes of workers. When workers were permitted for the first time to elect work-group and work-shop leaders in 1981, they tended to reject the incumbents – generally old workers with little formal education who had risen from the ranks – and to elect, instead, skilled workers or technical cadres.

There have been changes in hiring policy also. The *dingti* system, which had tended to turn state factories into family firms, was losing ground in the early 1980s to more open systems of recruitment, notably to the traditional Chinese practice of examinations for jobs. Older workers tend to dislike examinations and fear they will be increasingly used to determine pay rises. Factory engineers favour them, seeing them as a way of ensuring that they have better trained or more trainable workers, in an era when production techniques are to be modernized.

'The Four Modernizations' is a key phrase used almost everywhere in China. But much of the talk of modernization is still in the world of the ideal. Modern, obsolescent and obsolete machines are still everywhere to be seen side by side. This may turn out in the long run to be a strength. The Chinese

安全生产 人人有责

A poster proclaims 'Everyone has responsibility for production safety'. In the struggle to achieve greater output, safety is a serious problem.

are good at using and repairing old equipment and adapting it to modern needs, a set of talents whose value has come to be appreciated elsewhere in the world.

Some of the oldest, most worn-out machinery in China is to be found in the 'collective' (non-state) factories, whose numbers are growing. Already in 1981 some thirteen million people in the towns worked in them, and half the school-leavers in China were going into them. Some were merely branch factories of state enterprises, started in order to give employment to children who had not been provided for by *dingti*. Average wages in collectives were three-quarters of those in state enterprises and most of them offered no welfare benefits, though there was a trend towards them. Most were labour-intensive.

Some thirteen million country people, about five per cent of all workers in the countryside, were employed in nearly half a million small-scale collectives owned by brigades, communes, and country towns, all outside the state sector. With about thirty workers on average, jobs in these were much sought after. The wages were low compared with those of town workers but high compared with peasants working on the land.

Finally there are a small number of self-employed Chinese. According to official statistics there were as few as 150,000 in 1978; but there was a six-fold increase to 1,130,000 in 1981, a fifth of this made up of recent school-leavers.

An article in the *People's Daily* on 8 December 1982 said:

Workers employed in collective enterprises in cities and towns throughout the country now amount to 25.68 million . . . 23.5% of the total number of staff members and workers throughout the country. The collective economy has become an important force that should not be ignored in the national economy. Due to the long-term influence of leftist guiding ideology, a few comrades . . . at the mere rustle of leaves in the wind . . . will make an example of the collective enterprises by toppling a number of them. In Beijing, the proportion of the collective economy (not including the big collectives) is still very small. Judging from the total turnover of social commodities, it accounted for only 5.5% in 1980, 6% in 1981, and about 7% this year. But the collective economy has demonstrated its immense superiority; . . . it is flexible, mobile and highly adaptable. It assumes sole responsibility for its profits or losses and practises the system of distribution according to work, thus avoiding the malpractice of 'eating from the pot and receiving equal benefits'. It has very bright prospects.

Although the Chinese economy is still dominated by planning, and the operation of the plan is still primarily dependent on the central allocation of resources, there is no doubt that Deng Xiaoping and his government are determined to push China in the direction of contractual responsibility for small groups, not only in agriculture but also in industry. Meanwhile the difficulty of finding jobs in established enterprises, and the opportunities, in the new, free-er market conditions, for enterprise and flexibility have led to a significant growth in independent units, with low overheads and employing few people, often family members. These are conditions in which, outside China especially, the Chinese have often been conspicuously successful.

An idealized industrial landscape entitled 'Daqing flowers grown on the banks of the Yangtze River'. This is a reference to a famous oil field in Manchuria, Daqing, stories of whose development in the 1960s and 1970s were held up as models for industry elsewhere in China.

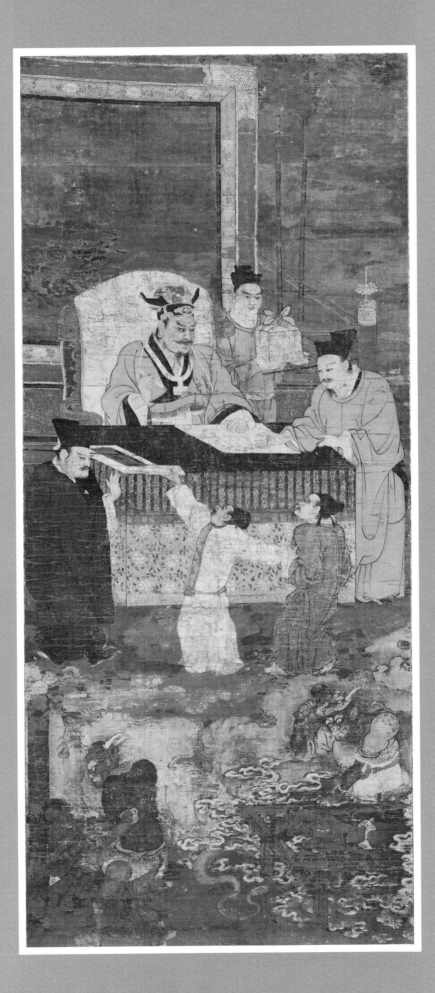

CORRECTING

CRIME AND PUNISHMENT

Two men and a woman approached a younger woman by a lake in Nanjing one July day in 1982. The older man, a judge, asked, authoritatively, 'Could you find a place with not many people where we can have a talk? Somewhere with a bit of grass?'

The lake from whose banks they were walking was on the outskirts of the city. Nanjing is one of the great cities of China, lying on the lower Yangtze River. It has a slightly French feel about it, with boulevards, cafés, and an easy-going, even pleasure-loving way of life. It was the capital of China in the nineteen-thirties. It is neither austerely administrative like Beijing, nor consciously international and potentially rebellious like Shanghai; simply independent.

It is also a place where the 'consumer revolution' has started. The shops on the leafy boulevards are full of tape-recorders and television sets. Crowds gather round the windows, and pack close round anyone who is evidently about to buy. A television set may cost half a year's income for a worker in a city, two years' for a peasant.

The judge was investigating a case of cat-burglary, involving the theft of both an imported cassette-recorder and a Chinese-made television set. His companions were the 'lay assessors' who would sit beside him at the trial, and together check the investigation made by the police, deliver the verdict, and also determine the sentence. There are no juries in China. The accused was the young woman's sister-in-law, Nie Chengying, a pharmacist working in a distillery.

'So tell me, what happened that day?' the judge asked the woman, as he and the assessors settled round her, almost as if to a picnic.

My sister-in-law came here one morning when I was at work. She was crying. She said she was ready to die: she was too ashamed to face anyone: and she felt sorry for the older and the younger generations of my family, for her mother-in-law and her child.

I thought to myself, 'People say that two kinds of scandal are most shameful. One is stealing, the other is the immoral relationship between man and woman.' What I was thinking then was that she might have done something immoral with another man. After all, she is young. So I asked her. She shook her head. I said, 'Have you done something wrong economically?' She kept quiet. Suddenly she asked me to go back to her home and fetch her child. She said that she wanted to see the child, otherwise she would kill herself.

I said nobody can guarantee they will never commit any errors. But if you can correct your errors you are still good. I told her that if she killed herself people would think that she died 'with a crime on her'. She agreed. She begged me to see if her husband would forgive her.

King Chu Jiang, one of the Ten Kings of Hell, listens to a protest in a Song Dynasty Buddhist painting.
The scenes of judgement in such paintings of the afterlife generally resembled court scenes in real life.

In the trial of Nie Chengying, a young woman accused of cat burglary and fraud, the public prosecutor rises to argue the state's case against her.

When I got to her house there were people from the Public Security Bureau there. They told me that my sister-in-law was a thief. I said she wanted to give herself up. I asked them not to wear uniform and not to have too many of them when they arrested her because it would be very embarrassing for her in front of other people. The Public Security people agreed. A team leader got her bike and rode with me to where she was waiting. We went to the local police station.

It transpired that Nie Chengying had a history of crime. The files of her work-unit led the judge and the assessors to interview her cousin, Nie Chenglin:

It was 1976; I was living with my parents but they were away. I put some money, about a hundred yuan, and a cheque in a wardrobe and left the key in the lock. When I came back it had gone. Nie Chengying's family and ours lived next door to each other and they could come and go as they pleased. I telephoned my parents and brothers who came back for a family discussion. My father asked my cousin's family about it. He said the culprit should confess. We had a big family meeting. No one confessed. Both my parents and Nie Chengying's parents talked to her but she still wouldn't admit it. Then I told her that I was going to ask the police to check the fingerprints. That made her confess.

We asked her why she had done it. She said she couldn't live on what she earned. We held a family meeting to educate her. When we asked her why she stole from relations, she said it was because relations would not suspect her. She knelt before my father and vowed she would never do it again. If she did it again she would be willing to go to jail.

Because it took her such a long time to confess I had already reported it to the local police, who suggested that I should see her work-unit, so I went to the factory and told their security people. When she admitted her theft she knelt down before both our fathers. Our grandmother died about 15 years ago. Everyone in our family is angry because she has damaged the family's reputation.

In China the family has generally been the most important social group and 'losing face' was something that affected the family first and foremost. A convicted criminal brought shame upon his family, neighbours and village. For the worst crimes in the past, collective punishment extended to all the members of a family. The idea of mutual responsibility can be traced back to very early times, and the Qin Dynasty (221-207 BC) made it a central feature of its system of government. This responsibility could take the form of mutual surveillance in the neighbourhood, or the liability of the village-head, who could be brought to court if somebody had, for example, failed to pay his taxes. The idea of collective guilt and the feeling of collective shame, however, could lead the family or the neighbours to conceal crimes. A further feature of Chinese law, therefore, was the practice of rewarding informants.

The purpose of the legal system in China has never been merely to prevent crime by locking up prisoners, or even merely to deter; it has always included the aim of reforming criminals. This has been seen as necessary for the restoration of the harmony of the social order. In China the individual has always been judged according to his frictionless functioning within society or in the small groups on whose cohesion that of society itself depends. Both traditional and modern legal philosophies are more concerned with society than with the individual.

During the formative age of Chinese philosophy, in the fifth to second centuries BC, many methods of achieving and maintaining harmony in society were proposed by the different philosophical schools. These ideas have been highly influential in Chinese history, and their influence has not vanished. Three schools of thought, Confucianism, Daoism and Legalism, each proposed a different way to achieve harmony.

For the Confucian thinkers society was hierarchical and stratified. The individual was seen as a part of various social groups – family, lineage or clan, and state – to which he had corresponding obligations. Harmony was achieved when each person fulfilled the appropriate duties of his station in life. This could be done by self-cultivation and by observing the accepted rules of social behaviour. Laws and punishments were necessary as a last resort, but were only a second-best solution. In Chinese antiquity laws were regarded as a means to correct the unenlightened, whereas the gentleman was guided in his actions by the unwritten code of propriety: 'Corporal punishments do not reach up to the gentry, the rules of propriety (*li*) do not extend down to the common people.' This distinction between two different codes of behaviour for those in command and for 'the masses', the one amenable to moral persuasion, the other governable only by force, has, with modifications, survived throughout Chinese history and is not extinct now.

Whereas the Confucians stressed the role of the social order, the Daoists emphasized the individual. They rejected the idea of rule either by propriety or by law. The Daoist ideal was to minimize intervention by the ruler and the state. All human interference with the ways of nature was regarded as intrinsically bad. For some Daoist thinkers crime and rebellion were themselves results of law and government action; the less administration there was, the less crime there would be. Such ideals could, in their extreme forms, end in anarchism.

A Qing Dynasty magistrate presiding in court in Shanghai

This picture of a magistrate's court was painted on the lid of a seal box of the Ming Dynasty (1368-1644).

Legalism was opposed to the two other schools. Whereas both Confucians and Daoists held a basically optimistic view of mankind, the Legalists had a bleak vision. Like the Daoists, but by different means, the Legalists tried to ensure a frictionless society in which the ruler would have little or nothing to do, because every infringement would automatically be compensated for by an appropriate punishment, applicable to everyone alike. This would lead to the disappearance of crime. Conflicts, disorder and crime could, in the opinion of the Legalists, be prevented only by written and unambiguous laws which were applied relentlessly. Rewards and punishments were the only means to keep the world in order, and everybody had to be made to observe the laws regardless of his social status. There was little room in Legalism for the idea of reforming a criminal; the aim of the law was prevention through intimidation. Confucianism, by contrast, allowed for the reform of a convicted culprit because man was thought to be capable of learning and re-education.

The history of Chinese law since the unification of 221 BC can be seen as an interplay between Legalist and Confucian systems of values. The common idea that the Chinese have always had a preference for dealing with breaches of order by mental or psychological means rather than by force is part of an ideal picture which has developed over the centuries inside China as well as outside, and which persists even today: a portrait of the Chinese as an essentially peaceful nation of farmers. 'One does not use good iron for nails, and a good person never becomes a soldier': this and similar proverbs have suggested that the Chinese people were essentially non-violent and unmilitary. Nothing could be further from the historical truth. The present frontiers of China are largely the result of conquest, not of peaceful expansion. The fact that the word for a justifiable war in ancient China was 'corrective action' (*zheng*), and the idea that the defeated enemy 'reverted to civilized ways' *(guihua)*, suggest the close relationship between the idea of the use of force on neighbouring states to subject them to civilization and the use of force on individuals to subject them to the requirements of the same civilization. To sentence a criminal and to wage a frontier war meant equally to re-establish order and harmony in the world.

Together with codes of acceptable social behaviour, written penal laws have existed in China since very early times. Fragments of Qin laws and ordinances came to light through excavations in 1982, and show detailed rules both on criminal matters and on the administration of the state. The Han Dynasty (206 BC-AD 220) had a complex code, only remnants of which have survived. The earliest fully preserved law code is the seventh-century *Tang Code with Commentaries* (*Tanglu shuyi*). The law codes of the Song (960-1279), Ming (1368-1644), and Qing (1644-1911) Dynasties are based on it; and it was also adopted by Korea and Japan.

Chinese laws have generally been very carefully worded. For each offence one and only one punishment was provided. The punishments varied from the lightest (such as ten blows with a cane) to execution by strangling or decapitation, the latter being considered more severe, because the body was mutilated. An even more extreme punishment, the death by slow slicing, was adopted later from the Khitans and preserved by the Ming and Qing Dynasties. The system of punishments included hard labour and exile, usually to a remote and dismal part of the empire such as the far north, or Hainan Island off the bleak granite southern coast, where the poet-administrator Su Dongpo was banished in the eleventh century for backing the wrong side twice at court.

In theory the magistrate who applied the law had no discretion in the choice of punishments once the facts had been established, though minors, aged and disabled persons and negligent offenders had to be granted a reduced sentence. However, edicts were constantly being promulgated by the imperial governments, supplementing the codes and giving rulings on matters that the original codification did not include. Chinese law was static only in its basic principles, and the spirit of the law changed considerably over the centuries.

Judicature was only one of the many duties of the county magistrates. They did not receive a formal legal training but were supposed to be familiar with the code, the ordinances and also collections of important cases which served as guidelines for subsequent judgements. Serious cases had to be sent to a higher court for review, and any doubtful case could be referred to higher authorities, up to and including the imperial court. Throughout much of Chinese imperial history capital sentences had to be confirmed by the emperor after several reviews.

Conviction by a magistrate normally had to be preceded by a confession. Confessions could, if necessary, be obtained by torture, and judicial torture could also be applied to witnesses. The court proceedings were always public, and so were torture, beatings and executions. There were no professional lawyers to plead in court and no institutionalized defence. Legal counsel existed, but only as an unofficial profession of advisers with no formal status.

The Chinese codes included rules on agrarian property, family law and inheritance. But most matters corresponding to civil law in the West were left to arbitration between the parties, usually within their native community or within guilds of merchants or craftsmen. Here as elsewhere the Chinese tended to rely on self-regulation within small groups and to resort to written law only for cases which were thought to have an impact on society as a whole because they violated generally recognized social values. The harshness of the law was mitigated by the frequent proclamation of amnesties. In some periods amnesties were so frequent that most capital sentences were never carried out. As a rule executions were allowed only in winter, because winter was dominated by the yin principle, the aspect of nature that concerned shadow, coldness and death. Sometimes, therefore, a convicted felon had to wait for many months in prison. If he was lucky, in the meantime an amnesty would intervene, giving a full remission of the sentence or a reduction in punishment. Under the Mongols in the thirteenth and fourteenth centuries it also became common to free prisoners at high

Buddhist festivals. Hard-line Chinese officials complained that such acts of clemency undermined the law.

Another mitigating aspect of the Chinese system was the relative weakness of the forces of the law. A magistrate had a very large area under his jurisdiction and a population sometimes of hundreds of thousands of people; there were perhaps a few dozen 'runners' (policemen), and close surveillance of the whole district was physically impossible. Basic law enforcement was a responsibility of members of the local population, who often had conflicting loyalties.

Such proverbs as 'In death avoid hell, in life avoid the law courts' may suggest that in all respects the common people avoided law if they could and preferred to settle their affairs out of court. But this is only partially true. In addition to his function as dispenser of punishment to criminals the magistrate also played an important role as mediator. Under the Song, for example, in cases concerning marriage, division of property and inheritance, the function of the magistrate was to negotiate an arbitration or to propose an equitable solution based on mutual consent between the litigants. Some farmers, as in most societies, constantly went to court over land-rights and made themselves a nuisance to magistrates by repeatedly filing suits against their neighbours or relations.

Even though the letter of the law allowed little individual freedom of decision to the magistrates, some had a reputation for being benevolent and lenient; others were notorious for cruelty and relentlessness. Some accepted bribes, whereas others remained incorruptible. Others again became famous for their achievements as investigators in difficult cases. Since trials were public, a lurid case might attract a huge audience. Detective stories or courtroom novels and plays were immensely popular in China, and were indeed first invented there. They featured clever and benevolent judges or cruel and corrupt magistrates, whose misdeeds were in the end avenged by the intercession of higher authorities. Justice wins in Chinese literature; the evil always lose. Judge Bao in the eleventh century, a legend for his investigative skill, became a kind of Sherlock Holmes of the bench in popular tradition. He is the hero of innumerable short stories and plays, and even became associated with the deity of justice in popular religion. There is a temple dedicated to him on the slopes of the holy mountain of Taishan. The popular Chinese conception of judgement after death was, like other ideas of the afterlife, extremely literal, and a reproduction of everyday life in much the same form. Thus a judge with instruments of torture on the table in front of him and 'runners' with thick bamboo canes ready to inflict punishment on their victim, were precisely what one had to expect in the hereafter, just as in court here on earth.

One appalling defect of the system of justice was that even innocent bystanders who might simply have witnessed a severe breach of law or order could be drawn into the proceedings and flung into prison for long periods awaiting the trial of the offender. Imprisonment was not normally regarded as a punishment in traditional China. Judicial torture might be used by the

Chinese magistrates on anyone concerned in a case, even as a witness or as the plaintiff. If two witnesses disagreed, both might be tortured. There was no presumption of innocence.

The execution of judicial punishment was left to 'runners' or, in prison, to professional executioners under only loose supervision from the magistrates. Gaspar da Cruz, a Portuguese Dominican, imprisoned in China in the sixteenth century, wrote of a scene of punishment, 'Many die after receiving fifty or sixty stripes, for they destroy all the giblets of the hams . . . And the beadles butchering, as they are commanded, the magistrates are altogether void of compassion, talking with one another, eating and drinking, and picking their teeth.'*

Despite the clear codification and exactitude of the punishments prescribed for each crime, designed to balance it accurately and thus to deter crime altogether, 'beadles' or runners could make nonsense of the system by doing their work with a severity proportionate to the bribes they received, beating ineffectually all those who paid them well, and flogging, in some cases to death, those who failed to pay them enough. The meticulousness of the laws seems to have carried over to their tariffs and charges. Fang Bao, a scholar-official imprisoned in the eighteenth century, wrote:

Persons who are to undergo the highest of all penalties [the death by slow slicing] are told, 'If you go along with us, we will stab you in the heart first. If you don't we will completely dismember your four limbs while leaving the heart still alive.' Persons who are to undergo strangulation are told, 'If you go along with us, we will cut your breath off at the first twisting. If you don't, only by applying a different instrument at the third twisting will you die.'*

As one of the runners explained, if they did not treat poorer people who could afford to give them only small bribes more cruelly, the system would break down because people would cease to dread the law.

Fang Bao wrote notes on his own incarceration and recorded his dismay at the divergence between the Confucian ideals he had believed in before his imprisonment and the realities of the system he discovered in jail. There were no windows in the cells, and at night prisoners were chained on a bench, side by side and unable to move. 'Every evening, when the locks are closed, all the urine and excrement are left inside to mix their vapours with the food and drink . . . Throughout the night living persons and those who have died sleep next to each other head to head and foot to foot without any means of turning away. This is why so many persons suffer contagion.'* Death was a normal consequence of imprisonment. Fang Bao wrote of the bodies of the dead being eaten by starving survivors. Prisons generally went unreformed because those officials who were jailed were too ashamed to publish accounts of their experiences, and the fact that much of prison life was organized by the jailers for profit and with indifference was incompatible with the ideal Confucian vision of the emperor and his officials always acting with 'benevolence'. When Fang Bao was released he paid to have windows put into his prison's cells.

The celebrated Judge Bao presides over a courtroom. The judge, who lived during the 11th century, was renowned for his acumen in dealing with complicated cases and became the hero of many popular courtroom plays and novels. This picture illustrates a Qing Dynasty drama.

In general, the idea of 'correcting' implies that certain people know what is correct and have the means to restore the correct order. In the old days these were the Confucian-Legalist educated elite, who watched over the orthodoxy of an ideology embodied in the classical books and the law codes. Today the scholar-officials' judicial and punitive monopoly, and the monopolists themselves, have changed; but the basic pattern has not. The Party knows what is correct and uses legal means to establish a social order where conflict is to be minimized.

When the Communist Party won power in 1949 it abolished all existing laws, including the modern codes introduced in the 1920s and 30s. The revolutionary People's Courts were not guided by any written laws but followed a policy of 'extirpating the feudal and oppressive elements' of the old order by arbitrary decisions. After a period in which many old scores were settled by violence, a legal system with some traditional elements and some resemblances to Russian models was introduced. The Russian system in its turn looked back to the Napoleonic code, the basis of French, German and Japanese law also. It is common to both the Chinese and the Napoleonic tradition that the judicial and investigative roles are united. Thus by the time a defendant comes to trial – when, under the Anglo-Saxon system, the case would be assessed from the start by a jury not previously exposed to the evidence – the verdict may well have been determined.

Some of the earliest legislation under the People's Republic dealt with land reform and with marriage law. In 1954 a new Constitution was promulgated which promised a separate legal system and a legal recognition of the rights of individuals. But by 1957, even though most large cities and some counties had lawyers' associations, there were still only 2500 lawyers, with another 350 part-time, for the whole of China. The Chinese have a long-standing distrust of lawyers. In the imperial past they were seen as tricksters and cheats who would rob the ordinary man of justice and help the rich to buy verdicts. Their profession conflicted with the Chinese sense that one should reach agreement through conciliation rather than advocacy. Mao Zedong, who in this as in other respects was in tune with popular feeling, personally disliked them. Between 1957 and 1972, China drew away from Russia and remained aloof from the world, and Mao Zedong instigated the Great Leap Forward and then the Cultural Revolution. The theory in those years was that the courts and the law should be 'open' to 'the mass of ordinary people', and that lawyers were not needed. In the Cultural Revolution judges, teachers of law and practising lawyers were among the first to be sent to the countryside and the last to return. All law schools were shut down. The courts and mediation committees were used as a forum for trying 'reactionaries', 'high-handed bureaucrats' and 'capitalist-roaders'. Law enforcement was placed in the hands of the Red Guards and the People's Militia. A new principle of legality was introduced, last heard of in 1918 in the USSR: 'revolutionary legal consciousness'. It meant that formal laws stood for nothing: mass trials and judgements were to be based not on codified principles but on what were called 'the political dictates of the

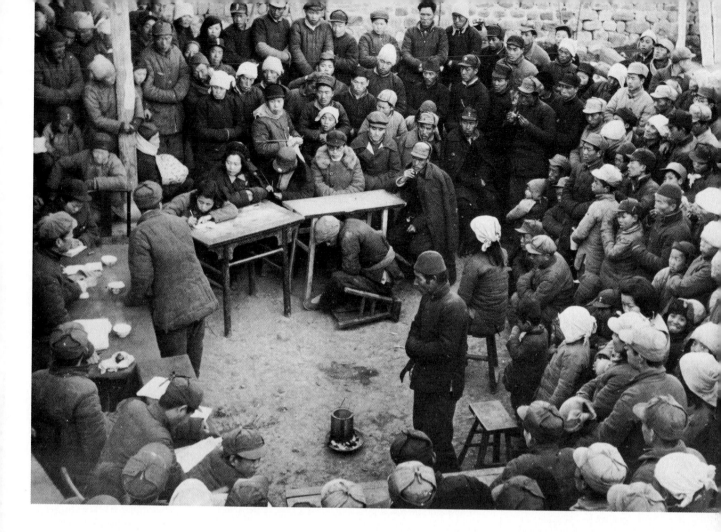

moment'. Towards the end of this period the People's Liberation Army was called in to restore order.

In the years 1972–6 the rebuilding of the legal system began. Law schools were reopened and there were discussions about the need for a new constitution. In 1976 Mao died. After the arrest of the 'Gang of Four' later in 1976 there was a resurgence of legislation and a return of codified rules. Mao's successors wanted to strengthen and stabilize the social order, and law was a means to this end. Even so, at first only a few hundred students received legal training, and these were almost exclusively taught commercial law, urgently needed because of the increase in trade with foreign countries.

A new Constitution came into effect on 1 January 1980, together with seven new laws: the Organic Law of the Local People's Congresses and the Local People's Governments; the Electoral Law for the National People's Congress and Local People's Congresses; the Organic Law of the People's Courts; the Organic Law of the People's Procuratorates; the Criminal Law; the Law of Criminal Procedure; and the Law on Joint Enterprises using Chinese and Foreign Investment.

The main immediate purpose of the new legal system was to remove the courts from random local influence and to subject them more closely to the control of the state. Its wider aim was to prevent a recurrence of anything like the Cultural Revolution. The laws also gave a framework within which

A People's Court in Henan Province during the 1950s tries a man accused of attempting to sell one of the female members of his family. In the early years of communist rule, cases were tried in such courts without reference to codified law.

The trial of the 'Gang of Four' in 1981 was a well-publicized demonstration of the new legal system, introduced at the beginning of 1980. Jiang Qing (Madame Mao) (centre) and her co-defendants were tried on a long list of charges. Several important new legal principles were demonstrated in the case, notably the exclusion from the courtroom of issues defined as political or ideological, and the importance of factual evidence in a trial.

private property and land ownership could be re-established on a limited scale; they provided some reassurance for intellectuals and technocrats persecuted in the Cultural Revolution and now needed for the 'Four Modernizations'; and they offered a degree of security for the foreign and overseas-Chinese investments the government was hoping to attract.

The efforts made by the state to publicize the laws demonstrate the importance it attached to them. All the leading daily papers published their full texts with explanatory comments; many papers opened special correspondence columns to answer questions about them; the Central People's Broadcasting Station put out special programmes on the Criminal Law every other day; and simple legal guides were issued by publishing houses.

In 1978 lawyers began acting as advocates in court in Beijing, and in April 1981 the Lawyers' Association and its advisory offices were reopened there for the first time since the Cultural Revolution. In 1980 the state increased the number of places in law schools by more than a thousand. Promising fourth-year law students were encouraged to undertake part-time legal work. Most of their older colleagues had practised before 1956, so that the average age of practising lawyers in China was still high. Lawyers remained paid employees of the state. Nevertheless this new body of legal professionals began to constitute a distinct force in society previously unfamiliar both to the people and to the government.

In late 1978, the Chinese courts began 'reviewing and redressing' cases tried during the Cultural Revolution and over the next three years 'reviewed 1,200,000 criminal cases' and retried and redressed 'more than 301,000 unjust, false and wrong cases involving more than 326,000 people.'*

The year 1981 started with the first major display of China's new legal system, the trial of the 'Gang of Four' (Jiang Qing, Zhang Chunqiao, Wang Hongwen and Yao Wenyuan). There was an extraordinary degree of detail contained in the charges. It was alleged that the accused had 'framed' and persecuted Party and state leaders and plotted to overthrow the political power of the dictatorship of the proletariat; that they had persecuted or suppressed large numbers of 'cadres' and 'masses', plotted to assassinate Chairman Mao Zedong and to engineer an armed counter-revolutionary coup d'état, and plotted armed rebellion in Shanghai. Altogether forty-eight separate counts were prepared by the Special Procuratorate under the Supreme Procuratorate of the Chinese People's Republic.

Several important legal principles were demonstrated in this case. The concept of 'proceeding from the facts' excluded issues of politics and ideology from the proceedings. A distinction was made between 'crimes' and 'mistakes', which helped to protect the record of Mao Zedong and also to shield his successor as Chairman, Hua Guofeng. And when Jiang Qing (Madame Mao) declined to recognize the court's authority, on the grounds that it was not in accordance with the philosophy of Mao, and tried to discuss politics and ideology from the dock – which would have been perfectly legal and indeed 'correct' under Mao – she was charged with contempt of court.

Jiang Qing and Zhang Chunqiao were given death sentences suspended until January 1983. Wang Hongwen was sentenced to life imprisonment and Yao Wenyuan was given twenty years. Six of their associates received sentences of from fifteen to eighteen years. In 1983 it was announced that Jiang Qing and Zhang Chunqiao had shown some change of attitude, and that while they would be kept in prison the suspended death sentences would no longer apply.*

The Chinese legal system is much concerned with 'changes of attitude' and the first step in a 'change of attitude' is generally expected to be confession. Most defendants confess before their cases come to trial. The authorities require a confession not merely as a confirmation of the conclusions of their investigation; in the modern legal system they are expressly forbidden to assume that a defendant is guilty merely because he or she has confessed. The confession is required for deeper reasons. Just as under the empire, so under the People's Republic, the harmony of the social order has to be re-established after the discord created by a crime. From the accused's point of view the process of confession signals his or her capacity to see the facts from society's standpoint and to engage in self-criticism, and thus in time to be changed in order to fit once more into society. Confession is also the way in which a lenient sentence can be obtained.

Thus the defendant has a motive for confession, irrespective of his or her guilt. Protesting innocence may show something at least as serious as the alleged crime: a mind not yet open to re-education. People sentenced to 'reform through labour' have in the past been told that protests of innocence, demands for proof and appeals showed a bad attitude; and an appeal against a sentence has been known to lead to its doubling.*

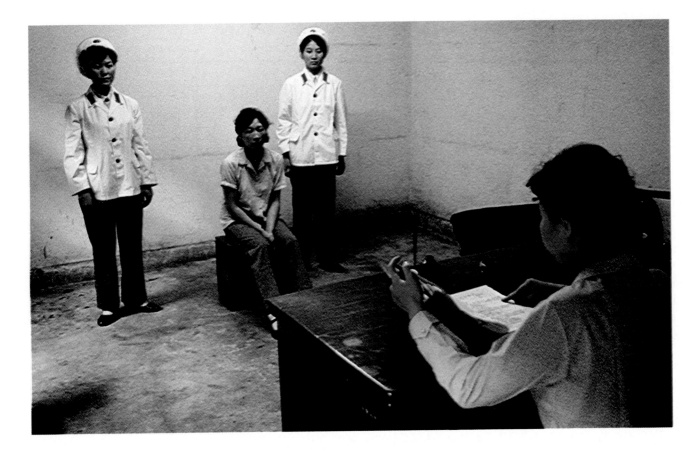

Handcuffed and flanked by two officers of the Public Security Bureau, Nie Chengying, a 28-year-old pharmacy worker, listens to her indictment at the People's Court in Nanjing. She has confessed to crimes of cat burglary and fraud. During her trial, seven days after the reading of the indictment, she will be represented by a defence lawyer, one of the major provisions of the new legal system introduced in 1980.

The legal authorities under the Deng Xiaoping regime, in stating that, 'many unjust, frame-up and wrong cases tried during the "great Cultural Revolution" resulted from judges readily believing fabricated or distorted evidence,' particularly stressed that, 'no conclusion can be reached on a case only on the strength of a statement made by the accused under examination but without other evidence.'*

The part played by confession and 'change of attitude' in the trial and sentencing of Nie Chengying, the young woman accused of cat-burglary, shows something of the operation of the Chinese system that is characteristic even of much more serious cases. When she was arrested Nie Chengying confessed to the police and said she regretted what she had done. The indictment, when she was accused, included details supplied in her confession.

'It has been discovered that the defendant Nie Chengying, at about 4 p.m. on 17 May 1982, took a brick and broke the window of her neighbour Sun Zhaoxun's flat, with the intention of stealing. At about 8 a.m. on 21 May, she propped a board between her lavatory and the broken window and crawled across into Sun's house. She stole a twelve-inch black-and-white "Pine Tree" brand television set which Sun had recently bought, a small Japanese Sanyo radio-cassette recorder, and a new woollen quilt.

'In about March or April of the same year, with a duplicate of the door key belonging to her neighbour at number 212, Fei Zeshan, she unlocked the door when no one was at home and went into Fei's flat. She stole Y130 of the People's Currency, 110 jin-worth of food tickets, a lady's overcoat of leopard fur, a pair of man's long trousers of fancy suiting, a pair of trousers of polyester fibre, two pairs of nylon socks, and other things. Since being arrested, Nie Chengying has confessed to other crimes. From 1980 to January 1982 she pretended she was going to buy bicycles and various other items and fraudulently obtained over Y1200 from five workers at her factory, including Wang Jialin and Pan Xiuhua. As she extracted money fraudulently from some people she returned money to others.

'The defendant has already confessed frankly. Her errors are comparatively severe. She has infringed the private legal property rights of citizens, harmed social public security and thus violated Article 151 of the Criminal Law of the People's Republic of China.

'I now announce to you under Article 26 of the Criminal Procedure Code of the People's Republic of China, that the defendant has the right to defend himself or herself in court, or alternatively can engage a lawyer or a member of his or her family. Which do you want to do?'

'I want a lawyer.'

'We will tell your husband to engage a lawyer for you.'

The position of the defence lawyer is ambiguous: he is an official, a member of the governmental authority that will decide on the sentence. That does not mean that he will not try to defend his client to the best of his ability, but his loyalties are to an order of society to which the individual must be expected to conform. When Nie Chengying's husband visited a local law office to engage a defence lawyer, he addressed him as a member of the official world that was ranged against Nie Chengying, and could exercise clemency.

'I hope the government will sentence her leniently, and give her a chance to turn over a new leaf. After all she's still young, isn't she? Please give her a chance.'

'Everyone should abide strictly by the law' [said the lawyer]. 'If anyone breaks the State's law, they must be punished by the law. She must draw a lesson from this case. Everything must be done according to the facts and under the law. I shall put forward all possible points favourable to her: everything that can reasonably be said in legal terms. All right. That's all for today.'

Next it was the turn of the judge and his two lay assessors to interview the accused:

'Our Court has formed a collegiate bench. My name is Tao Qibin. This is Zhang Zhigen and her name is Sun Liqiang. Today our main task is to interrogate you and check certain facts with you. If anything in your previous confession is not the truth, you may correct it. You can sit down. When you make your statement you must state thoroughly the time, place, methods, the whole process and result of what you did. Do you understand?'

Nie Chengying made her statement as she was asked, in great detail. She was a co-operative witness.

When the trial began, the Public Security Bureau mentioned that,

'After she had been arrested the defendant's attitude to confession of her guilt was on the whole good. She confessed nearly all the details of her theft. By following up her confession we got back everything she had stolen. Finally, after she had been arrested, her husband Lin Yongli on his own initiative returned all the money fraudulently obtained from other people by his wife.'

The members of the collegiate bench seemed concerned at the trial not only to establish what the defendant's attitudes to guilt and reform actually were, but to shape these attitudes by a variety of processes, including a moral harangue. The authorities seemed also, in a traditional Chinese way, to be reaffirming their own solidarity with the social order in front of each other, and reaffirming the harmony of the social order itself, which this crime had disturbed. For example, after the evidence had been heard, the woman lay assessor rounded on the defendant:

'Listen to me. You are young and you have already set up a happy family. Your family income is nearly a hundred yuan a month. You have a radio, a television set, a sewing machine, a bicycle and furniture. Under the present conditions of our country, you can be said to have everything you ought to have, as an ordinary family. You have that young daughter who isn't even three years old. The simple little thing asks for you every day. She cries for mother every day. But can she get mother-love from you? Think about it: in her childish heart, what sort of effect and anxiety will she be left with?'

As soon as her daughter was mentioned the accused girl broke down and started crying bitterly.

'Do you think about all these things? Do you consider that your aged father and your mother who suffers from hemiplegia cannot get comfort and care from you? Instead they have to worry and worry about you.
    'They often cry. You have not only failed to live up to the training and education given you by the country; you have also failed your husband, your child and your parents.'
    'Nie Chengying, the defendant, have you heard clearly?' [asked the judge].
    'Yes, I have heard clearly. All the crimes I have committed today have broken the law. No matter how the government decides to deal with me and no matter where I have to go from now on, I have to work hard with both my hands to wash off the crimes from me.'
    'Fine. Nie Chengying, the defendant, is everything you have said earlier about your theft and fraud the truth?'
    'It is all the truth.'
    'Is there anything else you want to say?'
    'No.'
    'The court investigation is now finished and the court debate commences. You can sit down. I call on Dong Xiujing, the public prosecutor, to state the case.'

Dong Xiujing was a woman in her early fifties who three decades earlier had studied at the Shanghai Law School. She began:

'This defendant's theft and her fraud have infringed the legal property of other people. They have directly influenced the economic life of the people and their socialist initiative to contribute heart and soul to the Four Modernizations, and they have broken the stability and unity of the social order. The fact that the defendant has embarked on the road of degeneracy and crime is the inevitable outcome of the fact that she has abandoned the working people's traditional virtues – hard work, plain living, industriousness, and domestic thrift – and that she has spent money without control under the guidance of a continuously developing greed, through the pernicious influence of the ten years of Cultural Revolution which has not yet been liquidated.'

'Breaking the stability and unity of the social order' is a markedly Chinese way of referring to a crime. The joining of traditional with socialist ethics is seamless.

The defence lawyer, when his turn came, argued more cogently on the defendant's side than perhaps his initial brusqueness to her husband might have suggested. Though his demeanour and attitude still plainly identified him with the authorities, ranged against the defendant, his arguments made an ingenious case, while conceding what it is wise in China to concede – the

matter of guilt – since only confession can lead to leniency. Those who had entrusted Nie Chengying with money, he argued, had given it to her voluntarily, and she had always had the intention of returning the money she had taken. So her behaviour did not really constitute the crime of fraud. She had merely delayed returning the money; but debtors often do this, and do not thereby become guilty of fraud.

After the speeches and the court debate were over the judge and assessors retired to deliberate together. When they returned, the judge pronounced:

'After discussion the Collegiate Judicial Bench has decided to sentence the defendant leniently. Under Article 123 of the Criminal Procedure law of the People's Republic of China, on behalf of the People's Court of Gulou District, I now pronounce the verdict on the defendant Nie Chengying's case.

'The defendant Nie Chengying committed a crime of theft and fraud and is sentenced to one year's surveillance. Under the Criminal Procedure Law of our country, the defendant can appeal to the Intermediate People's Court of Nanjing Municipality. Defendant Nie Chengying, do you hear this clearly?'

The defendant nodded. She could have been sentenced to five years in jail. Instead, she would now be watched over by the factory security section and made to repeat her story at countless corrective sessions. Part of the punishment would be the difficulties of her future relations with her neighbours and workmates and the shame of her entire family.

During her trial, Nie Chengying faces the judge and two lay assessors on the bench. The clerk of the court is on the right.

193

A conversation with other people in Nie Chengying's workshop after the trial suggested something of their attitudes to the prospect of a 'returned criminal' in their midst. People are no doubt doubly on their best moral behaviour when stating their intentions to foreigners: nevertheless the remarks made by those present contained some hints of shrewdness as well as displaying an ideal comradely tolerance.

'We shall help her to turn over a new leaf.'
    'Not only will we not discriminate against her, we have to give her warmth.'
    'Whether she comes back to this workshop is something the leaders will arrange. But if she comes back, we'll greet her. We won't discriminate against her. We'll make her feel the warmth of our group'.
    'And we won't be taken in again.'
    'We shall not be taken in, because we are experienced now.'

Thus after the trial, the restitution of the defendant to society was said to be part of their role by the people she had worked with before. The court system and the system of group solidarity are not separate from each other in China. And the activities of neighbourhood committees and mediation committees are still more obviously an extension of the general community vigilance that has been a feature of China since before the empire was founded in 221 BC. For codes of ethics and right behaviour have always been supported in China by the family and by neighbours.

The new legal system that has been emerging in recent years, with its centre-piece the codification of the 1980s, will like its imperial predecessors have to fuse the two ancient attitudes to law and order, those represented by Qin Shihuangdi and by Confucius. The emphasis given in current Chinese penal theory to the alteration of prisoners' attitudes can be seen in part as a reflection of the old methods of settling disputes by mediation and discussion to which the Chinese people have been long accustomed, but also in part as a new twist to the grip of the Legalist state on its subjects, extending now to their minds as well as to their bodies.

Like the legal system the Chinese prison system is much concerned with changes of attitude in prisoners. The walls of prisons may display slogans such as: 'Get to the bottom of your crimes', 'Criticize your crimes', 'Remould yourself quickly', and 'Make a start towards a new life'. One main means of reform in Chinese prisons is seen as physical labour. Prisons have small factories inside them, and sometimes factories themselves are converted into prisons. The prison authorities are free to put prisoners to constructive work rather than to jobs like rag-picking as there are no trade union protests. Prisoners may work in management, accounting, storekeeping and quality control as well as in production. Performance in menial jobs such as cleaning the lavatories, serving meals and fetching drinking water may also be used to judge willingness to reform.

While 'reform through labour' is an important aspect of prison life it is only one element of the system in most city jails. Each cell will usually house a group leader, who can earn remission by his conduct of 'study and criticism

sessions' with new prisoners. Such criticism sessions may involve intense and protracted psychological pressure from one or many people. In some respects the experiences of Chinese in prison resemble the experiences of all Chinese during the Cultural Revolution.

If labour and exhortation do not appear to be having much effect, the prison authorities have a number of additional devices at their disposal. These include solitary confinement, usually from three to seven days, with fourteen days normally the maximum; handcuffing; and putting prisoners in fetters.

There is also another kind of a penal system, the range of institutions called 'reform through labour' camps (*laodong gaizao*, usually abbreviated to *laogai*) and 'education through labour' camps and enterprises (*laojiao*).* Although 'reform', 'labour' and 'camp' all sound milder than 'prison', in practice *laogai* seems to have been far more dreaded.

Perhaps because, apart from a wave of releases at the end of the Cultural Revolution, few inmates have been able to leave China or even return home and tell the story of the labour camps, the facts about them have been little known. The Chinese Government has generally declined to comment on them.* One man who did emerge in 1964 told a story from his own experience which gives an indication, among other things, of the seriousness of the concern with reform that may be entertained by the camp authorities

Nie Chengying weeps as she is reminded by one of the lay assessors of the sorrow she has caused her family. Her sentence is lenient: she is to be placed under surveillance. She will return home and be watched over at work by the security section of her 'unit'. However, everyone will know of her crime, and her family is likely to feel deep shame at a collective disgrace.

and of what this may mean in practice. At an assembly a prisoner who had been a barber was brought out, chained and with his hands tied, accompanied by a man in a blue uniform. The brigade leader in charge of production addressed the prisoners:

'I have something awful to speak about. I'm not happy to do it and it's nothing to be proud of. But it is my duty and it should be a lesson for you. This rotten egg here was jailed on a morals charge – homosexual relations with a boy. He only received seven years for this offence. Later, when working in the paper mill, his behaviour was constantly bad and he stole repeatedly. His sentence was doubled. Now we have established that while here, he seduced a young prisoner nineteen years old – a mentally-retarded prisoner. If this happened in society, he would be severely punished. But by doing what he did here, he not only sinned morally but he also dirtied the reputation of the prison and the great policy of Reform Through Labour. Therefore, in consideration of his repeated offences, the representative of the Supreme People's Court will now read you his sentence.'

The man in the blue uniform strode forward and read out of the sombre document, a recapitulation of the offences that ended with the decision of the People's Court: death with immediate execution of sentence. Everything happened so suddenly then that I didn't even have the time to be shocked or frightened. Before the man in the blue uniform had even finished pronouncing the last word the barber was dead. The guard standing behind him pulled out a huge pistol and blew his head open.*

From the little official evidence available, eighty-three per cent of all prisoners in China were at one time kept in labour camps.* That was in the 1950s: no subsequent figures are known. Estimates of the numbers have varied from some thirty million – the 'five per cent who are against us' referred to in the past in Party pronouncements* – to a few hundred thousand, including over 100,000 political prisoners.* Life in them, according to reports, is hard: work – on construction, farming, mining, and such tasks – is exhausting; the diet is inadequate; and the discipline harsh. There are camps in most cities, and many in remote areas: near the Soviet border, or Qinghai in the far west, which was closed to foreigners until 1980. The latter province, according to an American – the son of a missionary doctor and a Chinese nurse, who spent twenty years in the camps without being tried or sentenced – 'was built up as a penal colony, a Chinese Siberia; one compound near Xining covered about five hundred square miles. In one camp in Sichuan a young man who had made a pun on Mao's name was incarcerated for eleven years, during which time his family was not allowed to visit him, though he was able to write to them.'*

The shift in line since Mao's death has led to some changes. Their extent is not certain. In theory it is no longer possible to be sent to any penal institution without trial. However, as late as 1978 a former teacher rehabilitated with 20,000 inmates of his camp saw about as many younger prisoners being driven in to take their places. The new legal system did not come into operation until 1980. Forestalling it, in 1979 a stiff decree dating originally from 1957 was reissued by the National People's Congress, re-establishing the system of 'education through labour'. Some who have experienced both this and 'reform through labour' have said that they found little difference.* Officially, however, 'education through labour' is less

severe. The Public Security Ministry's authorities can still send somebody to a labour camp without trial for 'education' but initially only for three years, with a limit of two years' extension if the person concerned does not show improvement in the view of the authorities. After five years, a trial becomes necessary. At the camps, there is said to be a wage of two yuan a week, no uniforms, permission for monthly visits from family and friends, and training in a trade. At the end of the sentence prisoners are allegedly found jobs, though these may be in the vicinity of a camp, and so may be in a remote area. There is some evidence of camp inmates near Beijing being found jobs recently.*

Education through labour, as re-established in 1979, is likely to be in part a measure designed to deal with the wave of juvenile lawlessness reported in

Convicts sentenced to 'reform through labour', in this case for minor offences, muster for the midday meal at a labour reform farm near Nanjing. The slogans on the wall are reminders of the principles of reform through labour.

Work in a tea plantation at the same labour reform farm for inmates who have committed minor offences.

the Chinese press, in the wake of the Cultural Revolution. Of the generation born about 1960, that succeeded the Great Leap Forward, their parents say 'Born in famine, raised in chaos.'

The evidence of disorder available in press reports in China may be evidence not so much of an increase in disorder, as of a new wish on the part of the government to see it reported. Most people would feel considerably safer walking the streets of Shanghai or Beijing at night than those of London, Paris or New York, and rates of reported crime in China, for what such vague measures are worth, appear to be somewhat lower those usually given for indictable offences in most European countries or in America.* Whatever the facts and the underlying reasons, the Chinese authorities were giving considerable publicity to problems of law and order in the early 1980s.* One article in Shanghai's *Liberation Daily** said:

Profiteering, smuggling, tax evasion, illegal price rises, market disruption, bribery, perversion of justice, leaking or selling economic or technological secrets, murder, arson, robbery, organized gambling, rape, gang rape, abducting women for prostitution, call-girl clubs, drug peddling, are all on the increase. Some people are engineering explosions and distributing leaflets to oppose the people's democratic dictatorship. Some are setting up illegal organizations, publishing illegal journals, spreading anti-party and anti-Socialist sentiments, and establishing secret ties with one another . . .

Sexual offences seemed to have become a particularly serious problem. In Shanghai, Beijing, Tianjin, Wenzhou, and other cities – almost certainly in all other cities – special security forces had been created to deal with 'terrorism and lawlessness'. The militia was no longer regarded as reliable, and had even been involved in some of the violence. The Beijing Government and the provincial administrations were also showing alarm at dangers to railways and power lines. A National Conference on Reform Through Labour organized by the Ministry of Public Security in 1981 reported that the current situation differed from that of the past, in that counter-revolutionaries were now few, ordinary criminals were in the vast majority, and most of these were young. They were 'influenced by Lin Biao and the Gang of Four', but were victims as well as criminals, 'while harming others, they were also damaging themselves'. They needed strict control but they also had to be treated with humanity and with concern for their welfare.*

It was constantly reiterated that the 'overwhelming majority of those who cause disruption are young people',* and it was suggested that this rising wave of juvenile rape, robbery and theft had no motive other than 'bravado, curiosity and mischief'.* Neighbourhood committees and local mediation committees were urged to take action by increasing their surveillance of young people and also by paying more attention to their leisure needs.

Two years later the authorities were announcing a surprisingly steep decline in the number of reported crimes, which was said to have gone down by fifteen per cent between 1981 and 1982 and to be still falling, though homicide, robbery and rape were still causing concern, and the emergence of hijacking was also perturbing the authorities.* It would seem probable that a very long time must pass before law comes to mean in Chinese thinking what it has long meant for the European peoples, protection for the individual, and the foundation of liberty. It is not at all apparent that the protection of the individual or his liberty has been, or really is now, a prime objective in Chinese social policy. Individualism has been denounced as a bourgeois vice. Liberty is usually conceived as a vague general good (for example in the use of the word 'Liberation' as the official term for the Communist Party's assumption of power throughout China in 1949), not as an individual right. It would seem more than likely that these fundamental differences will continue to modify any system of law designed in part on European models.

In general the purpose of law in China is and has always been twofold. On the one hand the authorities have tried to make the enforcement of law flexible and adaptable to circumstances. Education, mediation and the reform of offenders have always played a great role and do so still today. This can be seen as a continuation of Confucian ideas. On the other hand, law is and has always been also regarded as a deterrent. This is in conformity with Legalist thinking. The fundamental ideal which lies behind all law and order in socialist China, just as in the Confucian imperial order, is harmony in a world where ideally no infractions of rules should occur.

UNDERSTANDING

THE BODY AND THE UNIVERSE

Today, with one exception, there is no such thing as Chinese science or Western science, only science done by various people throughout the world in broadly the same way. The exception is medicine. Hospitals in China offer both Western and traditional Chinese methods of treatment; and in the traditional departments an ancient cosmology which is unique to China still shapes the practical details of diagnosis and treatment. Even though, like Western cosmology, it has changed radically over the centuries, certain principles have endured and have provided the framework for some impressive scientific and technological discoveries in medicine and, in the past, in other fields also.

In all societies sick or injured people appear to need to understand what is happening to them and to be reassured that their painful experiences can be fitted into a comprehensible pattern with a hope of cure. Chinese classical medical literature, which forms a vast corpus, sets out to give an integrated account of sickness and therapy in the context of the traditional Chinese view of the world.

The two fundamental terms in which the Chinese have for thousands of years understood the natural world are 'yin' and 'yang'. Thinking in yinyang terms means analyzing the universe into pairs of fluidly interacting opposites, such as shadowed and bright, decaying and growing, moonlit and sunlit, cold and hot, earthly and heavenly or female and male. Whether a thing is classified as yin or yang depends not on its intrinsic nature but on the role it plays in relation to other things. In relation to Heaven man may be classified as yin, but when paired with Earth he would be seen as yang. Heaven itself is the supreme embodiment of the yang aspects of the cosmos: ethereal, bright, active, generative, initiatory and masculine. Earth is seen as deeply yin: solid, dark, cool, quiescent, growth-sustaining, responsive and feminine. Men and women are not seen as exclusively yang or yin: each has only a predominance of the one aspect or the other, and the balance within them and between them may change. The relation of the two elements of a yinyang pair is not a static one, but is thought of as a continuous cycle in which each tends to become dominant and responsive in turn. This idea may ultimately have derived from the experience of day and night and the annual cycle of growth and decay in an agricultural community.

More complex cycles can be analyzed in terms of the 'five phases' (*wuxing*)

In a 17th-century painting Chinese of all ages study the yinyang symbol, an interlocking figure representing the two opposite but balancing aspects of nature. Though this particular symbol may be no more than a thousand years old, evidence of the idea of yin and yang is found among the earliest records of Chinese civilization.

of wood, fire, earth, metal and water. These have sometimes been translated as 'elements', but unlike the earth, air, fire and water of the ancient West they are not distinct and immutable constituents of the universe. The five phases are in reality a more detailed means of analyzing the cycle of the seasons than the yinyang pair. At the centre of a circle lies earth. The Chinese represent south – the direction of the sun at midday – at the top of their charts: thus above and correlated with the south is fire, displaying the fullness of the role of yang in the summer. On the left, correlated with the east, is wood, representing the phase of growth, the start of the yang half of the yearly cycle in the spring. To the right of earth, in the west, is metal (associated with cutting and destroying), representing the autumn as the start of the yin half of the cycle. Below, in the northern position, lies water, cold and inactive: the yin phase that culminates in the dead of winter. But the fullest development of the yin tendencies is always followed by the growth of yang activity, and so the cycle begins once more with the phase wood. Either in this or in some other arrangement, the five phase system can be applied to all phenomena in the universe: there is a detailed scheme of correlation which allocates all colours, sounds, times, seasons, flavours, organs of the body and much else besides to their matching phases.

An even more complex and versatile scheme of correlative thinking was based on the system of trigrams and hexagrams that culminated in the *Yijing* (*I Ching*), the *Book of Change*. A trigram is an array of three horizontal lines, one above the other, each of which may be either continuous (yang) or broken in the middle (yin). Since any line of a trigram may be chosen in either of two ways there are eight possible trigrams:

HEAVEN   THUNDER   WATER   MOUNTAIN
(QIAN)   (ZHEN)   (KAN)   (GEN)

EARTH   WIND   FIRE   LAKE
(KUN)   (SUN)   (LI)   (DUI)

All the combinations of eight trigrams used in pairs yield sixty-four possible hexagrams. It is around these that the *Yijing* was structured.

At some time in the first millennium BC this work seems to have arisen partly as a book of divination, and partly as a collection of wisdom. By 250 BC it had attracted a mass of explanatory material which made it the basis of an elaborate metaphysics, in particular the 'Great Commentary' which treated it mainly as a means of self-cultivation and self-examination. The Chinese have long recognized the value, and the difficulty, of understanding one's own condition through self-examination: as the polymath scientist Shen Gua wrote in the eleventh century, 'The human mind is by nature spiritually responsive, but since it is unavoidably burdened, one must, in

order to gain access to it, use as a substitute some thing that does not have a mind.'* The *Yijing* is used for divination by the selection of a hexagram through some random procedure such as shuffling and laying out stalks of the yarrow herb, or tossing coins. No hexagram is a static entity; each is taken as representing one particular stage in a continuous process of change.

The idea that change occurs as a result of natural, cyclic development is characteristic of traditional Chinese thought; the concept of determinate chains of cause and effect, which has been essential to Western thinking for many centuries, is alien to it. In about the year 300 Guo Xiang wrote, 'Heaven and earth and the myriad things change and transform into something new every day and so proceed with time. What causes them? They do so spontaneously . . . What we call things are all what they are by themselves; they did not cause each other to become so.'

It is this belief which, among ordinary people, expresses itself in the virtue of 'restraint' or 'forbearance' (*rennai*). The conviction that no state of affairs is permanent but that change cannot be forced is one of the foundations of the Chinese philosophy of life. It has obvious links with China's agricultural past. When the sun reaches its summit at noon, it begins to set; when the moon is full, it begins to wane; when a course of events reaches its most

The ceiling of a Daoist temple on Qingcheng mountain in Sichuan Province shows a yinyang symbol surrounded by the eight trigrams. The trigrams are a combination of three lines, either continuous (yang) or broken (yin). Combined in pairs, as hexagrams, they form the basis of the ancient Chinese book of divination, the Yijing *(I Ching) or 'Book of Change'.*

propitious or inauspicious point, it will change into its opposite. No amount of human precaution or intervention can alter the inexorable cyclical mutations of nature or human affairs. The lesson to learn is not to succumb to despair when confronted by misfortune and not to be complacent when fortune is favourable.

The Chinese regard health, in a universe of constant change, as a state of balance established between the body and the natural world as well as of balance between the different components of the body itself. They see illness as occurring when this balance is disturbed. Those illnesses caused by heat, overeating or 'overfullness' are yang diseases; those caused by cold or 'deficiency' are yin diseases. The task of the physician, as one early medical text puts it, is simply to 'eliminate overfullness and make up deficiency', thus restoring the body to balance; or, better still, to keep his patient healthy enough to resist the effect of any destabilizing factor outside the body. The human body is thought of as a system for dealing with vital energy, and to a traditional Chinese doctor all that needs to be done to intervene in the body's workings can be done either through the administration of drugs or herbs or through manipulation at the surface of the body.

The term rendered here as 'vital energy' is *qi*; it is a concept of great significance in Chinese cosmology outside the specialized realm of medical terminology. No modern Western idea corresponds very closely to the range of meanings of *qi*. It is not simply subtle matter, yet some thinkers held that matter was *qi* in condensed form. Hence some broad analogies have been drawn between traditional Chinese cosmology and modern sub-atomic physics, in which certain entities are conceived of as behaving in some respects as waves and in others as particles.

Qi is a central explanatory concept in the most comprehensive early medical document in China, the *Huangdi Neijing (The Yellow Emperor's Inner Book)*. It dates in its present form from about 50 BC, and summarizes the medical knowledge of the day. There are numerous references to the 'five yin systems' and 'six yang systems' of *qi* or vital energy, and it generally refers to them by the names of the organs associated with each, such as the liver, the heart and the spleen. The five yin systems store vitality in its various forms in the body, while the six yang systems assimilate and distribute vitality around the body. It is the harmonious and timely interchange of *qi* between the systems of the body that Chinese medicine defines as constituting health. The aim of the physician is to maintain this dynamic balance in the patient, and to restore it when it has been disturbed.

In assessing the patient's condition, Chinese medical practice makes use of a four-fold method of diagnostic observation. This begins with a visual examination of the patient, and in particular of his tongue. The next stage involves listening to the patient's breathing and to any other sounds such as coughing or groaning, as well as using the sense of smell on the patient's breath, body odour and excretions. The patient is then questioned on his medical history and present condition. The fourth and final stage is based on what can be learned by touch, including feeling the pulses. There is thought

Acupuncture and moxibustion are two ancient Chinese medical techniques, still in wide use today. Needles, with or without burning fibres of the artimesia plant (moxa), are inserted into particular points of the body according to a complex system of diagnosis preserved for over two thousand years. In this Song Dynasty painting a patient is held down by his companions while a country doctor applies the painful cure of moxibustion to his back.

to be a complex linkage between the pulses in different parts of the body and the state of the systems of energy, and the classical manuals distinguish more than twenty different sensations that the doctor must look for when feeling the various pulses.

The part played by yinyang cosmology and the system of five phases in Chinese medical examination may be illustrated by an incident in the great eighteenth century novel by Cao Xueqin, *The Red Chamber Dream*. A doctor is calling on the sick wife of a member of the wealthy Jia family. After a preliminary exchange of courtesies the doctor examines his patient by feeling the pulses in both her arms, comparing their rhythm with his own carefully controlled breathing. He then withdraws and gives his diagnosis in the following terms:

A rapid lower left-hand pulse means that a deficiency of energy in the heart is causing it to produce too much activity corresponding to the phase 'fire'; and the strong lower median pulse means that the energy of the liver is blocked, so that there is a lack of blood. A thin weak distal pulse on the right side indicates a gross deficiency of energy in the lungs; and a faint right median pulse lacking in vitality shows that the phase 'earth' in the spleen is being checked by the phase 'wood' of the liver.*

On the basis of this diagnosis the doctor gives an accurate prediction of the symptoms experienced by the patient: general lassitude and discomfort, insomnia and failure to menstruate. He laments that the case has gone so long without proper treatment, writes out a complex prescription for a herbal decoction, and takes his leave of a satisfied family, who are convinced that such a display of expertise means they have done their very best for the sick woman. She may have been neither better nor worse off than a contemporary patient in Europe, if it has been correctly estimated that the chances of improving after being treated by Western medical techniques before 1900 were about the same as the chances of improving without being treated.*

In the early twentieth century, many thinkers in China rejected traditional Chinese medicine, along with other aspects of the Chinese past, as 'the accumulated garbage of several thousand years'. Sun Yat-sen, the founding father of the Republic, was himself trained at a Western medical college, as was China's greatest twentieth-century writer, Lu Xun. Western medicine was only beginning to make an impact in China at the time and until then had in any case had few effective therapies to offer. It was when the newly-discovered germ theory of disease was applied to the Manchurian Plague of 1910-11 by Western doctors that their approach, with its 'specific' treatments as opposed to the Chinese 'holistic' way of understanding the body, began to be appreciated. It was at about the same time that some Western surgeons were tentatively accepted in China.

As the twentieth century went on, tides of opinion moved in different directions. The communists were attracted by the modernism of Western medicine, but in the 1930s and 1940s, while their bases were blockaded by the Nationalists, they discovered the value of traditional remedies as a means of treating their wounded when Western drugs were unobtainable. Some of their leaders were attracted to Chinese medicine as a store-house of national wisdom. When the communists came to power they increased training in both traditional and Western medicine, and a network of clinics and hospitals, which had been started in the 1920s and 1930s, was extended across the country.

Most production brigades now have rudimentary clinics, as do many neighbourhood and street committees in the cities. The pattern is far from uniform, and in the rural areas access to a hospital is often difficult. In addition 'barefoot doctors', now called 'rural paramedical workers', with some two years' training in traditional and Western medicine, are available to treat the sick in the villages, and may also staff small country hospitals. They are no longer expected to work part-time in the fields.

In Chinese hospitals the responsibility for feeding the patients is often left in the first instance to their families. In some cases, only those without families are fed by the hospital. The Chinese consider that what one eats is an important factor in health and neither in Chinese medical thinking nor in the lore of folk healing is there any sharp distinction between what counts as food and what counts as medicine: the same verb, *chi*, means to ingest both food and medicine. Different kinds of food have different properties: some are yang, some yin, and ordinary people are usually well aware of the difference and treat minor ailments accordingly. Fresh ginger, which is yang, may be eaten to treat diarrhoea and stomach-ache, thought to be induced by anything yin or 'cold', from a draught to an icy drink. Dandelions and turnips, which have yin properties, may be eaten for boils, pimples, mouth ulcers or abscesses, which are caused by 'heat'. One young

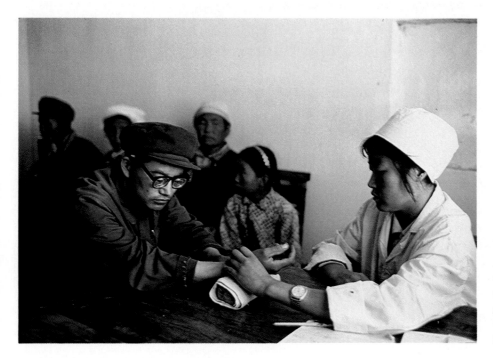

At the outpatient clinic at the Chengdu traditional hospital the initial approach is to assess the general wellbeing of the patient by close observation and taking of the pulse.

Chinese remembers as an adolescent rubbing the family rhinoceros horn on a file about a foot long and tipping the horn powder into a bowl for her mother in Shanghai, who took the powder with a sip of tea whenever her migraine became intolerable. Once when she herself was suffering from a severe headache she asked her mother's permission to take some of the white powder, but was refused: unmarried girls were not allowed to use rhinoceros horn since its very powerful cooling effects, unbalanced by the yang of contact with a man, could cause sterility.

Herbal remedies, usually prescribed in compounds, are still widely used in China today, and village healers and travelling stallkeepers, peddling herbs and other remedies at country fairs, still survive almost everywhere in China. A peddler may sell fifty or sixty different wares, such as tendril-leaved fritillary bulbs for rheumatoid arthritis, bear's paw and tiger's penis for tonic effects, an armadillo-like animal, the pangolin, to cure pustules, and 'antelope influenza tablets', containing horn powder mixed with honey, for a variety of ailments. The most versatile of all herbal remedies is ginseng, and it is still highly prized for its strengthening effects.

A section of a Ming Dynasty painting entitled 'The Garden for Solitary Enjoyment' shows a scholar reclining in his herb garden. Most Chinese think of food and medicine as closely related, and ailments are often treated in the first instance by an adjustment of the patient's diet. A large pharmacy may stock over 5000 types of herbs and dried roots, while street stalls sell a wide variety of medicinal foods of plant and animal origin.

The traditional Chinese hospital in the provincial capital of Sichuan, Chengdu, is a centre of the ancient arts. Besides a wide range of herbal and animal ingredients, its dispensaries contain at least one intermediary: a caterpillar which is allegedly a vegetable for half the year and an animal the other half. Such a hybrid, defying rigid definition, may perhaps make a special appeal to those who see the world in yinyang terms, and in the traditional medical restaurant not far from the hospital in Chengdu duck garnished with these 'caterpillar-herbs' is a speciality. It must be recorded that even Chinese visitors not familiar with the cuisine of the place seem to find the prospect of eating the dish faintly disquieting.

China has a long tradition of using massage and gymnastics to strengthen the natural powers of resistance and to deal with minor disorders. Manuscripts showing medical gymnastics were among the documents discovered in the Han Dynasty tomb, dating from 168 BC, recently excavated at Mawangdui. Ancient Chinese methods of relaxation as a means of therapy for psychosomatic ailments are currently arousing particular interest in the West. At one extreme, such practices have shaded off into the mystical activities of Daoist adepts who attempted to attain immortality through controlling the flow of their *qi* by breathing techniques: this was known as *neidan*, 'internal alchemy' as distinct from the *waidan*, 'exterior alchemy', which went on in laboratories. *Neidan* often included special sexual practices designed to build up a beneficial accumulation of *qi*, and a consciousness of the role of well-regulated sexual activity in maintaining health has long been a part of the medical thinking of ordinary Chinese people. A better-known feature of Chinese efforts to stay healthy is the large number of people in the cities whose day would be incomplete if it did not begin with a *taiji* exercise routine performed in a park or public garden.

The Chinese therapeutic technique most widely known in the West is 'acupuncture and moxibustion', *zhenjiu*. It is already described in the *Yellow Emperor's Inner Book*, and is known to have been in use as early as the second century BC, though seldom in isolation from herbal and other remedies. As in drug therapy the aim is to influence the flow and storage of *qi* among the systems of energy in the body. The theory underlying acupuncture and moxibustion is that there are on the surface of the human body a large number of well-defined points, known as foramina in the West and *xue* in Chinese, where the insertion of a fine needle, with or without burning fibres of the artemisia plant (*moxa*), is thought to be particularly able to affect the balance between the systems of energy. About a hundred such points are in use today, although several times this number are listed in ancient treatises. They are organized into a system of twelve main cardinal channels (*jing*) and fifteen main reticular channels (*luo*), together with numerous minor capillary channels. The system of channels does not correspond to any physical network such as that of the blood vessels or nerves; its object is to map out functional connections rather than physical links. Nevertheless the acupuncture points commonly used over the centuries correlate well with important nerves and nerve junctions near the surface of the skin.

The skin is the main point of entry for diseases in traditional Chinese pathology; after entry, a disease may be expected to show itself through the minor system of channels, followed by penetration into the major system and a deeper involvement with the central functions of the systems of energy. Treatment will be organized broadly in accordance with the supposed entry point of the disease, and the sites for acupuncture or moxibustion will be chosen in an effort to right the imbalances the disease has caused. Although the system of channels and spheres that explains *zhenjiu* therapy is alien to modern Western conceptions of physiology, the consensus of scientific studies is that in many instances the treatment itself can be shown to produce therapeutic benefits.

Some of the most familiar aspects of acupuncture today are recent developments, including its use in conjunction with Western-style surgery, which in the 1950s culminated in the technique known as 'acupuncture analgesia', whose main advantage over anaesthetics in operations was its lack of side effects. By the early 1980s some three million operations had been carried out using this method.

One possible explanation of the working of acupuncture analgesia is that it stimulates the production of endorphins, the body's natural opiates. Sceptical Western theories that the pain relief might be the result of patriotic preference for things Chinese have been harder to sustain since the successful production of acupuncture analgesia in animals.

Another innovation of the 1950s, based on French research, was the use of the ear as a main acupuncture centre. Only one of the body's traditional acupuncture points was located in the ear, but this is the place where the vagus nerve reaches the surface. It is one of the most powerful nerves in the body, and controls the heart, the stomach and the spleen.

Even today, despite the successful combination of acupuncture with surgery, a Chinese traditional doctor would be puzzled by the modern Western admiration for dramatic surgical intervention in the body and its internal functions; although as Chinese doctors have grown more familiar with surgery and have formed a clearer idea of what it can do, their objections have become less sweeping. For the Chinese doctor all the processes within the body can be affected without cutting into it, and cutting into it is at best dangerous and traumatic, and may be more serious still. In traditional Chinese morality the body is a precious gift from one's parents, and is in effect their very flesh and blood. In the *Book of Filial Piety* (*Xiaojing*), a Han Dynasty text ascribed to Confucius, it is written, 'We receive our flesh, bones, hair and skin from our fathers and mothers, and should on no account do anything to injure them.' It was this tradition that made decapitation and any form of mutilation a doubly appalling punishment to the ancient Chinese.

When the great general Meng Tian, who had built part of the 'Great Wall' for Qin Shihuangdi, received an order to commit suicide in a letter purporting to come from his ruler though in fact forged by his rivals, he attributed his fall to the fact that he had cut the veins of the earth while engaged in his wall-building. The earth was thought of as pulsing with vital energies (*qi*), circulating in much the same way as in the human body although on a larger and slower scale. In traditional Chinese cosmology man's fortune depended on maintaining proper relations with Earth and with Heaven: they were the two cosmic powers whose influence governed not only agriculture, then and now the predominant activity of the Chinese, but all operations of the natural world.

For instance it was of great importance where people chose to site their houses, their cities or their tombs. The *Yellow Emperor's Siting Classic* (probably written before 1000 AD) states that if the site is settled, then one's family will be prosperous and lucky for generations. If the site is not settled, then one's clan will decline. The selection of a burial site was even more crucial than the siting of a house. As one text put it, 'To bury is to take advantage of vital *qi*.' An ancestor well planted so as to have his spiritual power nourished by a reservoir of *qi* in the earth could be counted on to secure blessings for his descendants far into the future. Conversely if one chose the wrong place, the Earth might be displeased.

Archaeology and the study of ancient documents have revealed evidence of the caution with which choices of site were made. The ancient *Book of Documents*, describing the building of the Western Zhou capital in about 1000 BC, makes it clear that before the Duke of Zhou inspected the site he sent his grand guardian to consult the oracles about whether the location was appropriate. The oracles would have been questioned by means of a tortoise shell, prepared with conflicting statements about the auspicious or inauspicious nature of the site and pierced with a glowing iron so that the crack would indicate one statement or the other. Shang and Zhou Dynasty diviners also used the shoulder bones of oxen or deer for those purposes, and the split shells and bones bearing early specimens of writing were carefully preserved; hence the name 'oracle bones' for the shells and bones dating from the fourteenth century BC, first discovered at the end of the last century in an apothecary's shop being peddled as 'dragon bones', which confirmed much early Chinese history, thought to be mythological, including a list of rulers of the Shang Dynasty.

The techniques for making judgements on the location of dwellings and graves developed into a specialized discipline colloquially called, 'wind and water' (*fengshui*), usually translated as 'geomancy' or 'siting'. There are two basic approaches to the art of siting, and most practitioners have drawn on both as circumstances seemed to dictate. One was to make a 'fate-position diagram' to show the energetic forces of a locality, through consideration of its relation to the yinyang and five phases. In its other, more intuitive aspect, siting depended on the practitioner's skill in recognizing the way in which the physical configuration of the landscape revealed the flow and accumulation of *qi* in the locality, The imagery used in texts on siting is often explicitly physiological; according to the *Siting Classic*, 'The forms and configurations are considered to be the body; water and underground springs are the blood and veins; the earth is the skin; foliage is the hair;

Inscribed 'oracle bones' found at Anyang, in modern Henan Province, the site of the capital of the Shang Dynasty from the late 14th-century BC onwards. The inscriptions on the oracle bones are the earliest known examples of writing in China, and suggest a continuous evolution to modern Chinese script.

The 17th-century figure on the left shows the system of main and subsidiary channels, linking these acupuncture points, through which the vital energy (qi) was believed to circulate.

dwellings are the clothes; door and gate are the hat and belt.' The analogy between landscape and human body went further. The ideal topography for collecting *qi* was a coombe surrounded on three sides by hills. This was called *xue*, the same word as that used for an acupuncture point on the human body.

Even in nineteenth-century China fear of the dangerous consequences of cutting into the earth was still sufficiently widespread to serve as a focus of opposition to the laying of railway tracks or the driving of deep mineshafts: a local magistrate could refuse to accept the alien innovations, with their threat to the stability of the social order, by arguing that they risked damaging the local *fengshui*. In the People's Republic 'siting' has been suppressed as superstition, but there are reports that it is still practised, not merely privately but, for instance, to decide on sites for reservoirs.

The most drastic sign that the Earth is displeased is an earthquake, and China is an area that has many. The records of earthquakes in Chinese histories are the fullest and most continuous in the world, going well back into the first millennium BC. The world's first seismoscope was built in China, by Zhang Heng, in 132 AD. Today the Chinese government operates a large number of seismological stations, and although the largest role is played by modern apparatus and techniques, considerable attention is still paid to traditional lore when this is thought to have scientific value. Thus a small station manned by part-time workers as part of a mass-observation programme of earthquake study has not only ordinary recording instruments but also a herd of deer whose behaviour is constantly monitored. Another station keeps chickens: if they refuse to enter their coop a tremor is thought to be imminent. A similar warning would be taken from a sudden change in the level or muddiness of well water. Characteristically the Chinese policy is to use all predictive techniques in combination.

In early Zhou times, about 1000 BC, Heaven was probably regarded as a rather remote but nonetheless personal deity, whose strong disapproval of immorality might be shown by such portents as floods, droughts, thunder

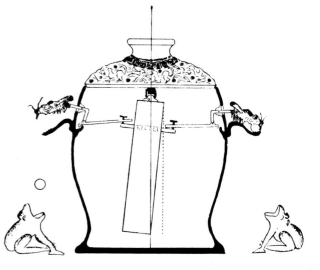

or eclipses. By the Han period (206 BC–AD 220) the aspects of personality had largely faded away, but Heaven remained a cosmic power with a strong concern for ethical behaviour. It was the emperor's unique role to ensure that the harmony of the powers of Heaven, Earth and Man was maintained, and if he fell short of this ideal through ignorance, weakness or deliberate fault then Heaven would be sure to respond with portents or disasters. If the empire was being well governed it was expected that Heaven would display a corresponding regularity in its behaviour. In the earliest periods for which such data have survived there were already astronomical officials charged with organizing the calendar. Acceptance of the emperor's calendar demonstrated his subjects' acceptance of his celestially ordained role in maintaining cosmic harmony; production of a rival calendar might be taken as an act of deliberate treason.

The Chinese calendar was not simple. Until the early twentieth century each month had to begin on the day of a new moon, while the year had to keep in step with the natural cycle of the seasons and so depended on the sun. Independently of these two irreconcilable cycles, the Chinese used a third and man-made division of time, a series of sixty-day periods which seem to have been counted off in unbroken sequence since as far back as the second millennium BC. A shorter, ten-day cycle, corresponding to the week, governed such matters as rest-days.

For the masses of the Chinese people the possession of an accurate calendar has always been seen as a vital necessity of everyday life: a marriage, a funeral, a business transaction or any other affair of importance could turn out successfully only if it was arranged to fall on an astrologically suitable day. At the beginning of each new year therefore it was the emperor's symbolic duty to promulgate an almanac informing his subjects precisely when in the sixty-day cycle each lunar month would begin, and whether this particular year was one in which it was necessary to insert an intercalary or 'leap' month to ensure that the solar cycle did not get too far behind the civil year of twelve lunar months.

From early in the Han Dynasty it is clear that pressures of imperial prestige were at work to drive astronomical officials to seek for a detail and accuracy in their predictions going far beyond anything needed for practical calendrical purposes. Official astronomical tables began to include rules for calculating planetary motion, and later on attempts were made to deal with the finer regularities of solar and lunar motion. It was particularly important to demonstrate the imperial authority and virtue by accurate forecasting of any unusual occurrence such as an eclipse. The peak of traditional Chinese mathematical astronomy was reached with the work of the Song and Yuan Dynasty astronomer Guo Shoujing, whose highly sophisticated system was officially promulgated in 1281. The giant measuring scale and tower he erected to observe the shadow cast by the sun at noon survives at Dengfeng (Yangcheng) in Henan, and later copies of his armillary sphere and other instruments are still preserved in Nanjing. These devices enabled him to calculate the solar year to within an accuracy of twenty seconds. The last

The giant tower built by the astronomer Guo Shoujing, in about 1276, for the measurement of the sun's shadow at the winter and summer solstice, still stands at Dengfeng (Yangcheng) in Henan Province. Using this tower, in 1283 Guo calculated the length of the solar year to an accuracy of twenty seconds.

great calendrical reform under the emperors took place at the beginning of the Qing Dynasty in 1644, and it was carried out by European specialists who had come to China as part of the Jesuit mission under the leadership of Johann Adam Schall von Bell. It is by means of the Jesuits' system that the date of the traditional Chinese New Year is still fixed today.

When the Jesuits gave the Chinese imperial court the by then slightly stale secrets of Western mathematics and astronomy, although the Chinese accordingly revised their calendar they evaded the larger lesson that the Jesuits hoped thereby to teach them: the idea that the cosmos itself is like one of the marvellous scientific instruments that they had brought with them from Europe, a brilliantly constructed machine made by a great Creator God who has imposed unchangeable laws of cause and effect on nature. Such an idea was alien to the Chinese. In the words of the French sinologist Jacques Gernet:

Their whole intellectual tradition held the Chinese back from thinking of the universe and the beings in it as machines. This simplistic conception was in complete contradiction to the idea that they had formed of nature as the autonomous source of all order, assuring the birth, growth and decline of all things . . . Nature could not be compared or likened to the artificial creations of man, necessarily inferior to this power of inexhaustible effulgence which revealed itself in even the knots of the bamboo and the shape of snow crystals.*

The most basic reality of the universe was the ethical order which found its fullest expression in a fully-developed human being living in a well-ordered society. Compared with the richness of ethics and cosmology the sort of order to be found in the non-human world was flat and colourless. The study

The oldest surviving star chart in the world, in a manuscript of about 940 from the Dunhuang caves in Gansu province. Although the purpose of astronomical observation was prediction, Chinese scholars have always been deeply interested in the past and in memorials of their predecessors: here the stars are drawn in three colours, white, black and yellow, to show which of three astronomers had determined their positions more than a thousand years earlier. These two segments include the constellations known in the West as Orion and Canis Major (left), and Canis Minor and Cancer (right).

An armillary sphere, an astronomical instrument for taking observations to determine the position of celestial bodies, from a Qing Dynasty painting. The Chinese have had armillary spheres for more than two thousand years, and over this period have thought of the heavens as spherical, and of the earth as flat with China at the centre both of the earth and of the celestial sphere.

(Right)
After her impressive early contribution to the world's science and technology, China became increasingly conservative and static until the impact of the West in the nineteenth and twentieth centuries. Despite early Chinese aeronautical inventions such as the kite and the 'bamboo dragonfly' – a prototype of the helicopter-top – the first aeroplane flight in China in 1911, commemorated in the painting opposite, was regarded by many Chinese with suspicion.

of books came to be seen as more important to educated men than technological skill or knowledge of the natural world. Increasingly, this tended to separate the literary elite and the artisans from each other.

If anyone were to ask what role China's pre-modern heritage plays in the practice of science and technology in China today, the answer would turn out to be fairly complex. Except in the case of the living tradition of medicine and the popular but not officially recognized science of siting, it is clear that the explicit intellectual structures of the past have not survived. In the case of astronomy and some other fields modern scientists are able to make use of ancient observations that have come down in the admirably systematic Chinese historical sources, but this cannot be taken as representing any real continuity with past practice. There is no discernible tendency amongst Chinese scientists to join Fritjof Capra and other Westerners in claiming that certain features of ancient Chinese thought strikingly anticipate some of the more abstruse insights of modern cosmology such as quantum physics. Nor is there any discernible evidence that the Chinese language – as is sometimes claimed – has a lesser capacity than any Western one for the expression of coherent logical or mathematical thought. Early Chinese achievements, for instance in algebra and in mechanics, are striking evidence against it.

Why the Chinese 'fell behind' in science and did not have a scientific revolution until the limited one of the late seventeenth century, when in many respects in earlier centuries they were in advance of the West in both science and technology, is a complex question that cannot be definitively answered. However, one partial explanation is China's lack of political variety. Whereas the diversity of Europe meant, at a crucial time, that ideas not acceptable in one place could be cultivated in another – for instance that Galilean notions of astronomy could be discussed in Holland when forbidden in Italy – the unity of China made for a single elite orthodoxy based on ethical foundations, from the thirteenth or fourteenth century on.

Orthodox neo-Confucian cosmology in theory provided a scheme into which all aspects of knowledge could be fitted; and in the eleventh century there were still men, such as the polymath scientist Shen Gua and the philosopher Zhu Xi, who had no trouble in reconciling a passionate interest in natural phenomena with their ethical concerns. But after their time the increasing emphasis on moral introspection made a variety of interests rarer.

In Europe the fact that specialists in different sciences and, later, practical craftsmen could come together in bodies such as the Royal Society of London or the Lunar Society of Birmingham has generally been held to be an important part of the explanation of the origins of the scientific revolution and the industrial revolution. In China, knowledge fell apart into specialisms which did not communicate with one another intellectually to any great extent, and were institutionally separate. A mathematical astronomer at court had little to say to an alchemist in a remote mountain abbey, and neither would have had much in common with a siting expert. Craftsmen and technologists were generally separated from all three; they were usually unconcerned with the largely contemplative culture of the educated.

One Chinese story dramatizes particularly well the contempt of the artisan for 'book-learning'. The *Zhuangzi*, one of the two prime texts of philosophical Daoism, tells the story of Bian the wheelwright, who rebuked the Duke of Qi for reading books which had nothing in them but the leftover dregs of dead men:

'When I read a book', the Duke said, 'what right do you have to criticize me? You'd better explain yourself, or you'll be dead yourself!' Bian replied, 'I look at it from the point of view of my work. When I'm chiselling a wheel, a stroke that's too slow may go sweetly but it won't grip, while a stroke that's too fast sticks and won't cut deep enough. When I'm getting it just right, my heart answers to what my hand is feeling. I can't explain what it is: that's just the way they work together. I can't explain it to my son, and he can't get it out of me, and that's why I still have to chisel the wheels myself at the age of seventy. Now the men of olden times have died and taken with them the things they couldn't pass on to us, so that's why what Your Grace is reading is only their leftover dregs.'*

Although practical craftsmen in China lived in comparative isolation from literate and learned men, some of their discoveries transformed the world that the scholars administered. Those discoveries in which the Chinese take the most pride, and which they call 'the four inventions' – the compass, gunpowder, paper and printing – transformed sea transport, warfare, and literacy, first in the East and then in the West. Already in the fifth and fourth centuries BC, the Chinese had discovered an efficient form of harness for horses, and with it revolutionized transport in China and, in time, the West. Other early inventions, from the wheelbarrow and the crankshaft to various kinds of water-pump, all demonstrate a grasp of mechanics and an inventiveness that are remarkable as well as remarkably early.

It was partly the importance of the art of siting, in which the magnetic compass has a central role, that led to its early elaboration in China. Some specimens of siting compasses bear up to twenty-four concentric graduated rings, used in making 'fate-position diagrams'. The earliest clear Chinese descriptions of the directional property of a magnetized iron needle occur in the eleventh century, at least a hundred years before the topic is mentioned in European records; and early texts show that the Chinese were even then aware of magnetic declination, the fact that the compass needle does not point to the geographic north. These discoveries played a major part in the success of the great Chinese maritime expeditions to India, to the Arabian Gulf and to East Africa under the Moslem eunuch admiral Zheng He at the beginning of the fifteenth century.

The earliest documents concerning gunpowder give advice not on how to make it, but on how to avoid making it. It appears to have been discovered in the course of peaceful concoction of elixirs by an eleventh-century philosopher who accidentally singed his beard. However the story that the Chinese subsequently used it only for fireworks is apocryphal: it was told by a Chinese emperor to a visiting Westerner as a self-deprecatory joke. In reality the Chinese used gunpowder from the first in warfare, mainly to explode in projectiles hurled by mechanical means or to frighten their enemies with noise and smoke. Its adaptation to the task of propelling

China's greatest contributions to science and technology in the past were the so-called 'Four Inventions': paper, printing, gunpowder and the magnetic compass.
Top: paper-making,
introduced to court in 105 AD by the eunuch Cai Lun, had been discovered by anonymous craftsmen probably at

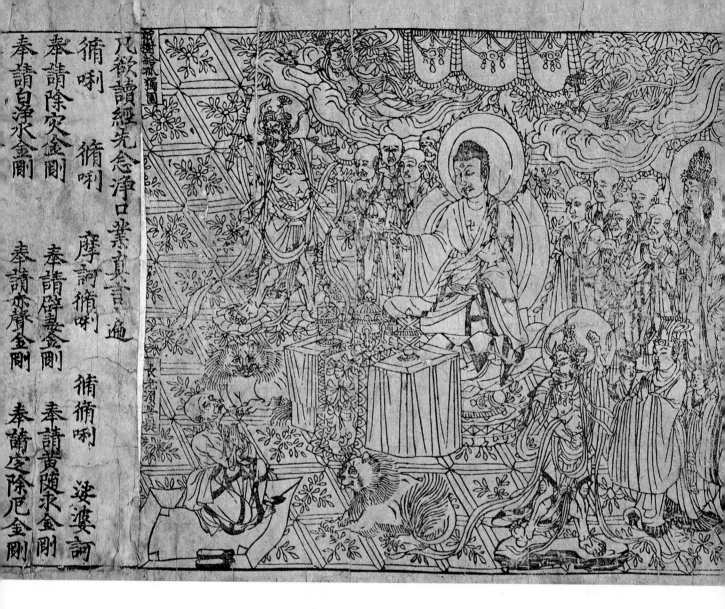

least two centuries earlier.

Left, middle: Gunpowder was apparently discovered in the course of alchemical experiments in the Song Dynasty (960-1279). This drawing, showing arrows being fired by gunpowder, is from a 17th-century treatise on the art of war.

Left, bottom: The Chinese discovered that when a lodestone, a piece of naturally magnetic iron ore, was placed on a polished bronze surface, it rotated to align itself north and south.

Above: The Diamond Sutra of 868 AD, a sacred Buddhist scroll, is among the oldest printed texts in the world, and the first with a printed date.

cannonballs seems to have been due in large measure to the Mongols, and to have been spread by them through Asia Minor to the West.

It is not perhaps surprising that two of 'the four inventions', paper and wood-block printing, concern bureaucracy closely . The invention of paper is traditionally ascribed to a court eunuch, Cai Lun, in the year 105, though recent archaeological discoveries have established that craftsmen had invented it at least two centuries before he introduced it to court and took the credit for it. Before this, and for some time after, the Chinese wrote their official records on bamboo strips which could be bundled together as in a mat to form long documents. When aesthetic considerations outweighed those of cost they used silk.

Wood-block printing followed in the eighth or ninth century. The first printed texts appear to have been Buddhist prayers; the multiplication of sacred texts, whether by copying or by printing, was considered virtuous in Mahayana Buddhism, a parallel to the mass-production of statuary in so-called 'Thousand Buddha Caves'. From the tenth century onwards,

Modern Chinese rockets being launched. There have been many campaigns for modernization in China since the 19th century. The current one, the so-called 'Four Modernizations', refers to agriculture, industry, science-and-technology and defence.

printing was used to transmit the standardized Confucian classical texts which formed the examination curriculum; and more than a thousand years ago the Chinese had invented that prime weapon of bureaucratic warfare, the pre-printed official form.

Early Chinese printing was mainly done by cutting an entire page onto a single block of wood; the great number of Chinese characters made this more economical even after the invention of movable type. A few experiments with pottery movable type were made in the eleventh century, and with metal type in the thirteenth century, particularly in Korea, where it was perfected some two hundred years later, about the time Gutenberg was first using it in Europe.

On 18 March 1978 Deng Xiaoping addressed a National Science Conference which celebrated the end of more than a decade of isolation in Chinese science:

In ancient times China had brilliant achievements in science and technology; its four great inventions played a significant role in the advance of world culture . . . But our ancestors' achievements can serve only to confirm our confidence in catching up with and surpassing advanced world levels and not to console us on our backwardness today. China must embark vigorously on the Four Modernizations of agriculture, industry, national defence, and science and technology. The 'Gang of Four' made the absurd claim that 'if the Four Modernizations are carried through, capitalist restoration will happen on the same day' . . . Their wild sabotage brought our national economy to the brink of collapse and was increasing our distance from advanced world scientific and technical standards.

For example, Deng said, an average farm worker in China was then producing about 1000 kilogrammes of grain a year, 'whereas in the United States the figure is over 50,000 kilogrammes. . . Independence does not mean shutting the door on the world, nor does self-reliance mean blind opposition to everything foreign.*

In a ministerial report following Deng's speech the Chinese government announced that China ought to specialize in agriculture, energy, materials, computers, lasers, space, high energy physics and genetic engineering.* The development of lasers in China has been impressive. Laser science is a young field in which China did not have to make up a backlog of decades of research before beginning to contribute to new developments. In other fields also, there is little doubt that China can call on an impressive reservoir of scientific talent. The fact that striking successes have been achieved by scientists who have left China to work in the United States and Europe suggests that, given comparable facilities, the Chinese can produce comparable results.

But there are obstacles to be overcome. One is the language barrier. International scientific information has to be channelled into domestic circulation through translation from other languages (in this case mainly English). One of the main purposes of the present Chinese computer development programme is to invent methods for automatic translation.

The flow of information from China to the rest of the world can be equally slow, though this has in the past been for political and administrative reasons as much as for linguistic ones. The delay in publication caused by the Cultural Revolution is probably the only reason why the Shanghai Institute of Biochemistry failed to be awarded a Nobel Prize for its successful synthesis of insulin in 1965.

Another obstacle is the fact that Chinese scientists are closely controlled by officials without scientific training. Bureaucracy has a moral authority in China that is often used, as in the past, to make people accept obstruction and inertia. The abiding emphasis on seniority makes it difficult for scientific organizations to get rid of incompetents. It is also complained that it is difficult to terminate research programmes that are not doing anything useful.

In addition, the ideology which the bureaucracy professes is based on a nineteenth-century mechanistic conception of science, in which 'the march of science' is portrayed as unfailingly progressive. The Chinese authorities find it difficult to deal with pollution or even to admit that economic growth may entail such costs. But the greatest difficulty facing the Chinese is probably the fact that they have had to begin their modernization programme from a weaker position than any other equally ambitious nation. As a poor country economically, China cannot afford mistakes of the kind that richer countries can write off daily without concern. Yet as a country with a rich intellectual inheritance, China may resent any sign of relative backwardness, and may feel tempted either to deny it or to attempt 'great leaps' to overcome it.

CREATING

INK BAMBOO AND ROCK

'When I first saw him,' wrote a contemporary about the poet, painter and scholar-official Su Dongpo (1036-1101), 'he was slightly drunk and said, "Could you paste this paper on the wall?" . . . Then he rose and made the bamboos, a bare tree and a strange rock.'*

Or as Su put it himself, writing about a similar occasion:

> When my empty bowels receive wine, angular strokes come forth,
> And my heart's crisscrossings give birth to bamboo and rock.
> What is about to be produced in abundance cannot be retained:
> It erupts on your snow-white wall.*

It is not surprising that scholar-officials often painted when under the influence of wine, or, as sometimes with Su Dongpo, when rising from sleep after drinking with friends, fellow officials who also might need to drink to release their creative spirit from its daytime restraints. Wine was part of the way of life of the scholar-official in the country, off-duty or in disgrace, and it has been connected with all the arts in China.

To retire from the court was the ambition or at least the consolation of many Chinese scholars. Yang Yun, a disgraced official of the Han Dynasty (206 BC-AD 220), described his country life in these terms:

When I have finished my work, I roast a sheep or bake a lamb, draw a pint of wine and console myself with it . . . My wife plays the zither very well. And I have a few slave girls and maids who can sing. When the wine has reddened my ears, I look up at heaven and, beating the measure on an earthen jar I start shouting 'woo woo'. Then I sing a song:

> . . . for enjoying this brief life,
> Why strive for wealth and honour?

On such a day, I straighten my robe and am happy. Swinging my sleeves I rock my head, tapping my feet I start to dance. And who shall say that such untrammeled amusement is not seemly?*

Many poets celebrated such moments of inebriation, notably Li Bai (Li Po) (701-62), who is said to have died when tipsy by falling out of a boat while embracing the moon's reflection in the water:

Huang Yongyu, one of China's foremost living artists, draws inspiration from the river and lake scenery in Hunan Province where he was born. He has made his own style out of a combination of Western influences with certain traditional Chinese techniques such as 'flung ink'.

An ink painting entitled 'Bamboo in the Wind' by the 14th-century artist Wu Zhen, shows the close relationship between such painting and calligraphy. The same brush can be used for both, and in either case the work is executed in a single flow, without hesitation or revision. Bamboo was a favourite subject for Chinese scholar-officials. Its pliancy and uprightness represented the spirit of the 'superior man' who could adapt to adversity and change without sacrificing his integrity.

With wine I sit
absent to Night, till
(Fallen petals
in folds of my gown)

I stagger up
to stalk the brook's moon:
The birds are gone
and people are few.*

The original Chinese form of this poem consists of only four lines of five syllables each and, like most Chinese poems, it rhymes. There is even more left to the imagination than in this spare English translation. Since there are no tenses, singulars, plurals, definite or indefinite articles in Chinese, each line is merely five monosyllabic words. The third line, which conveys the idea of moon and man keeping pace together as the poet follows its reflection along the stream, would be rendered literally as:

> Drunk
> rise
> pace
> brook
> moon

The reader has to do the rest by imagination.

Even Li Bai's contemporary Du Fu, the poet often contrasted with Li Bai for his sobriety, wrote a poem about getting drunk on the day he heard that the An Lushan Rebellion was finally crushed. These two, with Su Dongpo, are generally considered to be China's greatest poets. Su Dongpo was not himself a great painter: his influence on painting was through his writings on the subject, and through his grasp of the essence of creativity as it was experienced by other Chinese artists.

Both writing and painting in China can be done in ink with the same brush; and Chinese calligraphy is itself an abstract, painterly art. The convergence of the two from the Tang Dynasty onwards brought about a kind of painting that can be done in the same spirit as a piece of calligraphy, in a single flow, without interruption or hesitation and without revision; for in such art there is none of the possibility of painting over that oil-paint allows. One must thus have grasped, before putting brush to paper, the essence of what it is one is painting.

For the Chinese painter each living creature, each plant, and rock has its own vital force, *qi*, and the *qi* within the painter resonates or exchanges energies with this outer energy. Thus in painting bamboo one must first have the perfected bamboo in mind. Then comes the moment of complete concentration and at the same time complete abandon: 'When one takes up the brush and gazes intently one sees what one wants to paint. Then one rises hurriedly and wields the brush to capture what one sees. It is like the hare's leaping up and the falcon's swooping down; if there is the slightest slackening, then the chance is gone.'* Or as Su wrote about his friend Wen Tong (Yuko), who taught him to paint:

> When Yuko painted bamboo,
> He saw bamboo, not himself.
> Nor was he simply unconscious of himself:
> Trance-like, he left his body.
> His body was transformed into bamboo,
> Creating inexhaustible freshness . . .*

Bamboo painting, the closest of all forms to calligraphy, was a favourite genre for scholar-painters, both because it lent itself to the brush-strokes used in writing and also because it represented the spirit of the *wen ren*, the independent man of integrity or 'superior man', who bends but will not break, and whose uprightness is his most immediately obvious quality. Su Dongpo used to refer to paintings of bamboo as the 'gentlemen on the wall'. The *wen ren* represented the ethical ideal of the neo-Confucian scholar-official.

Su Dongpo was himself one of China's most famous, if not most successful, administrators. As a Confucian bureaucrat, he could call on a tradition of stately, lucid prose to address the emperor directly:

'My dominion over the mass of people', says the Book of Documents, 'is as precarious as the driving of a team of six horses with rotten reins,' meaning that no position in the whole land is as insecure as that of the ruler. When his people are united they become his subjects; when disunited, his enemies; and the space between union and disunion will not admit even the breadth of hair . . . It is entirely upon the allegiance of his people that the ruler depends. Popular allegiance is as necessary to the ruler as the root to a tree, as oil to the lamp, water to the fish or goods to the merchant . . . None but a madman who courted death and disaster would venture to give free rein to the desires of his own heart in defiance of the will of the people.*

Off-duty with music and wine, he can describe a moonlit expedition to the Red Cliff in a poetic prose of his own invention:

A cool wind blew gently, without starting a ripple. I raised my cup to drink to the guests; and we chanted the Full Moon Ode, and sang out the verse about the modest lady. After a while the moon came up between the Dipper and the Herdboy Star; a dewy whiteness spanned the river, merging the light on the water into the sky. We let the tiny reed drift on its course, over ten thousand acres of dissolving surface which streamed to the horizon, as though we were leaning on the void with the winds for chariot.*

Su was a strikingly gifted young man who had passed high into the imperial administration, and yet never seemed able to come to terms with its factional politics or the intricacies of its rules. In the alternations of imperial power politics he backed the wrong side almost consistently, and had a life of failed promise. He was banished to the south coast, and then to the island of Hainan, a place of exile then fever-ridden and not one where an ageing scholar-official could expect to stay alive for long. He turned increasingly in his old age to Buddhist ideas. He had had a religious mother and had been educated by a Daoist teacher and is a vivid example of a neo-Confucian in whose nature 'the three teachings' had flowed into one.*

His poetry reflects this versatile nature. It is thoughtful, almost 'metaphysical', and shows the concerns of an unquiet scholar-official; yet nature imagery can suddenly illuminate it.

> Do you want to know what the passing year is like?
> A snake slithering down a hole.
> Half his long scales already hidden,
> How to stop him getting away?
> Grab his tail and pull, you say? . . .
> I get up and look at the slanting Dipper.
> How could I hope next year won't come –
> My mind shrinks from the failures it may bring.
> I work to hold onto the night.
> While I can still brag I'm young.*

In another vein, his verse can present the suffering of the poor simply and dramatically, as in this poem put into the mouth of a farmer's wife:

> . . . My tears are all cried out, but rain never ends . . .
> We sold the ox to pay taxes, broke up the roof for kindling;
> We'll get by for a time, but what of next year's hunger?
> Officials demand cash now – they won't take grain;
> The long north-west border tempts invaders.
> Wise men fill the court – why do thing get worse?
> I'd be better off bride to the River Lord.*

Su tried to alleviate the sufferings he saw by writing memorials to the court, but to little avail. One great administrative achievement did crown his life: the draining and clearing of the great West Lake at Hangzhou, where he was prefect: a freshwater reservoir of immense size that defined the shape of the city, which then had a hundred thousand inhabitants but was soon to become the southern imperial capital of a million, when the Song court fled from the invading Mongols in 1126. The inhabitants blessed Su's memory, not only for the water in their wells, but for a causeway built for pleasure-strollers across the broad part of the lake: a touch that shows the hand of the poet-administrator, that uniquely Chinese phenomenon, at work.

The Chinese regarded the enjoyment of landscape painting as analogous to strolling across a lake or walking in nature. Although there is perspective in Chinese landscape painting it is a moving perspective, designed to allow a viewer to inspect a wide painting or a scroll, and to see each new scene as if he were in front of it. All the houses in any part of the painting are face-on to the viewer, and the receding lines run not to a single vanishing point but to a moving series of them.

Shadows are almost never found in traditional Chinese landscape painting. The Chinese painter did not limit his representation to a particular time of day any more than to a single point of view. The scholarly painter in particular sought to portray the inner spirit of *qi* of a scene, to fix an idea of its

essence. In the words of the polymath scientist and critic Shen Gua (1010-93), every element in painting should be considered 'much as we look at an artificial rockery in our own gardens. . . "from the angle of totality".'*

Landscape painting was the dominant pictorial tradition in China from the Tang Dynasty (618-906) onwards. Its theoretical basis was firmly established in the Five Dynasties and the Northern Song Dynasty when painters were seeking for a new realism. They concentrated on compositions with a few powerful motifs – a single mountain, a valley, a waterfall, and a group of trees – and portrayed them with carefully chosen texture-strokes (cun). The Song painter Guo Xi describes three ways of portraying mountains, using different kinds of strokes for 'high distance, deep distance, and level distance'. The first, which is the view of a mountain-top from below, has a 'clear and bright' tone; and the effect of height is achieved by expressing an upward force in the brush-strokes. 'Depth' is obtained by piling layer on layer; and an effect of 'level distance', looking across at a mountain from an opposite height, is obtained by the use of 'misty lines which gradually disappear.'*

The first of these three methods – high distance – was the dominant mode in this early period. One example is the hanging scroll 'Travellers Among Streams and Mountains'* by the early Northern Song artist Fan Kuan. The painting is simply but powerfully constructed in two halves. The lower third is a valley in which the landscape is shown in detail. A misty area separates this from the upper two thirds of the painting occupied by a massive centrally-placed mountain. The height and distance of the mountain compared with the foreground valley are indicated by a number of techniques: the prominence of the mountain's vertical ridges, the use of a single line for the waterfall, the short, broken texture-strokes depicting the rock surface, and the distant scrub on the mountain-top. There trees are shown as generalized masses of vegetation. By contrast, the valley-floor is portrayed meticulously: trees are individually depicted, and even realistic

details such as dead branches are evident. A stream is shown falling from one level to the next and its vivid portrayal justifies the remark made by Mi Fu (1052-1107) that 'in Fan Kuan's landscapes you can even hear the water.'

Landscape painting in China took two divergent paths from the Tang Dynasty onwards. They were classified much later as the 'northern' and 'southern' schools. A fine example of what was later to be called the northern school is an anonymous scroll called 'The Journey of Minghuang to Shu', representing the emperor's flight from the An Lushan Rebellion in 755. This school, whose influence persisted after its time among professional painters and court painters, painted landscape in a detailed way, and used colour, particularly delicate blues and greens.

The other tradition looked for its models to Su Dongpo's writings and, beyond them, to the Tang Dynasty poet-painter Wang Wei (669-759). It favoured a calligraphic, spontaneous style which left out everything but essentials. The fact that the scholarly tradition could be contrasted with that of the professional painters was, for the scholars, one of its appeals: for it was

A section from the handscroll 'Dwelling in the Fuchun Mountains' (1350), by Huang Gongwang (1269-1354). It is a classic example of what was later to be called the 'southern school' of Chinese landscape painting, which eschewed colour and omitted all that was not considered essential. It was favoured by scholar-officials who looked back to the ideas of Su Dongpo.

partly to distinguish themselves from the common people and from professionals that they stressed those qualities in the arts that to them were the hallmarks of the 'superior man'. The absence of detail – since detail was the way the professional painter showed his skill – was a way of saying gracefully that the scholar-painter was not a paid hack; he could even admit, as Su Dongpo did, that he was not very good at painting, that he always had a little awkwardness (*ruo*). After Su Dongpo and his circle laid down the theory of the amateur inspirational manner and defined it as the only appropriate one for officials, most scholar-painters from the next dynasty, the Yuan (1279-1368), onwards continued to follow them.

The classification into northern and southern schools of landscape painting was invented in the seventeenth century and was intended to reflect a certain disdain for the 'northerners'. It had little to do with geography, since a southern school painter might have come from the north, but referred at least in part to the distinction between northern or 'gradualist' Buddhism and southern, 'subitist' Buddhism. The former retained the original Indian idea that enlightenment comes only by a meticulous increment of one good deed on another. Similarly northern landscape painting is meticulous and detailed. In subitism – particularly prominent in Chan Buddhism, which is fused with Daoist ideas – enlightenment is believed to come in a flash, or not at all, and may be lost as rapidly as it comes. *

Some Daoist and Chan Buddhist painters used a technique known as flung ink; it reflected the distrust of conscious planning and control which they shared. They also sometimes specialized in dragon painting: the dragon

This rapid ink painting entitled 'Two Minds in Harmony', thought to be by the Song Dynasty painter Shi Ke, is an example of the spontaneity favoured by Chan Buddhists and Daoists. It is thought that the broad lines of the painting were drawn with a bunch of straw dipped in ink. The sage at rest on the back of a resting tiger illustrates an essential Daoist idea: that of harmony between man and nature.

could be the symbol of 'the *Dao* itself, an all-pervading force which momentarily reveals itself to us only to vanish again, and leaves us wondering if we had actually seen it at all.'* It is said of the dragon painter Chen Rong, a scholar-official of the thirteenth century, that he 'would give a great shout' when he was drunk, 'seize his cap, soak it with ink, and smear on the design with it, afterwards finishing the details with a brush'.*

Today the choice between meticulousness and spontaneity is still a real one to many Chinese artists. Some painters begin in the former way, then abandon detail and go for spontaneity, and for the 'marrow of the bone', as the modern painter Huang Yongyu puts it:

There are two approaches to painting mountains and rivers. One is to paint them in a very earnest and delicate way. This approach can also express the spirit, the particular atmosphere. Another approach is to paint their 'marrow' and ignore all the other, unnecessary things. I took the former approach as a basis and trained myself strictly. I painted very delicately, seriously and carefully with the former approach, so that I tempered myself. Then I tried to paint things in a simple way but the best way. In our history many distinguished painters painted traditional Chinese paintings in this way. I am more fond of this approach.

Huang Yongyu, who was born in Fenghuang, in Hunan, south of the

Yangtze, of the Tujia national minority, is one of the most famous living painters in China. He is the nephew of one of China's foremost writers, Shen Congwen, who has vividly described the life of the Yuan River people of this border area where the provinces of Sichuan, Hunan and Guizhou meet. As Shen put it in 1982, 'Our home town is a beautiful place with a lot of mountains and many rivers. You can hear the tigers roaring in the daytime. I found these much more interesting than studying.' Or as he wrote in his autobiography:

All day long I wandered along the mountains and the orange orchards, watching, listening, smelling – the odours of dead snakes, decayed straw, the skin of the butchers which always retained the scent of blood, and then the smell rising from the kilns after rain, where the porcelain was being fired – listening to the sound of a bat, the sigh of a cow when it is being felled, the rattle of the great yellow-throated snakes and the faint sound of fish jumping in the water. *

Shen's nephew Huang Yongyu followed a similar path in his youth. Although both his parents were schoolteachers he preferred the outdoor world and frequently escaped into the river and lake country, there delighting in the natural forms which today he represents in his own new version of traditional techniques, 'flung ink' being among them.

In Chinese painting pre-existing models have usually played a large part: every painting has been seen as an interplay between nature, the painter's feelings and the tradition that he has inherited. The painter approaches the work of the past much as a pianist in the West might approach the existing compositions of great masters. His new painting is a performance, and in order to prepare for that performance he will quite naturally practise by learning, and by rehearsing the performances of earlier painters.

In the seventeenth century in particular, collections of models for amateur painters were gathered together and published. Perhaps the most famous of these was the *Mustard Seed Garden Manual of Painting*, published between 1679 and 1701. The garden was named after that of Li Yu, the poet famous for his love of crabs. The manual was compiled by his son-in-law. Li's small garden at Nanjing was named after a saying, 'All Mount Sumeru in a mustard seed', which was a familiar metaphor for compression. Compression and miniaturization have had a particular appeal for the Chinese: they seem to enjoy as a repeated marvel the fact that it is possible to comprehend in the microcosm of a landscape painting the macrocosm of nature itself. Frequent references are made in eulogies of painters to their capacity to concentrate 'a whole panorama of 10,000 *li* into a single inch of silk'.

In the same spirit of delight in the relation between microcosm and macrocosm the Chinese early cultivated informal gardens that have much of the asymmetry and the contrast between verticals and horizontals that they love in landscape painting; and they have miniaturized even these, taking pleasure in arrangements of small stones and plants called 'tray scenery'.

The ideal Chinese garden has always involved an expanse of water, and has seldom been of a regular or symmetrical shape. The most celebrated examples of this art are the gardens of Suzhou; the ready availability of water in the level lake country near the mouth of the Yangtze makes the city specially suitable for such miniature landscapes. They are designed to be looked at from definite places along the way during a walk. Thus 'moon gates', circular openings formed to frame a view in a particularly delightful way, abound. Pavilions with intricately cross-latticed windows are built at appropriate viewpoints, and often someone will have written some verses and placed them there, much as, from the Song Dynasty onwards, an inscription might be placed in any empty space in a landscape painting. The novel *The Red Chamber Dream* describes a scene where Baoyu's cousin, who has been honoured by being made an imperial concubine, is allowed a rare visit home; an entire new landscape garden is created for the occasion, and Baoyu, the young hero, displays his skill and his knowledge of the classics by thinking of appropriate texts to attach to the various pavilions. The eighteenth-century European fashion for informal gardens in reaction against the symmetrical splendours of Versailles, which is sometimes credited mainly to the English, owes a direct debt also to China, for it was the Jesuits' accounts of Chinese gardens in the late seventeenth century that helped to create the fashion.*

Often tall, weathered limestone rocks have been erected by the water, or in small courtyards with a level floor of pebbles and little other adornment. These come ideally from one particular lake, Taihu. They can have the fantastical shapes of great mountains, and are usually set up to model just the kind of cliffs that landscape painters delight in depicting. A level expanse of earth or of water is yin; a mountain upthrusting to the sky is yang. The Chinese word for landscape painting in general is *shanshui*, which means literally 'mountains and water', itself a balanced yinyang pair.

Although in Chinese landscape paintings human beings are usually no more than small and almost irrelevant details, the Chinese have also had a rich tradition of figure painting. It is in fact more ancient than landscape painting, since one of the chief uses of painting in the earliest days was the portrayal of Confucian sages and other virtuous persons, and the illustration of texts of ethical exhortation. One source of inspiration to figure painters has been the wealth of Buddhist imagery from India. A great number of Buddhist wall paintings covered the inside of Chinese caves and temples from the fourth or fifth century onwards. They are still providing a point of departure for certain contemporary artists in China, the best known of whom is Kong Boji, who has drawn much inspiration from the Dunhuang grottos and other sites of Buddhist murals in north-west China.* In general the effect of Buddhist art is to create an immensely complex scene in which demons and immortals, men and beasts, intertwined and bound together, defy the laws of gravity and perspective. Buddhism in its early days was also the inspiration for what may be the only Chinese sculpture to display the human body in a sensuous way, as in India. As it became domesticated, such sculpture took on an increasingly Chinese restraint.

Figure painting executed for the court also tended to be detailed and, as might be expected, to pay close attention to matters like costume, posture

A 'moon gate' frames a striking view in a traditional Chinese garden. The ideal Chinese garden, besides such gates, and pavilions with elaborately latticed windows, contains a lake and tall rocks chosen for their irregular outline, to remind the spectator of the yinyang balance of nature, and of the mountains and water characteristic of landscape painting.

A detail from a handscroll attributed to the figure painter Gu Kaizhi (?344-406) entitled 'The Admonitions of the Instructress to the Court Ladies'. The poem which accompanies the painting laments that many know how to adorn themselves but few know how to adorn their souls.

A detail from another famous Chinese figure painting, 'The Night Revels of Han Xizai', who is shown seated here. The painting is attributed to the 10th-century artist Gu Hongzhong.

and the placing of figures in strict hierarchical order. One famous work that combines detail with a form of ethical exhortation, 'The Admonitions of the Instructress to Court Ladies', is attributed to Gu Kaizhi, a painter of the fourth century, and is regarded as the classic instance of a certain brush-stroke, the 'iron-wire line', a long, continuous, thin stroke for portraying the outline of figures. Perhaps the most famous of all court paintings, 'The Night Revels of Han Xizai' is attributed to Gu Hongzhong, a painter of the Southern Tang (923-936) period. Allegedly the emperor had heard of the un-Confucian behaviour of Han Xizai, his prime minister, after hours, when singing girls and revellers crowded the apartments of the languidly attentive gentleman portrayed in the painting. He is shown listening to one girl playing the lute while another peers from behind a screen. The contemporary version of the concealed camera, the court painter, was sent to record the scene in detail, so that the prime minister, arriving for an audience with the emperor, could suddenly be confronted with the image of his evening self.* But the painter has produced a work of art in which it would be difficult to identify his own sympathies as on the emperor's side rather than on Han Xizai's.

Figure painting is also an element in the many illustrations of poetry, folksongs and stories that Chinese painters have produced. Su Dongpo's prose poem 'The Red Cliff' was constantly illustrated by painters. In the poem the moon, the poet, his friends and their shadows are described at the outset of a journey as keeping each other company, and illustrations to it are among the only instances in Chinese painting where shadows occur. Chinese poetry and painting fed each other alternately with subject matter: a poet illustrating a painter's work, another painter illustrating that poem. Each might draw on music for added inspiration: to provide a verse form for a poem, through the invocation of some folk tune (as in a poetic form much used by Su Dongpo), or by suggestion to create almost a musical accompaniment for a painting, as in the lovely Yuan Dynasty narrative scroll, 'Songs of a Nomad Flute', which tells the story of a Han princess married to a barbarian and carried off to the north. Paintings were called 'silent poems' by Su Dongpo's circle, and the silence was waiting to be filled by musical suggestions, much as spaces were left in the paintings to be elaborated on by later commentators, perhaps with a poem, perhaps with a reference to another painting, to a melody or to an anecdote about the painter's life.

The stress on allusiveness and suggestion reflected the intimacy of communication among a small elite of scholars with a similar education, who needed only to hint at a literary or painterly allusion to be certain that their select audience would understand an entire poem or a painting and all the generations of accepted commentary on it from a title alone. It was the commentary in addition to the original that constituted the painting's meaning for those who were fully members by education of the Chinese literary culture. A commentary might be written on a painting by a friend, by a later connoisseur or even an emperor. The Qianlong emperor in particular was notorious for writing what Chinese connoisseurs say are undistinguished remarks prominently on many paintings.

The scholar-painters were often in danger from the court; and under the rule of the Manchus, and still more under the Mongols, they might be torn by conflicting loyalties to Chinese civilization and to an emperor who was a foreigner and yet who nevertheless held the strings of power and employment in the most rewarding career open to an educated man in China. The habit of obliquity and omission in painting could not only remind its conquered audience of their common civilization by its discreet hints at a culture the conquerors could not fully participate in, but could avoid the risks that an open expression of reluctant loyalty would entail. Thus the painter Zhao Mengfu, pressed by a Mongol emperor to work for him, succumbed, but left a discreet metaphor for his shame in a picture of a sheep and a goat – representing a captured Han Dynasty general, Su Wu, 'upholding the spirit of loyalty while herding sheep in the regions of Xinghai', as a later commentator explained – that meant a whole story of apology and regret to those in his confidence, and meant nothing, he must have hoped, to the emperor.

A detail from the painting 'Literary Gathering in Apricot Garden' by Xie Tingjun, showing scholars with a scroll in a garden.

Even under the native Chinese Ming Dynasty (1368-1644) a scholar-official might find every aspect of his painting or poetry scrutinized by eunuchs and censors for nuances that could be interpreted as subversive. One unfortunate Ming landscape painter was ruined because he painted a fisherman in one of his pictures wearing red, the colour that only an official should be allowed to be seen in. The habit of saying as little as possible, and so keeping clear of the court and all its ways, was thus wise.

Distrust on the part of artists and philosophers of those who wield power goes back a long way in Chinese history and mythology. When the Emperor Yao four thousand years ago became tired of governing, he is said to have looked round for a successor, and to have selected a sage called Chao Fu who 'in his distaste for human affairs had taken to living in the high branches of a tree, in a kind of nest he had formed for himself. The Emperor talked long about the glories of the "Dragon Throne" - "Why not leave your strange dwelling for the splendours of the Royal Palace?" Yao's words passed him by like the wind; at his departure Chao Fu washed his ears.'*

In the same immemorial spirit of detachment, the writer Shen Congwen, uncle of Huang Yongyu the painter, distances himself from the capital today:

I have never believed in power. I don't like it and I don't have the ability to fight for it. I think wisdom is more important than power. I want knowledge, so I read a lot of books and try to write in many different ways. If I am successful I don't care, but if I fail I think it is inevitable. Politics changes too fast. It changes every two or three years, and before a writer has his book published the situation has already altered. The writer's work should cover every aspect of humanity. It is wrong to follow a certain regime too closely. If one follows too closely, it will become a kind of burden.

In his early years, and with a similar detachment, Shen Congwen had ignored the fluctuations of life in a commercial society:

Huang Yongyu, like many other leading artists and writers, was sent to the countryside during the Cultural Revolution and, when he returned, was accused by Jiang Qing (Madame Mao) of having insulted her by painting a picture of an owl with one eye shut. After the arrest of his accuser, he painted one every day.

Teachers in Qinghua University who came back from America could earn four or five hundred yuan, but as a professional writer I could get no more than forty yuan. So my life was very hard and tense. But I didn't care and I always felt that I could control myself . . . So far I have written seventy books, yet I haven't got any income. The dealers made a fortune. I didn't care. I used to say 'It doesn't matter.' I always thought the main thing I wanted was to work.

During the Cultural Revolution humiliations and hardships were imposed on him. Again he exhibited the same spirit of detachment and restraint. And when, after the Cultural Revolution, he was 'rehabilitated', he simply 'washed his ears': 'Chairman Mao called me to an interview and told me that they wanted me to write. But I didn't. Isn't it nice to be in demand? But demanding cannot produce written works.'

Most of the other leading writers and artists of China also suffered in the Cultural Revolution. Ya Ming, the leader of the Nanjing school of painting, among the most prominent of the established painters recognized by the authorities in the 1980s, had his house ransacked by Red Guards, robbers, minor artists and dissidents; some of his paintings subsequently turned up on the Hong Kong art market. He was sent to do hard labour in the countryside.* Yuan Yunsheng, who was later to paint some famous murals at Beijing Airport, was sent to the countryside with other Fine Arts Academy teachers. The writer Lao She, two days after being criticized and beaten up by a mass of Red Guards, was discovered drowned in a pond; it is not known how he died. The young painter Tang Muli had to watch his father, the film director Tang Xiaodan, being beaten by Red Guards in front of a crowd of 10,000 people.*

Huang Yongyu spent three and a half years doing hard labour on a farm, together with colleagues from the Beijing Central Academy of Fine Arts. His creativity was not suppressed:

If during the daytime we couldn't paint, because in the daytime we had to be criticized, we had to attend meetings and to be denounced, then sometimes at night I used to paint from two o'clock till dawn. Therefore many and many of my paintings were done at that time. They were very serious and concentrated paintings. Meanwhile I developed a skill that whenever I heard somebody coming towards my room, within a few seconds I could change my room into one which looked as if nobody had been painting there. At that time I painted about one or two hundred paintings. Anybody could realize that such a situation was abnormal. Such a situation could not last. We were full of this kind of hope and so we went on with our work confidently.

In 1974 Huang Yongyu was attacked by followers of Jiang Qing (Madame Mao), who raided the Beijing Hotel while he and other painters were decorating it. Jiang Qing had been infuriated by an owl with one eye shut that Huang had allegedly painted to insult her. Doing things 'with one eye shut' is certainly a Chinese phrase referring to corruption in high places; but much more was read into it than that. The owl was said to be a 'black painting': it demonstrated that the painter wanted 'to restore the capitalist road' and it revealed his support for Prime Minister Zhou Enlai, Jiang Qing's greatest opponent.

To the surprise of many artists and party members, Huang Yongyu was chosen after the death of Mao to execute one of the works of art for his mausoleum in Tiananmen Square. It is a vast tapestry made from an oil sketch, a panorama of the great mountains of China assembled in a sea of mist. Many officials of the Communist Party came to peer at the work in the six months it took to execute it, and Huang Yongyu spent a time of considerable anxiety before it was completed.*

At least one of today's prominent young painters, Luo Zhongli, was once a Red Guard himself. Having expressed suitable shame at this aberration, he has gone on to become famous for a work that is almost hyper-realist in style, 'My Father'. He teaches at the Sichuan Art College, where he was a pupil. The forms of art taught in the school and the range of works on exhibition give a broad impression of the styles now available to a young Chinese painter.

The college is divided into two: a traditional Chinese department and a Western department. Students study both approaches. In the traditional department the techniques taught to young painters include the entire curriculum of inherited principles, brush-strokes and conventions of representation, headed by the venerable 'six principles of painting' first laid down in the second quarter of the sixth century and unaltered in wording since, though they appear to have meant rather different things to different painters over the centuries:

Luo Zhongli's 'Faithful Souls' (top) is a visionary painting commemorating a young girl who died in a demonstration in 1976 in honour of Zhou Enlai and against the regime of Mao and Jiang Qing.

1. 'Harmony of spirit, motion of life' [the picture coming to life through the *qi* of the painter and the *qi* of what he paints being in accord].
2. A strong bone-structure in the brush-work, [as a way of expressing this vital energy].
3. Faithfulness to subject-matter.
4. Likeness in colour.
5. Placing with care.
6. Preserving and transmitting the ancient models by copying.

To put into practice the second principle Chinese painters have been able to call on a whole range of different 'texture-strokes' (*cun*): for example the 'axe-cut', a rugged chopping stroke; the 'hemp-fibre' and 'dragon-vein' strokes for a more relaxed and graceful kind of drawing.* Other strokes include 'rain-drop', a vertical stroke squared off at each end, used by Fan Kuan for the mountain in the scroll 'Travellers Among Streams and Mountains'; and 'crab-claw branches', a method of portraying trees in winter, with the ends of the branches curling over.

Every element that can occur in a traditional Chinese landscape painting has long had an almost calligraphic, accepted way of rendering it: a single brush-stroke for a bamboo leaf, two hooked strokes for a face, a set of rapid angular lines for a leafless tree. Houses, bamboos, and the fishermen, herdboys and contemplative scholars who formed the main repertoire of amateur landscape painting had all been illustrated by manuals in the later part of the Ming Dynasty and the early Qing, as had the established methods of drawing birds, flowers and other conventional subjects. They did not

A detail showing the use of the 'axe-cut' texture-stroke, a bold stroke painted with the side of the brush, from 'Scholar by a Waterfall' by the Southern Song painter Ma Yuan (active 1190-1225).

Detail from 'A Buddhist Temple in the Mountains', attributed to Li Cheng (10th century) shows the crab-claw method, said to have been originated by him, for depicting trees in winter.

seem conventional in any pejorative sense to the Chinese of the Ming Dynasty, nor do they in the art schools of China, it seems, today.

In the Western department of the Sichuan Art College the main influence used to be from no further west than Russia. Soviet realism has formed a style for some dramatic statements of protest, not so much against capitalism recently as against the excesses of the Cultural Revolution: for example a striking picture of a professor outside his smashed laboratory, looking in at his ruined work as he tends an odd goat or sheep.* A more conventionally Stalinist work shows a stern father in military uniform looking on approvingly as his son, with shaven head, having betrayed the state by committing some crime, is about to be carried away in a lorry for execution. In these works the Victorian materialism of Karl Marx's legacy and the art teacher's need to show his mastery of detail combine to give an even-handed precision to the rendering of every object in the picture. The contrast with the selectiveness of Su Dongpo and the spontaneity of 'flung ink' technique is complete.

Russian influence is apparently not considered as unfashionable in contemporary art schools as the naïve poster painting done in the communes in the Cultural Revolution and at the time lauded as the new kind of people's art. The Huxian Production Brigade was allegedly the originator of this style; it was subsequently imitated all over China. But now anything that reminds people of the 'Terrible Ten Years' is out of fashion, and it is not represented in the repertoire of styles taught. The ebullient charm of some of these paintings, such as those by Zhu Shouzhen of Jinshan County, makes an immediate appeal, like the dances and games performed for visitors by the smiling kindergarten children of China; and like them it leaves a question about what lies behind the optimistic, flat surface.

Other pervasive models for young Chinese painters would seem to include the work of Andrew Wyeth, Bonnard and the nineteenth-century French masters of domestic realism. There would appear to be an influence almost of the late Sir Russell Flint or the Coca-Cola poster on many painters. One example is the rendering of the main figure, in a painting by Luo Zhongli, of the ascension, apparently into heaven, of a girl killed in a provincial demonstration in 1976 against the regime of Mao Zedong and Jiang Qing. The most famous such demonstration, which took place in Tiananmen Square in Beijing*, inspired another painting, 'Protecting the Wreaths', by Ai Xian, which manages to fuse the heroic revolutionary tradition with the almost chocolate-box approach to the painting of the young girl in its centre.* After the years of Cultural Revolution during which only political dogma was allowed to inspire works of art, and in which differences in the appearance of the sexes were minimized in both art and dress, the Chinese do not appear at present to distinguish very strongly between a beautiful painting of a face and almost any painting of a beautiful face.

A recent development in art schools has been the restoration of nude painting, which is not traditional in China. In the 1920s and 1930s the nude

was permitted to some extent in art schools, and the practice continued for a
time after 1949, but it was banned as alien to China during the Cultural
Revolution. Since then the late Prime Minister Zhou Enlai's notes on the
Venus de Milo and other works of classical sculpture, made on postcards
when he was a student in Paris, have been published, and this has helped
slightly to make the idea of the nude less unrespectable. But there is still a
widespread feeling that it should be only for the minority, for the art school
or for the laboratory; a fear that nudes will be too arousing if shown in
public. When the painter Yuan Yunsheng, born near Suzhou in 1937,
portrayed some nude and half-nude figures in his murals 'Water Festival:
Song of Life' for the Beijing Airport, an official storm arose.* The festival he
had portrayed was the annual celebration of a 'national minority' in the
south-west, and it is said to be by no means unlike the scene in the painting.
However the representatives of the minority, after saying they quite liked
the pictures, were enjoined to remark officially that they were insulted by
them. The paintings had been unveiled at the opening ceremony of the
airport on 1 October 1979 as part of the celebrations of the thirtieth
anniversary of the People's Republic, and were clearly seen by many Han
Chinese Communist Party officials as a deep embarrassment to China, much
as if Queen Victoria had attended a silver jubilee performance at the Albert
Hall and had been asked to watch, as the opening show, the Folies Bergères.

   The Chinese sometimes attempt to explain the virtual absence of nude
painting in their tradition by saying that they have always had a strong sense
of physical modesty, and that they have generally been more interested in the
character of a person than in appearances. The literature of China bears this
out, for it probably contains less sensuous poetry and prose than that of any

An illustration to a 17th-century edition of the satirical novel Jin Ping Mei *shows Gold Lotus, her maid Spring Plum and young Chen enacting what they have just studied in the silken frieze. Despite an unusual degree of physical modesty, and the absence of nude painting from the accepted genres of their art, the Chinese have until recently adopted a notably frank attitude to sexuality, and have made unashamed use of illustrated books in lovemaking.*

other culture. But the Chinese have always been quite frank about sexuality, at least until the last few decades. There have also been many illustrated books of a broadly pornographic nature in China. An otherwise decorous painting may show a woman or a man studying such pictures without apparent shame or furtiveness, while frequent references in poetry and prose suggest that erotic scrolls played an accepted part in lovemaking. In the Ming Dynasty novel *Jin Ping Mei*, which may have been written as a satire on an enemy of the author but in most respects, allowing for a degree of exaggeration, is realistic rather than pornographic in the sense of being intended to arouse desire, scenes of lovemaking are described with a notable frankness, and one of them in particular, an encounter between the concubine Gold Lotus, her maid Spring Plum and young Chen, who has been in love with Gold Lotus for two years, involves an unembarrassed reference to such works of art:

After they had drunk themselves into the mood, Gold Lotus removed all her clothes: young Chen and the maid followed her example; all three rejoiced in their rosy nudity, unimpaired by a thread of clothing. Now Gold Lotus took her place in one of those comfortable armchairs which were designed especially for drunken old gentlemen. Then she ordered Spring Plum to bring the silver lamp nearer, and to take from the picture-chest the silken frieze which had once adorned the chamber of an emperor . . . Snuggling close together, they examined, by the light of the lamp, the four-and-twenty sections of the frieze, in which were depicted, with perfect art, the most varied modes and phases of the sport of love. After they had gazed their fill they left the armchair for the wide cushions of the couch, in order to rehearse the pictorial lessons on their own persons. And the three abandoned themselves to the unutterable blisses of their passionate reunion. *

But in scholarly or court art since the Han Dynasty there has certainly been no nude painting.

Yuan Yunsheng has not been in favour in China since the unveiling and partial reveiling of the airport nudes some of whom subsequently appeared repainted with rather more on. Huang Yongyu, equally, is not one of the painters generally held up as a model in art schools. He has lived in Hong Kong and visited America, and has absorbed Western influences, combining them with inherited Chinese techniques. The painting 'Red Lotus' for example, which portrays one of his favourite subjects, the water plants of the Hunan marshes, owes a debt both to abstract expressionism and to Chan Buddhist 'flung ink' technique.

But though Huang has absorbed abstract expressionist ideas from the West, pure abstraction makes no appeal to him. After he visited the Whitney Museum in New York he said he could see no meaning in the abstract art there. Chinese painting, in seeking what he calls the 'marrow', may come close to abstraction, but it never seems to seek for a completely non-figurative approach. The title of a Chinese painting is always essential to it. The same is true of the title of a piece of music. Lin Hua, a composer working in Shanghai, though he uses Western instruments and Western forms like the string quartet, looks back to Tang poetry for some of the titles and literary suggestions that give the depth of meaning he wishes to convey in his music. One of his compositions, 'Seeing a Friend off in Yangguan' is based on a poem by the man often named by later critics as the forefather of the southern school of landscape painting, Wang Wei (669-759). The composition evokes the poem by its title without needing to go into detail, because the composer is confident that his listeners share a common culture with him, and from the title alone will understand a whole range of allusions to the poem, even to the form of the original, which he has echoed in the three-part structure of his own composition:

According to Wang Wei, who wrote the poem, he saw his friend off in Yangguan three times, and each time in a different way. His friend was about to leave; he felt very sorrowful. Even so, still he tried his best to restrain his passion. Especially in the end, he wanted to say something, but he didn't. I think that the main difference between Chinese and Western modes of thinking lies in this. In composing I must take into account the characteristics of Chinese people. Our aesthetic standards stress quiet elegance and implication. Everything is expressed through suggestion. If a Westerner describes his feelings he speaks them out thoroughly. But the Chinese are different. If a Chinese wants to say something, he restrains himself; that is to say, he intends to speak out something, but he might stop.

The way in which a poem or a picture may echo each other and give rise to a composition which may perhaps in turn inspire another poem or another picture is characteristic of Chinese art. It is particularly characteristic of that tradition created by the scholar-officials; and as there have been two traditions of painting in China, so two traditions have also developed in music, one for the scholarly elite and the other related to the popular arts. The scholar would take his lute and play as he sat by himself or as he accompanied the recital of poetry, which the Chinese tend to chant in a sing-song voice. This lute music was an austere and simple art, as slender as that of the line-painting that constituted the scholarly art of landscape. There was also a court tradition of ceremonial music, using full orchestra, and this in turn was related to the more popular narrative arts through opera, which in China has always been a popular form not restricted to elite audiences.

Just as every painting in China portrays a scene or tells a human story, so Chinese music is generally programme music, not in the sense of describing a particular scene or event but rather because it expresses the composer's inner response to it. For Lin Hua this is another essential difference between Western and Chinese methods of composition:

Westerners stress their respect for objective things and stress description, while we Chinese put the stress on the expression of the subjective sentiment. One of my compositions is called 'Shepherd Boy and Spring Rain'. If a Western composer were writing it he might tend to imitate the sound of the rain. But this is not the same in China. My composition puts the stress on the expression of the subjective feeling. The spring came to the countryside; I seemed to smell the scent of the earth which had been turned over and it seemed to be between raining and not raining. I did not consider description; I wrote of my feelings at a particular time.

Today all Chinese artists – musicians, writers and painters, and more obviously the practitioners of the newer electronic arts – have to make their own fusion of such dense traditional influences with modern and international techniques and ideas.

Seated figures embracing carved from a section of bamboo by Wang Keping (born 1949). As a member of the Xing xing *(Star-star) group, Wang Keping is generally labelled a 'dissident': the protests he has made are for a greater degree of freedom for practising artists. He is self-taught, and generally works in wood, in bold figurative forms.*

TRADING

INTO THE FOUR SEAS

Having learned that the world was round, Chrisopher Columbus set out westward, bound for the East, impelled by the idea that fabulous fortunes could be made through trading with the Orient. This belief – about China in particular – survives today in the continent he discovered on the way. However, not only in America but also in Europe it has now taken a new form. Instead of being seen as a rich source of luxuries to import to the West – silk, tea, works of craftsmanship – China in the twentieth century has been viewed as a vast mass-market: a thousand million mouths. Many businessmen have had fantasies such as, 'If only each Chinese could be persuaded to drink one bottle of Coca-Cola a year,' or 'Could the Chinese not be encouraged to buy the European butter-mountain?'* If wishes were cassette-recorders the Chinese would have music wherever they went; but China's numbers do not constitute a massive source of purchasing power as long as people do not have the money and the foreign exchange to buy.

China is still at a comparatively early stage of development and is a largely self sufficient continental economy. Though her Gross National Product is the sixth largest in the world, roughly equal to that of France, her imports and exports together account for less than a fifth of it, though the proportion has been growing.* And there is another obstacle. That 7.5% is watched carefully by officials with a keen sense of tradition, whose predecessors have long regarded trade as despicable (under the empire), or (under the People's Republic) as reactionary in so far as it involved the profit motive.

A folk story is told in London of a company that tried for years in the nineteenth century to be allowed to build a railway in China. At last permission was granted, and the Chinese even said they would buy the railway. When it was built there was a grand ceremony: the Chinese officials arrived in their sedan chairs, received the documents handing over ownership of the permanent way, and gave a signal. Labourers with crowbars lined the track to the horizon and immediately dug it up. 'But you could get so much more quickly from one place to another if you had our railway,' said the engineers. 'Why', said the Chinese officials, 'should it be better to be in another place? And also, why quickly?'*

Chinese trade has traditionally been under the centralized control of a bureaucracy; and not just of any bureaucracy, but of the most ancient and most precedent-bound bureaucracy in the world. And the Chinese

*Shanghai is China's largest city, major port, and centre of foreign trade.
Its main thoroughfare, Wai Tan, formerly called the Bund,
recalls its status as one of the five Treaty Ports opened for foreign trade in 1842.*

247

A detail from a thirteenth-century handscroll showing 24 stages of silk-making. The detailed production techniques were secret. Finished silk was a major export for many centuries, travelling along the famous 'silk road' through central Asia, and eventually, by sea, to Europe.

government has not always been content with controlling trade; at various periods, usually for strategic reasons, it has suppressed it. The age-old antagonism between the entrepreneurial merchant and the state official, which is worldwide, has resulted, among the Chinese, in only a few victories for the traders; and they have occurred either when the bureaucracy was weak, when it was evaded, for example by piracy or smuggling, or when it was powerless because traders had emigrated.

The Chinese have earned a reputation as 'the most businesslike nation on earth', mainly through the activities of the overseas Chinese. But the practices of a nation's emigrés are no sure guide to their way of doing business at home. How far will China's mercantile qualities flourish among the mainland Chinese, in their external or in their internal trade, now that the state has decreed that its subjects should export, and since the death of Mao has tentatively relaxed its grip on some of their internal market activities also? And how successful will Westerners be in trading with the Chinese?

Ancient institutions and attitudes and time-honoured ways of dealing with life persist in China. In relation to the outside world one great myth in particular has remained dominant: that China has always been surrounded by culturally inferior 'barbarians'. This is a survival of ideas originally developed more than two thousand years ago; in fact all China's immediate neighbours had literate cultures from the eighth century AD onwards. A consequent idea, that no form of international relations save nominal 'submission' to China was possible, again goes against much historical precedent but was deeply entrenched in the Chinese official mind for many centuries. Nevertheless the Chinese government has never been able to ignore trade for long, if only because trade has always been closely intertwined with matters of diplomacy and war.

As far back as the Zhou Dynasty (1027-256 BC), traders became essential to the Chinese through their command of horses. The Chinese were threatened by nomad tribes from the north, riders who could shoot accurately with a bow from the back of a galloping horse. To protect themselves from these flying archers Chinese rulers built walls along the frontier; and here great markets were installed where the Chinese could barter their agricultural products, much needed by the nomads, for the horses, which were greatly prized by the Chinese. The horse-traders enriched by this wall traffic became the first powerful merchants. They acquired political influence with their immense profits. It is believed that Lü Buwei, whose native state of Zhao exported horses, and who was Qin Shihuangdi's first prime minister, was a horse dealer.

As the state's power grew the merchants, like the horses they traded, were harnessed. Foreign trade became the prerogative of the emperor. One way of subordinating the traders was to humiliate them. In Han times, it is said, they had to wear distinctive clothing, including a white turban inscribed with their name and trade; and in order to render their appearance even less dignified they were required to wear one white and one black shoe. They were not allowed to ride horses and were not eligible for the examinations which in time became the only path to public office; they were subject to taxes, but were prohibited from owning land. The scholar-officials, the farmers and artisans were all placed above them in the social order.

However, as in most aspects of Chinese life, there was a strong, balancing counter-current. The emperors themselves, as consumers of the rare and exotic, directly encouraged trade in such goods. As China developed and the population grew, local self-sufficiency became less feasible and inter-regional trade became necessary. Commercial specialists appeared in order

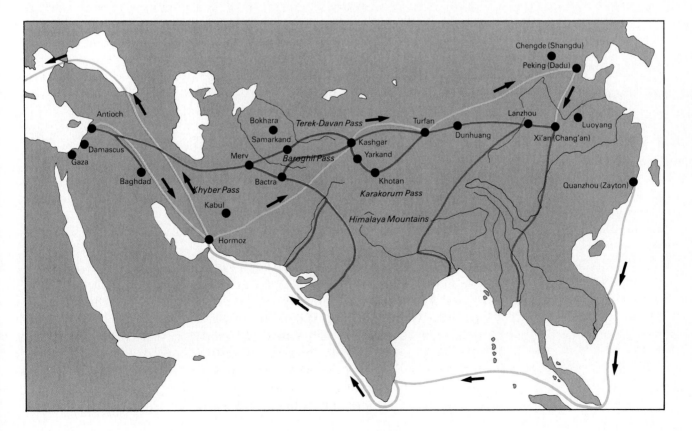

SILK ROUTE AND MARCO POLO'S JOURNEY

A detail from a scroll painting of the 10th century showing a party of horsemen. Horses from the vast pastures and breeding grounds of Mongolia and central Asia were among the few things that the self-sufficient Chinese could not produce at home, and this demand provided an early impetus for trade.

to supply what could not be obtained locally. And the imperial court was always aware of the links between trade and diplomacy, and of the military and political advantages that could be gained from foreign demand for Chinese goods.

One of the earliest stories of mercantile diplomacy is that of Zhang Qian, who was sent by Emperor Han Wudi to western Turkestan in 138 BC, to try to forge an alliance against the northern barbarians, the Xiongnu. His diplomatic mission was unsuccessful but he impressed the emperor with the magnificent horses he brought back with him; and trade with the north-west flourished in successive reigns. Caravans moving along the central Asian 'Silk Route' were to be important over the next 1500 years for both China and the West.

Not long after Han Wudi had sent Zhang Qian to central Asia, he

Merchants from Iran, central Asia, India and even the Byzantine empire conducted business in the market places. Chang'an, the capital of China during the Tang Dynasty, was then the largest city in the world, and people of many races are represented in the terracotta tomb figures of the time. The bearded figure above is probably an Iranian trader.

conquered south China, including the ports of Guangdong Province and those of modern North Vietnam. There he inherited the ancient trade with South-east Asia and the lands to its west. Soon Indian and Middle Eastern traders reached the China coast. Meanwhile Buddhist missionary monks had followed the caravan routes from central Asia and in time, as alien rulers conquered north China, monks rather than Confucian officials began to be employed in the service of government. In Buddhist monasteries on trade routes merchants could deposit money and goods for safekeeping, and the monasteries became important repositories of capital. They gained increasing influence over economic affairs, accumulating large quantities of metal which they stored in the form of bronze statues of the Buddha.

As trade expanded, Chinese metal currency became an obstacle to trade. The long strings of copper cash used for transactions were difficult and expensive to transport from one region to another, and some provinces which suffered from an adverse balance of trade would find themselves emptied of copper cash. Independent military governors sometimes prohibited the export of copper from their territory and thus brought an end to trade. To resume trading, merchants prepared deposit certificates. This practice was soon adopted by the imperial court, which issued its own deposit certificates for a charge of three per cent. Merchants began to deposit their copper cash with a government agency in exchange for a certificate, which they could put into circulation like money. It was from these certificates that the Chinese invention of paper money originated.

With Buddhism also came a trade in devotional objects, notably drugs and incense woods, and also a wide range of foreign ideas. Zoroastrians, Nestorians, Manichaeans and Muslims brought to China their goods and their notions of good and evil. The Chinese traditionally tolerated the religions and customs of others, and allowed them to live in their own way in the capital and in the great trading cities.

After the An Lushan Rebellion of 755, the military governors of the

The Ming emperors succeeded in obtaining tribute from countries as remote from China as modern Malaysia and Sri Lanka. This contemporary picture shows some exotic envoys offering gifts to the emperor.

行圖
真跡

This painting of a boat loaded with
marketable produce illustrates the
way in which agricultural progress
led to a flourishing internal
commerce in the Song Dynasty. It
also emphasizes the central role of
water transport at that time and
since.

frontier provinces of China grew more powerful in relation to the court. They declined to remit to the central government the grain and silk that they had levied as taxes. This forced the emperors to extract more of their taxes from state monopolies yielding cash. The first was salt; then, to make the tea trade a source of revenue, the state set up a commissariat to buy tea from the producers and supply it only to those traders in possession of a state licence. The two state monopolies, salt and tea, both progressed most rapidly in Sichuan, a major tea-producing region as well as an important source of salt. The relationships between officials and merchants fostered by the state monopolies led to increasing corruption.

It was in the Song Dynasty (960-1279) that Chinese internal trade expanded most dramatically. The state depredations on it also expanded. Chinese merchants had by then developed a long tradition of sensitivity both to market needs within China and to bureaucracy and its arbitrary demands. Their lowly social status made them seek protection from politically influential families. Whom they knew (in modern terms *guanxi*) was more important than knowing which administrative code was applicable to their case. As long as they were able to invoke official patronage, whether through bribes and purchases of court titles or through kinship connections, they could expand their trade beyond district and provincial boundaries. Once they were established in this way, their own extended family supported networks of trading enterprises and outlets. Their skill and experience might even lead to their whole district taking over certain lines of business across the country. Famous examples included the Huizhou merchants of Anhui Province who dominated wholesale trading and several state monopolies; the Shanxi bankers of north China who were renowned for their financial skills; and, not least, the Xiamen (Amoy) merchants who were active in any trade that depended on coastal and maritime transport.

During the Song Dynasty, social mobility greatly increased, and many of

Fragments from a hand-painted wallpaper made for the export market during the early Qing Dynasty illustrate stages in the manufacture of porcelain. The first picture shows supplies of petuntse being delivered to the kilns. After being ground down it was used as a glaze which gave a hard, fine finish. In the middle picture a merchant examines pieces of porcelain before collecting a consignment for an important customer. In the last picture (right) porters carry away the porcelain in baskets strung on shoulder poles.

the newly rich preferred to live in the cities rather than on their lands. With the concentration of absentee landowners, officials and rich merchants, the cities grew to become more sophisticated centres of commerce where luxuries of many kinds were demanded. Amusement quarters sprang up everywhere, with wine and tea shops, restaurants specializing in different types of cuisine, and courtesan houses such as the famous 'flower boats' *(hua chuan)*. There were also so-called 'tile-districts' *(washe)*, with theatres, puppet shows, storytellers, fortune-tellers and other entertainments. The main streets were lined with shops selling not only local silk, but also leather goods from the north, spices, ivory, sandalwood, gems from Annam and other luxury articles. Street stalls peddling market produce and religious objects abounded. Most of these commercial activities were carried out by private traders.

When north China was lost to the Jurchen Tartars, and the defeated Song escaped to Hangzhou to set up their Southern Dynasty (1127-1279), there was a new concern with overseas ventures. It was then that the sea routes from the southern and south-eastern ports finally replaced the Silk Route through central Asia as the main lines of foreign trade. Arab merchants in particular sought to expand their sea trade with China, and Quanzhou, which the Arabs – and Marco Polo, following them – called Zayton, became the leading port.

By the time the Mongols conquered south China in 1278 a flourishing over-sea trade had been established. Enough sea-power had grown out of that trade for Kublai Khan to launch the first two great naval expeditions in east Asia: to Japan and to the island of Java in Indonesia. When the country was once more united in 1368 under a Chinese dynasty the first Ming emperor, Hongwu, reacted strongly to the recent memory of Mongol discrimination against the Chinese, and pursued a policy of tight restriction on all dealings with foreigners, insisting on submission from China's neighbours. He sent envoys to the peripheral states of Korea, Japan, Annam and Tibet to announce his accession and to invite tribute. The Japanese, whom Kublai Khan had failed to conquer with his fleet, sent a frosty reply: 'There is more than one ruler on earth.' Others, without the sea to protect them, found outward submission to China less troublesome or more lucrative than protest. The Chinese emperors heaped presents on those who brought them tribute, often of greater value than the tribute articles they received, and emissaries were able to trade for themselves unofficially on the side.

The third Ming emperor, Yongle (1403-25), set out to incorporate the south Asian countries into his tribute system, and thereby to display China's supremacy for the benefit of Tamerlane, whose Mongol armies now threatened China in the west. Between 1405 and 1433, China sent out seven maritime expeditions, led by a Moslem eunuch, Zheng He. Chinese vessels sailed far down the east coast of Africa. Several Chinese reached Mecca. One at least of Yongle's objects was achieved: China was recognized as a great power throughout southern Asia.

A proverb of the time said, 'People hate their rulers as animals hate the net of a hunter.' One way to escape the net of a covetous government and corrupt officials was to resort to illegal trade. Along the eastern coast Chinese merchants collaborated with Japanese smugglers, and some Chinese who were at odds with the government became smugglers themselves. Contraband was so profitable that many officials were secretly involved in it. As early as 1387 the Chinese government began building fortifications along the coast, but since it was impossible to garrison the whole coastline, illicit trade continued. So many Chinese profited from this pirate trade that later, in the seventeenth century, the government ordered the coastal settlements to be transferred inland and all dwellings within ten miles of the coast to be razed.

The first Europeans to arrive in Chinese waters, the Portuguese, were thought to be pirate-merchants like the Japanese when they sailed up to Guangzhou in 1514. Their manner of arrival fed these suspicions. Before the city walls the leading Portuguese ship fired a cannonade, which the captain subsequently said had been meant as a salute. There was a strict prohibition on the carrying of armaments in Guangzhou harbour. Chinese outrage increased when a second fleet of Portuguese refused to obey local regulations, and were reported to have carried off Chinese youths as slaves. The Chinese expelled the Portuguese, forbidding them to return, and ordered local Chinese not to trade with them. But the Portuguese built an island fortress armed with cannons outside the river mouth, and from there continued as before. In 1557 the Chinese, to keep them under some form of control, gave them permission to base their trade in the small peninsula of Macao, whose narrow isthmus was then walled off so that the Chinese could at any time curtail its food and water supply. Ironically, the Portuguese claimed that they were given Macao as a reward for helping the Chinese get rid of the Japanese pirates. Since China had by this time broken off all relations with Japan and had strictly forbidden any trade between the two countries, the Portuguese were able to act as middlemen, exchanging Chinese silk, porcelain and gold for Japanese silver. But before long the Tokugawa Shogunate in Japan imposed its own policy of exclusion, aimed at the Portuguese and Spaniards, and Macao's fortunes rapidly waned.

The Manchu rulers who conquered China in 1644 decided on an even tighter control of foreign trade than their predecessors. At the moment when the maritime nations of Europe were sponsoring their subjects' expansionist trade, the rulers of China, like those of Japan, decided to hold merchants in check more rigorously even than in the past.

From the eighteenth century onwards, however, China faced a new form of European mercantile expansion. When the British public acquired the habit of tea-drinking the East India Company set up a trading post, or 'factory' as it was called, in Guangzhou. The trade based here was known as 'junk' trade, named after the Malayan word for a seagoing ship, and was derived from the old trade between Chinese and South-east Asians. The Qing court in Peking, in order to regulate and control this traffic in the distant south, appointed a dozen or so merchant firms and gave them the monopoly of the Guangzhou trade, putting them under the eye of a high official who collected taxes from them. The English called them 'co-hongs', derived from *gonghang*, 'officially authorized merchant firms'. They traded with the British East India Company and with a number of freelance merchants, of which the most prominent was the firm of Jardines.

The position was unstable. Britain wanted tea and silk from China, but the Chinese traders required nothing from Britain except payment in silver. To improve the balance of trade it was important for the British to find a product which the Chinese lacked. This proved to be opium from India. The opium poppy had long been known in China and was used as a medicine, especially for cholera. The habit of smoking opium had been introduced into China in the seventeenth century, and addiction was sufficiently widespread for the Qing government to ban the sale and smoking of the drug in 1729. Other

The design on this late 18th-century bowl made for the export trade shows the 'factories' of foreign traders in the port of Guangzhou (Canton).

imperial edicts followed in quick succession, prohibiting its import or domestic production, but to little avail. Both British opium importers and Chinese distributors made huge fortunes. The distributors' network was so extensive that no official could control them. Their well-armed smuggling boats, called 'fast crabs' or 'scrambling dragons', were manned by sixty or seventy oarsmen; they collected the opium chests from the foreigners' receiving ships, which were heavily armed floating warehouses stationed outside Guangzhou.* The imperial government drew no revenue from this trade, which enriched only the smugglers, the local officials who connived at it and the Shanxi bankers, who were financing the smuggling.

In 1834 the East India Company was abolished and the British government sent Lord Napier to Guangzhou to supervise the triangular Britain-India-China trade in place of the Company. Napier was assigned the all but impossible task of persuading China to trade with Britain on equal terms, and, like Macartney in 1793, he failed.

The Qing court was divided over what to do about opium, and there was a considerable body of opinion in favour of legalizing it, but after much debate it was decided that the trade should be eradicated. The man chosen to execute this policy was Commissioner Lin Zexu. He reached Guangzhou in the spring of 1839, and the measures he took to suppress the trade, besides writing an eloquent letter to Queen Victoria which was never delivered, included the confining of the British in the 'Thirteen Factories' zone and the confiscation of their opium. These could be argued to be acts directed against the British government, not merely against British traders; they led to a declaration of war on China. The Qing Dynasty's decrepit ships were no match against a well-equipped British navy. The Treaty of Nanjing, signed in 1842, ceded Hong Kong to Britain and opened five ports to British trade and residence: Guangzhou itself, Xiamen (Amoy), Fuzhou (Foochow), Ningbo (Ningpo) and Shanghai. British subjects living in the five treaty ports, and those Chinese they employed, were put under the jurisdiction of the British consul, not under Chinese law: they had what was called 'the right of extraterritoriality'. The other great powers subsequently acquired similar rights for themselves.

After the Treaty of Nanjing, Shanghai quickly displaced Guangzhou as China's main trading centre. Situated fifty-four miles from the Pacific and twelve miles from the Yangtze River, it lies in the heart of the tea and silk region. Chinese merchants flourished in Shanghai, some in the new role of 'compradors'. These were employees of foreign firms who dealt with other Chinese merchants on their behalf. Under the right of extraterritoriality they could claim exemption from Chinese law; each was governed only by the law of the nation he dealt with. Free from the interference of Chinese officials, the compradors developed into capable entrepreneurs, forming the elite of the newly emerging Chinese capitalists in Shanghai. They moved enthusiastically into modern banking, shipping and industrial development.

Chinese merchants studied Western laws and institutions and recommended reforms in China so that they could compete more

effectively. They expected their government to appreciate their efforts as patriotic and to foster them. But during a period when the imperial system had decayed and the majority of officials were conservative, traders were given little support. The days of private enterprise within China were brief and troubled. The merchants were caught between foreign capitalists backed by superior power on the one hand, and on the other a Chinese reaction against capitalism itself, which was identified with aggression against Chinese sovereignty.

After the fall of the Qing Dynasty in 1911 China was too fragmented for a strong centralized state to emerge, and the provinces once more came under the rule of military governors or bandit chieftains who were termed *dujun*, 'warlords'. Each milked his territory for revenue and fought the others for supremacy. But at first, as China's political system disintegrated, the economic power of the capitalists centred in Shanghai grew, aided by the difficulties caused to their competitors, the Western traders, by the First World War. On 23 June 1923 the Shanghai General Chamber of Commerce declared its independence of the government in Peking, and established a Committee of Popular Government composed of its own members. But by 1924 foreign competition was returning to Shanghai, and the Chinese capitalists' prosperity rapidly declined.

An anonymous painting of the mid-19th century shows the stages of tea production, from the preparation of hillside plantations (top) to the loading of tea chests onto boats at the wharf. After picking, the leaves are rolled by hand, dried, sorted, and fermented or steamed. In the foreground, the leaves are being packed into tea chests, weighed and sold to three foreign merchants in top hats. Tea exports to Britain rose from 30 million pounds in the 1830s to a peak of 150 million pounds in the 1880s.

The workshop of a state-run pottery in Foshan, near Guangzhou. This pottery specializes in traditional and modern figures, and in various traditionally-glazed shapes. Nearly all its output is exported.

Meanwhile they were being threatened from another quarter. In Shanghai there was a larger working class and more established trade unions than elsewhere, and also a small but growing communist party. The merchants backed the man who promised them the extinction of the communists, the humiliation of the foreigners and the defeat of the warlords: Chiang Kai-shek. He subdued his northern rivals in 1926, then attacked and all but destroyed the Shanghai communists in the following year. But far from favouring the capitalists in Shanghai he turned against them. They had recently handed him ten million dollars; he demanded thirty million more. Those who refused payment were arrested. The major banks were put directly under the control of the government; members of Chiang Kai-shek's wife's family were installed in leading posts in government while simultaneously occupying commanding positions in finance; and China returned to the imperial tradition of bureaucratic state capitalism.

Throughout the first part of the twentieth century, China's relationships with Japan remained her most important overseas preoccupation. They deteriorated through the 1930s into open conflict. Between 1937 and 1945 the war against the Japanese killed at least twenty million Chinese and almost entirely destroyed the modern sector of the economy. Then came the civil war, with millions more dead and further physical destruction. When the Chinese Communist Party won its dramatic victory in 1949 it inherited internal chaos and external hostility. The Western powers imposed a trade embargo. China's response was to implement a closed-door policy of her own against the West.

Meanwhile, to satisfy her need to industrialize, she turned to the Soviet Union to provide her with technical assistance and industrial plant. Today the Chinese feel that they paid a high price for Soviet assistance, both in the products taken from them in exchange and in political subordination to the Soviet Union. But in 1949 Mao Zedong had no choice. Although he was critical of Soviet policies, notably in agriculture, he needed heavy industry and only the Soviet Union had the planners, the technicians and the working models of central planning that he could call on. Almost as soon as he gained power in China he flew to Moscow to arrange the best terms he could get. The links between the two countries produced the most remarkable transfer of resources between nations ever seen up to that time.

Mao now needed to persuade the Chinese that the Russians, whom they had traditionally disliked, were their friends, and that the Americans, whom they had generally liked, were their enemies. The job was done thoroughly and was made easier by the fact that in the following year, 1950, the Americans and the Chinese were fighting each other in Korea.

In 1958-60, as Mao and Khrushchev, Stalin's successor, grew apart, the Soviet Union withdrew its technical assistance and abandoned 161 out of the 291 planned joint projects. The Chinese now sought economic independence through a policy of 'self-reliance': they would manufacture all the products they needed and rely only on their own resources. Where trade was indispensable, the slogan was 'Import whatever is needed to reduce imports, and export only what is needed to pay for imports.' But China could not manufacture capital-intensive goods more cheaply than Japan and the West, and she began ploughing back into heavy industry so great a proportion of her resources that consumption was held back, and as population increased, except between 1961 and 1965, living standards stagnated.

Such foreign trade as there was after 1949 was organized from Beijing, with buying and selling taking place passively in Guangzhou twice a year under the supervision of a vice-minister from the capital. For more than twenty years China's foreign trade was conducted exclusively by a dozen national import and export corporations. Chinese producers and foreign buyers were never in direct contact with each other, and the local provinces and central ministries had no right to handle their own import and export business. In the mid-1970s Jiang Qing (Madame Mao) argued against the sale of China's raw materials, especially oil, to foreigners, and effectively blocked imports for a year.

When Mao Zedong died in 1976 and his successor Hua Guofeng, who wanted fast growth and heavy industry, was overthrown in December 1978, the new leaders moved towards a series of major economic readjustments. At home they aimed at reducing capital construction to raise consumption; agriculture and light industry were given priority over heavy industry. They also ruled that market forces should be brought into play to a greater extent, and that fewer economic matters should be dealt with by Party officials. In July 1979 a system of limited devolution based on east European models, and already tried out in Sichuan by Deng Xiaoping's rising younger ally, Zhao Ziyang, was put into practice through China. A number of state-owned enterprises were allowed to retain a fifth of the profits which they would normally have remitted to the central government. Capitalists who had been dismissed in the Great Leap Forward and disgraced in the Cultural Revolution were rehabilitated, given back-pay and encouraged to contribute their skills as managers and as entrepreneurs, particularly to the building of new enterprises, in conjunction with overseas Chinese, directed towards the outside world.

China's foreign trade system was radically changed with the adoption of what were called 'open door economic policies'. Provinces, ministries and factories were given extensive and independent powers not only to conduct, but actively to go out and seek, foreign trade. To promote production for export, provinces and enterprises were allowed to retain two-fifths of their foreign exchange earnings. Some enterprises were allowed to negotiate foreign trade contracts directly, although final approval by central government was still required. The Bank of China made available two billion yuan in foreign exchange for the expansion of enterprises producing for export, and in 1980 China joined the World Bank and the International Monetary Fund.

But the expansion was followed by a rapid tightening up, starting in late 1979. By the end of 1980 the economy was officially stated to be 'in dislocation'. Inflation was growing. Enterprises all over China had surged forward with investment plans, in ignorance of the fact that there were either too few raw

为实现新时期的总任务而奋斗

A poster urges the Chinese people to use all their resources to achieve advances in the field of science and technology.

materials to complete their projects, or too little power to run them once they were completed. The percentage of Chinese investment tied up in uncompleted projects, already causing concern, increased. Since the prices of necessities had been kept artificially low by subsidies, and those of luxuries kept artificially high, there was a natural tendency on the part of managers, made responsible for the first time for profit and loss, to produce luxuries rather than necessities. And so great was the pent-up demand for foreign-made products – both machinery for investment and consumer durables such as television sets and cassette-recorders – that there was a particularly heavy expansion in the demand for imports, which after a series of bad harvests requiring the import of grain, led to a threatening balance of payments problem.

Since 1949 China had gone through several cycles of capital investment followed by periods of retrenchment. Each time that investment had been cut back, imports from abroad had also been cut back. When, after the launching of the most ambitious cycle in early 1979, the administration so rapidly slowed down later in 1979 and again in 1981, and agreed purchases were postponed, the confidence of many foreign traders and suppliers of machinery was badly damaged.

But while the economy faltered there was no collapse: and relatively liberal market policies continued, though on a tighter rein. The Responsibility System, extended to agriculture, was introduced in a variety of ways into industry. Foreign trade was not centralized to the extent that it had been before 1979, and important segments of China's manufacturing industry, chiefly textiles, were encouraged to continue to adapt to foreign markets and fashions.

In the early 1980s China had a surplus on her trade with developing countries, with the socialist bloc and with Hong Kong, to which she was supplying food, water and power. This went to pay for her deficits with the advanced industrial economies, particularly Japan and the United States. Since 1979 she has tried to reduce her deficit with the advanced countries by encouraging her trading partners to accept barter deals, joint ventures and 'compensation' schemes. 'Compensation' is a kind of submerged barter whereby foreign companies provide technology, equipment and essential capital goods for a factory in return for a share of its output for an agreed number of years, after which the factory and the equipment revert to Chinese ownership and control.

China has also introduced 'Special Economic Zones'. There are three of these in the province of Guangdong, bordering on Hong Kong, and one in Fujian, across the water from Taiwan. They are zones into which ordinary Chinese cannot penetrate – guards at the frontiers with China proper allow in only people employed in the zone – but from which it is comparatively easy to trade in both directions with Hong Kong. Foreigners can live and do business in them, and to some extent can be governed by their own laws and financial practices, remitting money abroad in their own currency after they have paid tax. The zones are in some respects like the Treaty Ports and foreign concessions of imperial China.

The main, though undeclared, political objective behind the policy of Special Economic Zones seems to be the easing of reunification with Hong Kong, Macao and Taiwan by the integration of their economic systems with China's; but the areas have evidently also been chosen with an eye to encouraging investment by overseas Chinese, most of whom originated in these provinces. So far most foreign investments in China have been made either by overseas Chinese or through them.

The government faces a traditional problem today in attempting to regulate the traders and entrepreneurs within its territory. The overseas Chinese in Guangdong and Fujian who invest in the Zones could turn into another set of compradors, a privileged capitalist class able to exploit East-West connections to their personal advantage while avoiding the restrictions of central government control. Many of their investments have been made in export industries, which are heavily concentrated in the coastal industrial areas. These have long been richer than the rest of China, as well as much more influenced by the West. Shanghai, for example, has the highest wages in China, provides one eighth of China's industrial output, produces one fifth of all exports, handles a third of total freight and is both the largest and the most cosmopolitan city in China. Its economic preponderance and rivalry with the capital have led to political problems for Chinese governments in the past, and could easily provide more.

There is nevertheless no sign of any diminution in the government's eagerness to develop industry round Shanghai, or to invite overseas Chinese participation in China's export industries and coastal development. As Xu Muqiao, Deng Xiaoping's leading spokesman, has said, 'We do not advocate the restoration of capitalism, yet we should not be overly afraid of it. It is all right to have a bit of capitalism since it is not time to exterminate capitalism yet.'

The 'yet' is worth noting. It could be a mere obeisance to Marxism. But it could signal a determination on the part of the leaders not to lose in the long run the traditional control that they and their predecessors have exercised over both Chinese merchants and foreigners within their territory.

Yet China cannot ignore the rest of the world, and she cannot any longer deal with outsiders simply on her own terms. To develop or even to survive economically and militarily in a rapidly changing world, she must import technology whether she likes it or not. But trade brings ideas as well as goods. Just as Buddhist monks followed the central Asian caravans along the north-western trading routes and helped to change the beliefs of China, so today the Western films and television programmes that the Chinese watch and the songs they listen to on their new cassette-recorders spread messages of a different, more prosperous way of life, associated with an economic system that is neither socialist nor traditionally Chinese, and with forms of political liberty that are alien both to Chinese tradition and to socialist practice.

China's historical success has perhaps been in maintaining the control of a state with limited aims over a society with limited expectations. In recent decades limited personal expectations survived partly because of the importance of the family and the preponderance of concern for children and posterity in China; but partly also because the population was kept in ignorance or misinformed about the world beyond China's frontiers. Today, with Western products displayed in the shop windows and with Western images flooding people's imagination through films and television, it is uncertain how long a large proportion of the people will rest content with a life's ambition bounded by a bicycle, a sewing machine, a cassette recorder and a nine-foot-square room.

Not only are economic expectations being adjusted upwards; the state with limited aims has been replaced. The Communist Party is not, like the old imperial government, concerned with maintaining a status quo. It promises dramatic material progress, and professes a creed of revolution. The two foundations of the old political order have both been disturbed.

What the outcome will be cannot be predicted. Only one thing is reasonably certain. Just as the Chinese transformed the Buddhism they imported from India by fusing it with their native beliefs to form Chan Buddhism, so, to the extent that they import consumerism from the West, they are likely to transform that also. Will Chan Consumerism be the next teaching of China to 'flow into one' with the others?

A large billboard in a Shanghai street tempts passers-by with an advertisement for Lucky Cola – 'cool and tasty, fragrant and invigorating' – the cheaper, Chinese version of Coca-Cola.

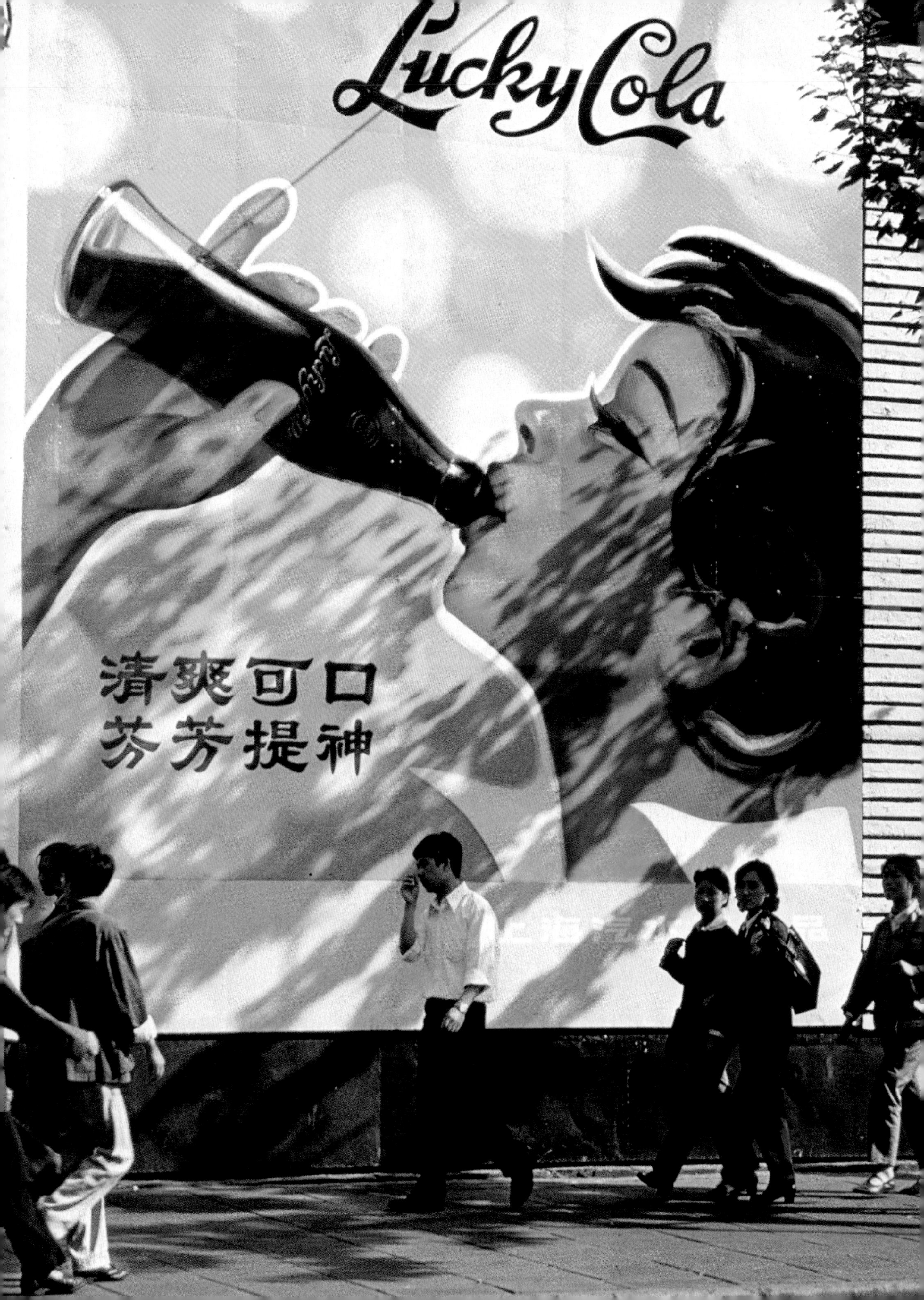
Lucky Cola
清爽可口
芬芳提神

NOTES

Bibliographical details are given in full for the first entry in each chapter.
Thereafter abbreviated details are given.

REMEMBERING

Page

5 *** . . . laden with goods.** See pp.122-3.

8 **'. . . shook the four seas.'** Sima Qian, 'The Hereditary House of Chen She', *Shiji*, 48; see *Records of the Grand Historian of China*, translated by Burton Watson (New York and London, Columbia University Press, 1961), Vol.1, p.31.

8 **'. . . ten thousand generations.'** Ibid., Vol.1, p.32.

18 **'. . . responsible for their conduct.'** 'The Letters of Père D'Entrecolles from Ching-Te Chen', reproduced in Bushell, *Description of Chinese Pottery and Porcelain: a translation of the Tao Shuo*, and cited in Soame Jenyns, *Later Chinese Porcelain* (London, Faber & Faber, 1959), p.14.

18 **'. . . become a bandit.'** Hsiao Kung-chuan, *Rural China: Imperial Control in the Nineteenth Century* (Seattle, University of Washington Press, 1960), p.464.

20 **. . . returned from hunting.** Susan Naquin, *Millenarian Rebellion in China: The Eight Trigrams Uprising of 1813* (New Haven and London, Yale University Press, 1976), p.176.

20 **. . . Taiping rebel armies.** Jacques Gernet, *A History of Chinese Civilization*, translated by J.R. Foster (Cambridge and New York, Cambridge University Press, 1982), p.545.

21 **'. . . navy, police and postal systems.'** John K. Fairbank, Edwin O. Reischauer, Albert M. Craig, *East Asia: Tradition and Transformation* (Boston, Houghton, Mifflin Co., 1973), p.632.

21 **. . . wangguao miezhong . . .** Stuart R. Schram, 'To Utopia and Back: A Cycle in the History of the Chinese Communist Party', *The China Quarterly*, No.87 (September 1981), p.410.

23 **'. . . to take control of China.'** Paul S. Reinsch, *An American Diplomat in China* (New York, Paragon, 1922), p.129.

24 **'. . . incurable disease.'** Peter Fleming, *One's Company* (London, Jonathan Cape, 1934), p.185.

27 **'. . . 20,000,000 people perished . . .'** Philip Short, *The Dragon and the Bear* (London, Hodder and Stoughton, 1982), p.165, citing Sun Yefang in *Economic Management*, February 1981.

27 **'. . . ants starting to move.'** Miriam London and Ivan D. London, 'The Other China – Hunger: Part I – The Three Red Flags of Death', *Worldview*, Vol.19 (1976), No.5, p.5.

27 **'. . . belly is tight.'** Schram, 'To Utopia and Back', *China Quarterly*, p.430.

27 **'. . . Overtake Britain in fifteen years . . .'** Liu Shaoqi, speech to the Second Session of the Eighth Congress of the Communist Party of China, May 1958, cited in Schram, 'To Utopia and Back', *China Quarterly*, No.87, p.420.

27 **'. . . buried 46,000 of them.'** Mao Zedong, speech to the Second Session of the Eighth Congress of the Communist Party of China, May 1958. For the revival of this remark in the campaign against Lin Biao, who interrupted Mao to oppose Qin Shihuangdi, see *Peking Review*, Vol.33 (1974), p.11.

27 **'. . . even Confucius.'** Speech by Mao Zedong at the Leshan Party Congress, cited in Jurgen Domes, *The Internal Politics of China, 1949-1972*, translated by Rudiger Machetzki (London, C. Hurst & Co., 1973).

30 **'. . . from this injury.'** Ken Ling, *Red Guard: From Schoolboy to 'Little General' in Mao's China* (London, Macdonald, 1972), p.238.

BELIEVING

35 **. . . in a different body.** (e.g. Cao Xueqin, *The Story of the Stone*, translated by David Hawkes (Harmondsworth, Penguin Books, 1973), Vol.1, p.275.)

40 **'. . . stirred up heaven and earth.'** Jia Yi, 'The Faults of the State of Qin', appended to Sima Qian, *Shiji*, 48, and Liu Xiang, cited and translated in J.J.L. Duyvendak, *The Book of the Lord Shang* (London, Probsthain, 1928, 1963), pp.2-3.

41 **'. . . but there are no words.'** 'Drinking Wine', No.V, translated by the author.

52 **'. . . the frenzy stopped.'** H.H. Dubs, trans., *The History of the Former Han Dynasty* (Baltimore, Waverley Press, 1938-55) and H.H. Dubs, 'An Ancient Chinese Mystery Cult', *Harvard Theological Review*, 35 (1942), p.223, cited in Susan Naquin, *Millenarian Rebellion in China: The Eight Trigrams Uprising of 1813* (New Haven and London, Yale University Press, 1976), p.288.

52 **'. . . the golden lotus.'** Daniel L. Overmyer, 'Folk Buddhist Religion: Creation and Eschatology in Medieval China', *History of Religions* 12 (1972) No.1, pp.60-2, cited in Naquin, *Rebellion*, pp.9, 10.

55 **'. . . earliest practice is followed.'** K.C. Chang in K.C. Chang, ed., *Food in Chinese Culture: Anthropological* *and Historical Perspectives* (New Haven and London, Yale University Press, 1977), p.45

57 '. . . cold pig's head.' Guo Moruo, '*Makesi jin wen miao*' ('Marx visits the ancestral temple of Confucius'), dated 17 November 1925, in Lin Wu-chi, *Readings in Contemporary Chinese Literature* (New Haven, Yale University Press, 1953), pp.7-17, cited in Wolfgang Bauer, *China and the Search for Happiness*, translated by Michael Shaw (New York, Seabury Press, 1976), pp.382-6, translation slightly amended.

65 . . . scathingly suggest. e.g. cartoon from *Beijing Review*, 22 June 1981.

MARRYING

67 . . . of the curses. C. Fred Blake, 'Death and Abuse in Marriage Laments: the Curse of Chinese Brides', *Asian Folklore Studies*, Vol.37 (1978), No.1, p.13.

68 '. . . sets no store.' Arthur Waley, *170 Chinese Poems* (London, Jonathan Cape, 1969), p.46.

70 . . . caused no injury. Bodde and Morris, *Law in Imperial China* (Cambridge, Harvard University Press, 1967), p.37.

70 . . . the death by slow slicing. Anon., 'Fifteen Strings of Cash' in *The Courtesan's Jewel Box*, translated by Yang Xianyi and Gladys Yang (Beijing, Foreign Languages Press, 1981), p.46.

70 '. . . to the end of her life. *Liji* I (Sacred Books of the East, UNESCO), Vol.28, p.457.

74 . . . had correspondingly increased. Arthur Wolf, in Margery Wolf and Roxane Witke, eds., *Women in Chinese Society* (Stanford, Stanford University Press, 1975), p.89.

77 . . . not universal. Ibid., p.111.

77 . . . as sister to brother. Ibid., p.128.

78 . . . preferable to their own. Cheng Tcheng, *Ma Mère et Moi* (Paris, Editions Victor Attinger, 1929), reprinted in Cheng Tcheng, *Ma Mère et Moi à travers la Première Révolution Chinoise* (Paris, Editions Etente, 1975), p.99.

78 . . . complain of this . . . Susan Naquin, *Millenarian Rebellion in China: The Eight Trigrams Uprising of 1813* (New Haven and London, Yale University Press, 1976), p.48.

78 '. . . It's still early!' Shen Congwen, 'An Amorous Boatman and an Amorous Woman', from *Recollections of West Hunan*, translated by Gladys Yang (Beijing, Panda Books, 1982), p.59.

82 . . . Responsibility System . . . See LIVING.

82 . . . Maoping in Zhejiang Province. Ibid.

83 '. . . Cannot be condoned.' *The Book of Songs*, translated by Arthur Waley (London, George Allen and Unwin, 1969), No.104, p.96.

84 . . . had them killed. Sima Qian, *Records of the Historian*, translated by Yang Xianyi and Gladys Yang (Beijing, Foreign Languages Press, 1982), pp.28-9.

84 . . . attend a meeting. R.H. Van Gulik, *Sexual Life in Ancient China* (Leiden, E.J. Brill, 1961), p.63.

84 . . . punished by death. See CORRECTING.

85 '. . . of the West.' Van Gulik, *Sexual Life*, p.76, citing H.H. Dubs, trans., *The History of the Former Han Dynasty* (Baltimore, Waverley Press, 1938), Vol.III, p.8.

85 '. . . to obtain longevity.' Ibid., pp.77-8, citing *The Dynastic History of the Later Han Period*, chapter 110.

85 '. . . on this subject.' Ibid., p.47.

85 '. . . in my bosom.' Ibid., citing Sima Xiangru, *Meirenfu*, preface.

88 '. . . has dared to enter this house.' Translated by Phillip S. Y. Sun in 'The Seditious Art of the Water Margin – Misogynists or Desperadoes?', *Renditions*, 1 (autumn 1973), p.100.

89 '. . . ignoring him.' Cao Xueqin, *The Story of the Stone*, translated by David Hawkes (Harmondsworth, Penguin Books, 1973), Vol.II, (1977) pp.150-1.

MEDIATING

104 . . . 'special school' . . . 'The Harbin Prison – A Special School', *China Pictorial*, 1982, No.12, pp.28-31.

107 *'. . . the benefits of forbearance.' Patricia Ebrey, *Family and Property in Sung China: Yuan Ts'ai's Precepts for Social Life* (Princeton, Princeton University Press, forthcoming).

EATING

111 '. . . ransom money for my life.' Li Yu, based on translations by T.C. Lai in T.C. Lai, 'Some Chinese Food for Thought', *Renditions*, No.9 (spring 1978), p.58, and by Nathan Mao in Li Yu, *Twelve Towers* (Hong Kong, The Chinese University Press, 1975), p.xxvii.

111 . . . 'He did not eat much.' *The Confucian Analects* (*Lun Yu*), translated by James Legge (Oxford, Clarendon Press, 1893), pp.200, 468-70, cited by K.C. Chang in K.C. Chang, ed., *Food in Chinese Culture: Anthropological*

and Historical Perspectives (New Haven and London, Yale University Press, 1977), pp.37, 52.

112 '. . . starved to death on the road.' Miriam London and Ivan D. London, 'The Other China – Hunger: Part I – The Three Red Flags of Death', *Worldview*, Vol.19 (1976), No.5, p.9.

112 '. . . so strange a kind of fishing.' Galeote Pereira, 'Report', in C.R. Boxer, ed., *South China in the Sixteenth Century* (London, Hakluyt Society, 1953), pp.42-3.

114 . . . still living. Jacques Gernet, *Daily Life in China on the Eve of the Mongol Invasion 1250-1276*, translated by H.M. Wright (Paris and London, George Allen and Unwin, 1962), p.53, citing *Meng liang lu*, XII, 5, pp.234-5.

114 '. . . which meat produces.' Lai, 'Food for Thought', p.60.

115 . . . 'phases' in nature . . . See UNDERSTANDING.

115 . . . cormorants. Jia Ming, *Yinshi xuzhi*, cited by F. Mote from *Yinquan pulu*, compiled by Yang Chia-lo (Taipei, 1968), in K.C. Chang, ed., *Food*, p.201.

115 '. . . by lighting a fire.' Lai, 'Food for Thought', pp.60-1.

118 '. . . steam till tender.' Ibid., pp.47-68. Cf. Arthur W. Hummel, ed., *Eminent Chinese of the Ch'ing Period* (Washington, US Govt Printing Office, 1943), pp.955-7.

119 '. . . charred leftovers in the wok.' Yuan Mei, *Sui yuan shi dan*, cited in Lai, 'Food for Thought', pp.51, 53.

119 '. . . than to have no soup.' Lai, 'Food for Thought', p.61.

119 . . . there were cults of tea-drinking . . . Edward H. Schafer in Chang, ed., *Food*, p.123; Michael Freeman in Chang, ed., *Food*, p.156.

120 . . . drunk frequently. Gernet, *Daily Life 1250-76*, p.139.

124 . . . punishable by strangulation. *The Tang Code*, translated with an introduction by Wallace Johnson (Princeton, Princeton University Press, 1979), Vol.I, p.72.

124 . . . his favourite concubines. Aisin-Gioro Pu Yi, *From Emperor to Citizen – the Autobiography of Aisin-Gioro Pu-Yi*, translated by William J.F. Jenner (Beijing, Foreign Languages Press, 1964), Vol.1, quoted by Jonathan Spence in Chang, ed., *Food*, p.287.

124 . . . is in short supply. London and London, 'Hunger in China: "The Norm of Truth"' in *Worldview*, Vol.22 (1979), No.3, p.16, and 'Hunger in China: The Failure of a System?' in *Worldview*, Vol.22 (1979), No.10, p.47;

Vaclav Smil, 'Communist China's Food: Still a Long Way to Go', in *Issues and Studies: A Journal of China Studies and International Affairs*, Vol.XVI, No.4 (April 1980), p.41; Hsû and Hsû in Chang, ed., *Food*, p.309.

124 '. . . persimmons from Songyang.' *The Baihua ting (Pai-hua t'ing)*, translated by Stephen H. West, 'Studies in Chin Dynasty (1115-1234) Literature', PhD dissertation, University of Michigan, 1972, cited by Frederick W. Mote in Chang, ed., *Food*, p.235.

125 '. . . dismiss him altogether.' *Meng liang lu*, XVI, 4, p.267, cited in Etienne Balazs, 'Marco Polo dans la Capitale de la Chine', *Oriente Poliano* (Rome, Istituto Italiano per il Medio ed Estremo Oriente, 1957), p.149, and in Gernet, *Daily Life 1250-1276*, pp.50-1; see also p.137.

125 '. . . two-legged mutton.' Gernet, *Daily Life 1250-76*, p.135, citing *Jile bian (Chong jiao shuo fu* edition), XXVII, f.14a-b.

125 '. . . burn it in lamps.' Pearl S. Buck, *All Men Are Brothers* (London, Methuen, 1933), p.186.

125 . . . enemies in anger. Ssu-ma Kuang, *Ciqitongjien* (Tokyo, Hobunken, 1892) 214:7a; 224:5a; 226:5b, cited by Edward H. Schafer in Chang, ed., *Food*, p.135.

126 . . . close to starvation. London and London, *Worldview*, Vol.19 (1976), No.5, pp.4-11.

126 '. . . ground pumice.' Peking Unitd International Famine Relief Committee, *The North China Famine of 1920-21, with special reference to the west Chih-li area* (Peking, 1922), p.13, cited by J. Spence in Chang, ed., *Food*, p.261.

126 . . . ground together. London and London, *Worldview*, Vol.19 (1976), No.5, pp.8, 11.

LIVING

136 '. . . in [the plain of] Chengdu.' Sima Qian, *Shi Ji*, chapter 29, cited in Joseph Needham with the collaboration of Wang Ling and Lu Gwei-djen, *Science and Civilisation in China* (Cambridge, Cambridge University Press, 1971), Vol.4, Part 3, p.288.

141 '. . . forever watering.' Shiba Yoshinobu, *Commerce and Society in Song China*, translated by Mark Elvin (Ann Arbor, University of Michigan Center for Chinese Studies, 1970), p.55.

141 . . . **'yellow soil plateau' of the north and west**
. . .The six provinces of the *huang tu* are Qinghai,
Ningxia, Gansu, Shanxi, Shaanxi, and Nei Monggol
(Inner Mongolia). They cover about 200,000 square
kilometres. See London and London in *Worldview*,
Vol.22 (1979), No.10, p.44.

144 '. . . **We got orders.'** London and London, 'The Other
China – Hunger: Part 1 – The Three Red Flags of Death',
in *Worldview*, Vol.19 (1976), No. 5, p.5, citing a peasant
originally from Guangdong.

144 . . . **did not follow him.** Speech to Leshan Party
Congress, July-August 1959, cited in Jurgen Domes, *The
Internal Politics of China 1949-1972*, translated by Rudiger
Machetzki (London, C. Hurst & Co., 1973).

144 '. . . **peasants are only peasants.'** First and Second
Zhengzhou conferences, November 1958 and February-
March 1959, cited in Stuart Schram, 'To Utopia and
Back: A Cycle in the History of the Chinese Communist
Party', *The China Quarterly* No.87 (September 1981),
pp.424-5.

145 . . . **farmland in that time.** The official statistics are:
17m hectares of farmland reclaimed, 29m lost for various
reasons, including the construction of roads and
buildings: total in 1957, 111.33m; total in 1982, 99.33m.
Per capita farmland in 1957, 0.18 hectare; in 1982, 0.1
hectare: cited from the State Statistical Bureau by Frank
Ching, 'China Reports Gains In Nutrition, Food
Output', *The Asian Wall Street Journal*, 22 July 1982.

146 . . . **Y100 a year per head** . . . United States Foreign
Broadcasting Information Service, cited in London and
London, additional references and notes to 'Hunger in
China: The Failure of a System?' in *Worldview*, Vol.22
(1979), No.10, privately circulated, note 5.

146 '. . . **with little result.'** *People's Daily*, 26 November
1979.

146 '. . . **the poorer one becomes.'** *People's Daily*, 26
November 1978; New China News Agency report, 20
March 1979, recorded by United States Foreign
Broadcast Information Service, 23 March 1979, item Tl,
cited by London and London in *Worldview*, Vol.22
(1979), No.10, p.44.

147 . . . **deserting their fields.** Party Central Committee
and Cabinet instruction on 'The Halting of the Outflow
of the Villages', *People's Daily*, 18 December 1957, cited
by London and London in *Worldview*, Vol.19 (1976),
No.6, p.44.

147 . . . **'big chopsticks.'** Cited in London and London,
Worldview, Vol.19 (1976), No.5, p.9

147 . . . **Anhui and Jiangsu.** e.g. *People's Daily*, 18
December 1957, Anhui People's Broadcasting Station, 2
September 1968, reported in *China News Analysis*, Hubei
People's Broadcasting Station, 4 June 1972, cited by
London and London in *Worldview*, Vol.19 (1976), No.6,
p.44.

147 . . . **the word 'famine' itself.** London and London in
Worldview, Vol.19 (1976), No. 6, p.44; Vol.22 (1979),
No.3, p.14; Vol.22, No.10, p.45; and additional notes,
xerox n.15, citing New China News Agency, 3
November 1978, *People's Daily*, 21 November 1978 and
Yunnan Provincial Party Committee broadcast, 3 March
1979, FBIS, 6 March 1979.

WORKING

162 . . . **and avert discontent.** *China News Analysis*, 19
November 1982, p.5.

169 '. . . **spontaneous combustion.'** *Economic Management*
(1982), No.12, p.11.

172 . . . **education and employment** . . . FBIS/176/T1,
China Daily, 11 September 1982.

172 . . . **built for workers** . . . SWB/FE/6853/BII/7, China
Daily, 8 October 1981.

172 . . . **occupy peasant land** . . . SWB/FE/6950/BII/16,
New China News Agency (C), 1 February 1983.

172 . . . **shield their children from punishment** . . .
SWB/FE/6840/BII/15, NCNA(C), 19 September 1981.

172 . . . **to build private houses** . . . FBIS/176/Tl, China
Daily, 11 September 1981.

172 . . . **social and public services.** SWB/FE/6977/BII/13,
Guizhou, 27 November 1981.

172 . . . **to move to the city** . . . (e.g. SWB/FE/6984/BII/
16, Anhui, 27 November 1981.)

172 . . . **'cadres' of high rank.** SWB/FE/6982/BII/4.

CORRECTING

185 '. . . **and picking their teeth.'** Gaspar da Cruz,
Tractado, cited in C.R. Boxer, ed., *South China in the 16th
Century* (London, printed for Hakluyt Society, 1953),
p.179.

185 '. . . **will you die.'** Derk Bodde, 'Prison Life in
18th-Century Peking', *Journal of American Oriental
Society*, Vol.89 (1969), p.321.

185 '. . . persons suffer contagion.' Ibid., p.319.
188 '. . . more than 326,000 people.' Jing Hua, President of the Supreme People's Court, report to Sixth National People's Congress, 7 June 1983, cited in BBC, Summary of World Broadcasts, FE/7372/C/2, 29 June 1983.
189 . . . would no longer apply. Ibid.
189 . . . lead to its doubling. Fox Butterfield, *China: Alive in the Bitter Sea* (New York, Times Books, 1982), p.363.
190 '. . . without other evidence.' Jing Hua, report to Sixth National People's Congress.
195 . . . camps and enterprises. cf. Huang Huoqing, Procurator General of the Supreme People's Procuratorate, report to Sixth NPC, cited in BBC, SWB/FE/7372/C/10-11.
195 . . . declined to comment on them. (e.g. Butterfield, *China*, pp.362, 356-6.)
196 '. . . and blew his head open.' Jean Pasqualini and Rudolph Chelminski, *Prisoner of Mao* (New York, Coward, McCann and Geoghan, Inc., 1973), p.187.
196 . . . kept in labour camps. *People's Daily*, 7 September 1954.
196 . . . Party pronouncements. Pasqualini and Chelminski, *Prisoner of Mao*, p.11.
196 . . . political prisoners. Philip Short, *The Dragon and the Bear* (London, Hodder and Stoughton, 1982), pp.113-16.
196 '. . . able to write to them.' Butterfield, *China*, p.366.
197 . . . found little difference. Ibid., pp.362-9.
197 . . . being found jobs recently. Xinhua, broadcast 25 June 1983, cited in BBC, Summary of World Broadcasts, FE/7372/CS.
198 . . . in the early 1980s. (e.g. BBC, SWB/FE/6868/BII/14 Zhejiang, 20 August 1981; SWB/FE/6759/BII/l Wenhui Bao, 17 June 1981; SWB/FE/6621/BII/6, Hainan, 30 December 1980.
198 . . . or in America. SWB/FE/7359/C/4. Figures of 7 to 8 per thousand are given, without a definition of 'crimes'.
198 . . . Shanghai's Liberation Daily . . . BBC, SWB/FE/6622/BII/1, 9 January 1981.
199 . . . and power lines. BBC, SWB/FE/6855/BII/7 NCNA (C), 11 October 1981.
199 . . . concern for their welfare. BBC, SWB/FE/6837/BII/7, NCNA (C), 9 September 1981.
199 '. . . are young people' . . . BBC, SWB/FE/6788/BII/3, NCNA (C), 24 July 1981.
199 '. . . curiosity and mischief.' BBC, SWB/FE/7053/BII/9, 22 June 1982, Beijing Wenzhai.
199 . . . perturbing the authorities. SWB/FE/7359/C/5.

UNDERSTANDING

203 '. . . that does not have a mind.' Cited by Nathan Sivin in 'Why the Scientific Revolution Did Not Take Place in China – or Didn't It?', *Chinese Science*, Vol.5 (June 1982), p.50.
206 '. . . of the liver.' Cao Xueqin, *The Story of the Stone*, translated by David Hawkes (Harmondsworth, Penguin Books, 1973), Vol.1, p.225; translation modified by Christopher Cullen.
206 . . . without being treated. Joseph Needham, 'The Roles of Europe and China in the Evolution of Oecumenical Science', Presidential Address delivered to Section X (General) on 31 August 1967 at the Leeds Meeting of the British Association, cited in *Advancement of Science*, September 1967, p.90.
214 '. . . shape of snow crystals.' Jacques Gernet, 'On Joseph Needham's Interpretation of the Comparative History of Science in China & Europe', *Festschrift for Dr. Sun Keun Lee* (Taegu, Yeungnan University, 1974), p.227.
218 '. . . leftover dregs.' *Zhuangzi*, cited in Liu An, *Huainanzi*, translated by Christopher Cullen, cf. A.C. Graham, *Chuang Tzu: The Inner Chapters* (London, George Allen and Unwin, 1982), pp.139-40.
221 '. . . to everything foreign.' Deng Xiaoping, 'Speech at Opening Ceremony of National Science Conference', 18 March 1975, *Peking Review*, No.12, 24 March 1978, pp.9-18.

CREATING

223 '. . . and a strange rock.' Mi Fu, *Huashi* (Wangshi huahuan 10), 16a, cited and translated in Susan Bush, *The Chinese Literati on Painting*, Harvard-Yenching Studies, XXVII (Cambridge, Mass., Harvard University Press, 1971), p.35.
223 '. . . on your snow-white wall.' Su Shi, *Jizhu fenlei Dongpo xiansheng shi* (*Collected Poems*) Sibu congkan edn. V.11.21b, cited in Bush, *Literati*, p.35.
223 '. . . is not seemly?' R. van Gulik, *Sexual life in Ancient China* (Leiden, E.J. Brill, 1961), p.67, citing *The Dynastic History of the Former Han Dynasty*, ch.66.
224 '. . . and people are few.' From *Li Po and Tu Fu*, poems selected and translated by Arthur Cooper (Harmondsworth, Penguin, 1973), p.111. The poem is said by its translator to be a 'reply' to a famous spring

poem by Meng Haoran (689-740), a contemporary much admired by Li Po.

225 '. . . then the chance is gone.' Su Shi, *Jingzhi Dongpo wenji shihuan (Collected Prose)*, Sibu congkan edn. IX, 49, 1a-2a, in Bush, *Literati*, p.37.

225 '. . . inexhaustible freshness . . .' Su Shi, *Collected Poems*, V.11 28b, in Bush, *Literati*, p.41.

226 '. . . the will of the people.' Su Dongpo (Su Shi), 'Letter to Emperor Shen-tsung [Shenzong]', translated by J.K. Rideout in Cyril Birch, ed., *Anthology of Chinese Literature* (Harmondsworth, Penguin, 1967), pp.375-6.

226 '. . . winds for chariot.' Su Dongpo, 'The Red Cliff, I', translated by A.C. Graham in Birch, ed., *Anthology of Chinese Literature*, p.385.

226 . . . had flowed into one. George C. Hatch, 'Sushih', in Herbert Franke, ed., *Sung Biographies* (Wiesbaden, Franz Steiner, 1976), pp.904, 947-9.

226 '. . . brag I'm young.' Su Dongpo, 'Seeing the Year Out' (1062), *Su Tung-p'o [Su Dongpo]: Selections from a Song Dynasty Poet*, translated and with an introduction by Burton Watson (New York, Columbia University Press, 1965) p.5.

227 '. . . bride to the River Lord.' Su Dongpo, 'Lament of the Farm Wife of Wu', Ibid., p.40.

228 '. . . from the angle of totality.' Tsung Pai-hua, 'Space-consciousness in Chinese Painting', *Sino-Australian Cultural Association Journal* (1949), p.27, translated by E.J. Schwartz, cited in Michael Sullivan, *The Arts of China* (Berkeley, Los Angeles and London, University of California Press, 1977), p.163.

228 '. . . gradually disappear.' Guo Xi, *An Essay on Landscape Painting*, translated by Shio Sakanishi (London, John Murray, The Wisdom of the East Series, 1935), p.46.

228 . . . 'Travellers Among Streams and Mountains' . . . In the National Palace Museum, Taipei, Taiwan.

231 . . . as rapidly as it comes. Michael Sullivan, *Arts*, pp.216-19.

234 '. . . seen it at all.' Ibid., p.179.

234 '. . . with a brush.' Ibid., p.179.

235 '. . . fish jumping in the water.' Shen Congwen, 'Autobiography', cited in introduction to Shen Congwen, *The Chinese Earth* (New York, Columbia University Press, 1982), (reprint of George Allen and Unwin edn., 1947), stories translated with an introduction by Ching Ti and Robert Payne, p.9.

236 . . . to create the fashion. Maggie Keswick, *The Chinese Garden* (London, Academy Editions, 1978), pp.15-16.

236 . . . in north-west China. Joan Lebold Cohen, *Painting the Chinese Dream* (Northampton, Mass., Smith College Museum of Art, 1982), p.16.

238 . . . of his evening self. Sullivan, *Arts*, p.158.

239 '. . . washed his ears.' Chiang Yee, *The Chinese Eye* (London, Methuen, 1960), p.70.

240 . . . in the countryside . . . Sullivan, 'New Directions in Chinese Art' in *Art News*, Vol.73 (September 1974), p.40.

240 . . . a crowd of 10,000 people. Cohen, *Painting the Chinese Dream*, p.39.

241 . . . before it was completed. Ibid. p.14.

241 . . . graceful kind of drawing. Chiang Yee, *The Chinese Eye*, pp.154-5.

242 . . . an odd goat or sheep. Sullivan, 'New Directions', p.54.

242 . . . in Beijing . . . Jonathan D. Spence, *The Gate of Heavenly Peace* (London and Boston, Faber and Faber, 1982), p.356.

242 . . . in its centre. See Sullivan, 'New Directions', p.48.

243 . . . official storm arose. Cohen, *Painting the Chinese Dream*, pp.18-19.

244 '. . . their passionate reunion.' *Chin P'ing Mei: The Adventurous History of Hsi Men and his Six Wives*, translated from the German of Franz Kuhn, with an introduction by Arthur Waley (London, The Bodley Head, 1959), p.652.

TRADING

247 '. . . butter mountain?' *Europe and China*, May 1983, pp.11-12.

247 . . . has been growing. Foreign trade was 11% of GNP in 1978. By 1982 it had risen to 18%. Part of the growth is due to reclassification. Source: State Statistical Bureau, *China Statistical Abstract 1983* (Beijing, State Statistical Publishing House, 1983).

247 '. . . why quickly?' Folk memory appears to have embroidered some real events surrounding the opening of a tramway at Shanghai.

258 . . . stationed outside Guangzhou. John K. Fairbank, Edwin O. Reischauer and Albert M. Craig, *East Asia: Tradition and Transformation* (Boston, Houghton, Mifflin Co., 1973), pp.274-5.

ILLUSTRATION CREDITS

American Heritage 217
Ash Films 102, 106, 115
Berry-Hill Galleries, New York 259
Terry Boxall v
British Library 183, 214, 218, 244
British Museum 43, 51, 52, 53, 73, 119, 121, 122-3, 200
Camera Press 63
Jean-Loup Charmet 20, 21, 166 (top)
Cleveland Museum of Art 95, 248
Constance and Brian Dear *endpapers*
Paul Dinnage Collection 167
Mike Fox 7-8
Freer Gallery of Art 22, 46-7, 86-7, 133
Stanley Gibbons (Philatelic Advisers) 218
Torre Gill 127, 149, 150, 158, 222, 241
John Hillelson Agency/Eve Arnold 116, 207, 240, 243
John Hillelson Agency/Bruno Barbey 78-9, 112-3
John Hillelson Agency/George Gerster 33
John Hillelson Agency/Hiroji Kubota 81, 128, 229, 265
John Hillelson Agency/Marc Riboud 1, 4, 6-7, 26, 82, 98-9, 143
Stephen Kibble and Robin Harvey xiv, 117, 135, 170, 249
Seth Joel 251
Keystone Press Agency 30
Patrick Lui vi
Patrick Lui and Associates (Patrick Lui, David Wong, Simon Yeung and Barry Chung) 34, 42, 50, 64, 97, 105, 107, 114-5, 136, 137, 151, 155, 156, 160-1, 169, 163, 172, 180, 190, 193, 195, 197, 198, 203, 215, 246
Matheson Archives 256
Metropolitan Museum of Art 241
Peter Montagnon 90
Mottahedeh Collection 254-5, 257
Musée des Deux Guerres Mondiales 71, 126

Museum of Fine Arts, Boston 44, 49, 178, 224, 250
National Palace Museum, Taiwan 110, 205, 228, 231
J. Needham, *The Shorter Science and Civilisation in China*, CUP 212
Nelson-Atkins Gallery of Art, Kansas City 36, 84, 224, 228
Polytechnic of Central London 57, 63, 101, 174, 175, 176-7, 262
Popperfoto 33 (bottom), 69, 126, 166 (bottom), 187
Private Collection, London 68
Private Collection, Oxford 245
Patrick Procktor ii
Réunion des Musées Nationaux 138-9
Royal Geographical Society 68
Science Museum 210
Skira Archives/Commission for Protection of Cultural Properties, Tokyo 234
Society for Anglo-Chinese Understanding 25, 31, 63, 188, 211, 220
Victoria and Albert Museum, London 70
Vision International/Simon Holledge 171
Vision International/Paolo Koch 2-3, 28, 100, 120, 260
Wellcome Institute for the History of Medicine 221
Wango Weng 24
Wango Weng/Museum of Fine Arts, Boston 12, 14-15
Wango Weng/Brundage Collection 251
Wango Weng/Musée Cernuschi, Paris 117
Wango Weng/Cleveland Museum of Art 208
Wango Weng/Hong Kong City Museum 17
Wango Weng/National Palace Museum, Taiwan 13, 16, 38, 92, 130, 216, 239, 252
Wango Weng/Nelson-Atkins Museum, Kansas City 132, 232-3
Wango Weng/Fang Chao Ying Collection 19

INDEX

page references in italics refer to illustrations

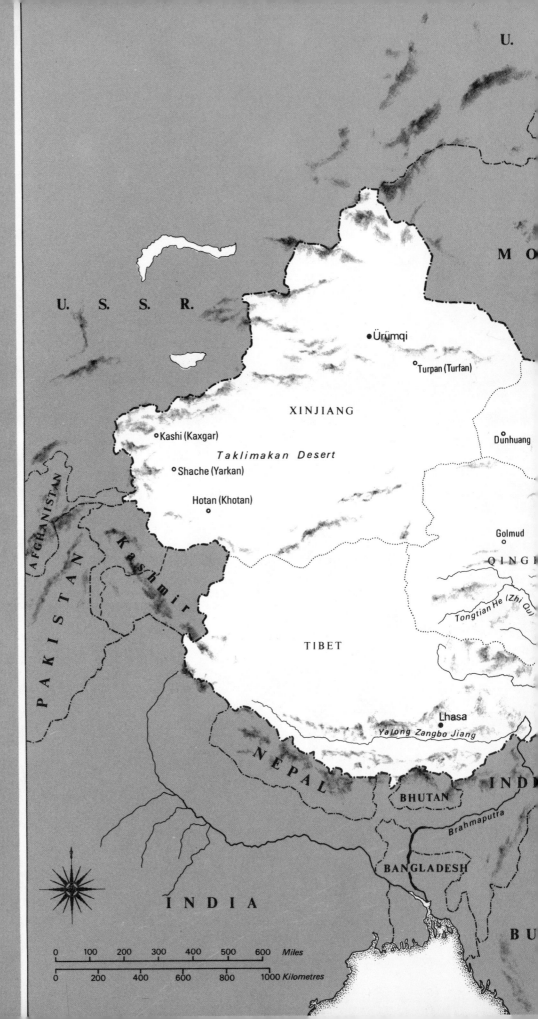

Prehistoric/Legendary Period
to c.16th century BC
Xia (c.21st century–c.16th century BC)

Shang
c.16th century–c.11th century BC

Zhou
c.1027–256 BC
Western Zhou (1027–771 BC)
Eastern Zhou (771–256 BC)
Spring and Autumn Period (771–476 BC)
Warring States (475–221 BC)

Qin
221–207 BC

Western or Former Han
206 BC–AD 9

Xin
9–23

Eastern or Later Han
25–220

Three Kingdoms
(Shu, Wei, Wu)
220–65

Northern and Southern Empires
265–589
Six Dynasties (Western Jin, Eastern Jin,
Former Song, Southern Qi, Southern
Liang, Southern Chen) (265–589)
Northern Dynasties (Northern Wei,
Northern Qin and Northern Zhou)
(386–587)

Sui
590–618

Tang
618–906

Five Dynasties
(Later Liang, Later Tang,
Later Jin, Later Han, Later Zhou)
906–60

Northern Song
960–1126

Southern Song
1127–1279

Yuan or Mongol
1279–1368

Ming
1368–1644

Qing or Manchu
1644–1911

Republic
1911–49

People's Republic
1949–